D0109298

THE
ENGLISH
IS
COMING!

How One Language Is Sweeping the World

LESLIE DUNTON-DOWNER

ILLUSTRATIONS BY MARY RHINELANDER

MAPS AND GRAPHS BY KRIS GOODFELLOW

A TOUCHSTONE BOOK

PUBLISHED BY SIMON & SCHUSTER

NEW YORK   LONDON   TORONTO   SYDNEY

Touchstone
A Division of Simon & Schuster, Inc.
1230 Avenue of the Americas
New York, NY 10020

Copyright © 2010 by Leslie Dunton-Downer
Illustrations copyright © 2010 by Mary Rhinelander

All rights reserved, including the right to reproduce this book or portions
thereof in any form whatsoever. For information address Touchstone Subsidiary
Rights Department, 1230 Avenue of the Americas, New York, NY 10020.

First Touchstone hardcover edition September 2010

TOUCHSTONE and colophon are registered trademarks of Simon & Schuster, Inc.

For information about special discounts for bulk purchases,
please contact Simon & Schuster Special Sales at
1-866-506-1949 or business@simonandschuster.com.

The Simon & Schuster Speakers Bureau can bring authors to your live event.
For more information or to book an event contact the
Simon & Schuster Speakers Bureau at 866-248-3049
or visit our website at www.simonspeakers.com.

Designed by Ruth Lee-Mui

Manufactured in the United States of America

1   3   5   7   9   10   8   6   4   2

Library of Congress Cataloging-in-Publication Data
Dunton-Downer, Leslie.
The English is coming! : how one language is sweeping the world /
Leslie Dunton-Downer ; illustrations by Mary Rhinelander ;
maps and graphs by Kris Goodfellow.
p.   cm.
"A Touchstone Book."
1. English language—Globalization.   2. English language—Foreign
countries.   I. Rhinelander, Mary F.   II. Goodfellow, Kris.
PE1073.E549   2010
420.9—dc22   2010025230

ISBN 978-1-4391-7665-8
ISBN 978-1-4391-7672-6 (ebook)

For my mother

CONTENTS

Introduction: Magic Glasses   ix

Hello?   xix

1. GLOBAL ENGLISH   1

   Robot   18

   Bikini   23

   Shampoo   28

   Jazz   34

   Cocktail   39

   Made in China   45

2. A FAMILY PICTURE OF ENGLISH   50

   Film   72

   Credit Card   79

   lol   82

   Blog   86

   Disco   90

   Star   93

3. MADE IN ÆNGLISC   99

   Business   117

   Parking   122

T-shirt   126
FREE!   131
Bank   136
STOP   143

4. MADE IN ENGLYSSHE   151
Check   172
Penthouse   176
Cookie   181
Taxi!   185
Job   189
Fun   193

5. LINGUA FRANCA AND ENGLISH   198
Stress   214
SAT   218
Relax   225
Safari   230
Deluxe   235
O.K.   239

6. FUTURE GLOBAL ENGLISH SPOKEN HERE   244
Bye   293

Acknowledgments   295
Notes   299
Index   313

INTRODUCTION

Magic Glasses

Word-loving people seem to know who they are early in life. They're the kids who find dictionaries at least as absorbing as children's books. And instead of asking parents or teachers why the sky is blue, they ask why the sky is called blue.

Where I spent my first years, in Santa Cruz, California, the most alluring language was to be found in the colorful compound words that cropped up everywhere. At school, there were *earthquake* drills and field trips, say, to a classmate's family *strawberry* farm. Our house sat in a *redwood* forest populated by *bobcats*, *mushrooms*, and what my German-speaking grandmother thrillingly referred to as *Wildschweinen*, "wild pigs," disappointingly called "boar" in English. A family friend, Jack, had what he called his *surfshop*, a smelly but exciting beachside design lab of sorts, where he was working on a *sharkproof* rubber wet suit, striped to mimic a poisonous fish he said even sharks refused to bite. (Sharks, it turned out, weren't fooled by Jack's invention.) Then, in 1966, a new TV series certified that compounds were truly wonderful and could even be created from scratch. My little brother was mad for the superhero protagonist's *Batmobile* and beguiling *Batcave*. For me, the show was all about *Batlanguage*.

These compounds were spellbinding verbal objects, two-part words that were so much more than the sums of their parts, equally satisfying to break down into their component pieces for closer examination and then put right back together. Some were easy to decipher, like *earthquake*, clearly what you get when the *earth quakes*, which it often did along the San Andreas Fault. Or *redwood*, obviously so named because the tree's *wood* and bark were *red*. Or at least reddish. But others were more mysterious, like *mushroom*. What was the story here? Were mushrooms called that because they grew in *rooms* full of *mush*? Or because there was *room* for *mush* to gather in the gills on the underside of their caps? The dictionary said that *mushroom* came from the French *mousseron*. Impossible. I had learned from my French-speaking mother that *mushroom* was *champignon* in French. Now she was insisting that *mousseron* had to do with *moss*. But that didn't answer my question. Besides, all I could hear in her mysterious French word was a hint of chocolate *mousse*.

For the time being, the whole idea of anglicized pronunciations of foreign terms was just too weird and complicated. *Mushroom* would have to remain its more manageable intriguing self, a word calling out to be loved for its divisibility. The same went for my favorite: *artichoke*.

Artichokes were great suppertime treats in our household, and happily, we lived near the self-proclaimed Artichoke Capital of the World, Castroville. When our parents drove us out to the farmers' fields, we traveled on dirt roads sprouting vibrant, hand-painted billboards. Many of them depicted cute, anthropomorphized artichokes, some smiling cheerfully, as if eager to be ripped from their native fields, taken in a car to some strange house, steamed in a pot, and devoured. A few were given speech bubbles saying things like "Best Artichokes Here!" The yummy plants seemed to have been named for the dazzling *art* that they'd spawned. But what about *choke*? Was it because you could grab the thick stem under the human-head-like bulb of spiky leaves and appear to be *choking* it? Or maybe it had to do with the hairy stuff in the middle of each artichoke, the stuff our mom scooped out so we wouldn't *choke* on it. When I asked my teacher for help, she showed me how the dictionary gave the word's origins going through several languages and back to one I'd never heard of, Arabic. But I found it hard to believe this version of the *artichoke* story, especially since I had seen the Artichoke Capital of the World many times with my own eyes. Surely the vegetable had been named in the *art*-filled fields of Castroville, not in the place that Mrs. Greider was indicating on the far side of the globe mounted on her desk.

My California *Batchildhood* ended abruptly in 1970, when my father moved our family to Colombia. He had a new job there, with the Peace Corps, and I soon forgot about compound words to embrace my own new task: learning Spanish.

Accompanying my father, I traveled to places in the Amazon and the Andes where people spoke languages so isolated from the rest of the world that few outside their small populations understood them. These groups of people were often visibly disadvantaged, lacking things that we in California, and even in Bogotá, could take for granted—like a doctor to treat a bad earache. It naturally appeared that not all languages were created equal: the more widely recognized ones, like my English and budding Spanish, or my mother's French, allowed their speakers to interact with a wider world, and to reap the benefits offered by life in a bigger and more broadly distributed population of speakers.

Our expat life in Latin America also proved that English had a special place even among the larger languages. In foreign capitals like Colombia's, educated people who were fully engaged with the world were likely to speak some English, whereas only oddballs and academics bothered to learn uncommon tongues such as Páez, spoken in the Andean region of Cauca. On the other hand, most native English-speaking adults visiting our household, even those whose jobs took them to countries where English was not officially spoken, turned out, far more often than not, to be monolingual. In their views a second language, whether spoken in huge parts of the world or not, was unnecessary. Any person one might wish to speak to was bound to know some English in the first place.

Ignorance of other languages was also seen as a perk of American superpowerdom, whose representatives in any case seemed to visit foreign countries more to talk than to listen. This was, after all, the Cold War era. Apart from English, the only major languages on the average Westerner's awareness map were those of allies in Europe. And maybe Japanese. And Russian. But the Soviet Union was then so closed to the world that—barring a plan to defect to or spy on the Eastern Bloc, or to head a Colombian guerrilla movement funded by Moscow, or to succumb to an overpowering desire to read Tolstoy in the original—it was rare for someone to see much point in learning Russian as a second language.

One American who had taken the time to master the Spanish I was just beginning to learn was Paul, a handsome and sweet Peace Corps volunteer. He worked to organize relief for victims of a cataclysmic earthquake in Peru. At age nine I developed a hopeless crush on him and was mesmerized by everything he did or said. When my father announced a field trip with Paul and a friend of Paul's, an American anthropologist, I petitioned night and day to be included. At the time, nothing compared with the company of the perfect Paul. But in the end, the indelible parts of the ten-day excursion were spent talking with his friend the anthropologist.

The man was living with a group of Andean Indians who spoke Aymara, and he had learned their language to study their way of life. I asked if he would have bothered to know a weird language if it hadn't been for his job. He thought about it awhile and finally said yes, he would, because knowing this other language was like being given a pair of magic glasses. If you put on the glasses, you would see new things about reality, things that had been concealed when you were looking at the world through your English-speaking eyes. And once you had the glasses, you could put them on whenever you liked, to experience the world in a different way. I must have rumpled up my face or told him that I didn't get his idea, because he went on to give an unforgettable example.

"You know how, in English, when we speak of the future, we picture it as something that lies ahead, physically? And that what has already happened, what is past, is thought of as what's *behind* us?" *Yes, that seemed obvious.* "Well, in the Aymara language, people speak of time the other way around. What has already passed is in front of you. And what's unknown for the moment, the future, lies behind you." *But,* I objected, *if you're walking forward, you're walking into the future, because you're advancing, going ahead!* Paul's friend was sympathetic. "You see things that way. And so do I, when I'm speaking English. But someone else could say that no matter how fast you walk or even run ahead, whatever you see with your eyes has already occurred by the time you see it. Even if your feet move like crazy, you're just moving faster toward what has already taken place."

I tried pirouetting quickly a few times, to see if I could catch a glimpse of things to come. "In the village where I live, there's a girl about your age, Alaya. If I told her that you and I think of the future as being in front of us, she would be just as surprised as you are by her way of seeing time."

What about magic glasses for English? What does our language have that's a fun thing to know? The budding anthropologist had a ready answer. "All languages have their own special ways of shaping our experience of the world. But English glasses aren't so magical, because so many people speak English."

Hmm. So any language that gains huge numbers of speakers can kiss its magic glasses good-bye? I could see the point Paul's friend was making. Unusual ideas—like the Aymara's one of the future's being behind us—wouldn't be so surprising, or have the potential to be so illuminating, if a zillion people had already accepted them as self-evident. But does a language only provide magic glasses if hardly anybody speaks it?

Over the years since that eye-opening conversation, I came to see that Paul's friend was wrong. English, for all its widespread familiarity, has always furnished its speakers magic glasses. And it now furnishes them a new pair that has only recently come into existence. The magic glasses of English enable speakers to behold the world on a global scale, and to shape life on our fast-changing planet in a language that is, itself, changing quickly.

How *does* today's world appear through the lenses of a language whose scope is nothing less than global? And what about the future?

Today English outsizes even the most widely used languages of the past. Since the rise of modern technologies of communication, beginning notably with the telegraph and the telephone but hardly ending there, English has been adopted throughout the world to become *Global English*, a language of unprecedented, planetwide recognition and use. Perhaps it would make more sense to say *Global Englishes*, since there's no one particular version of the language that speakers learn or use. Employed variously throughout the world, English has attracted hundreds of millions of new speakers and is slated in coming decades to become the common language of hundreds of millions more.

Some actively seek proficiency in English to gain access to global realms of activity, from education and web surfing to diplomacy and business. At the other end of the spectrum, Global English consists of words and phrases that an astonishing portion of Earth's population now knows by osmosis. Many of these pieces of language are already elemental building blocks in the daily lives of countless nonnative speakers of English. They're also essential terms for millions who don't really speak English but nonetheless recognize words and phrases in it. These expressions work as cultural portals, points of entry into a planetary realm of life, a realm that is for now the exclusive preserve of English.

It is a momentous time to be a speaker of this language. With its current status as the world's default common tongue, English is poised to be significantly transformed over the next few generations. Already, worldwide, the language claims more nonnative speakers than native speakers. In China alone, more people have acquired ability in English than speak it as a mother tongue in the United States. Those Chinese-speakers for whom English is a foreign language are bound to change the look and sound, and even the meaning, of many Global English words and phrases, and ultimately of English itself.* Other major languages including Spanish, Hindi,

---

*By "Chinese-speakers" I mean people who speak Chinese, rather than "speakers who are Chinese nationals" or "speakers who identify themselves as ethnic Chinese" or "speakers who reside in China." Throughout this book, I hyphenate similar phrases to clarify that we're talking about speakers of a language (English-speakers, Swahili-speakers, and so on) rather than passport holders of certain nations or members of ethnic groups. In the latter cases, no hyphens are used. So, "French speakers" refers to speakers who are French, while

Bengali, Portuguese, Russian, and Arabic, will likely also lead English down new paths.

What kinds of unexpected insights into the world will Global English be newly equipped to offer once its nonnative speakers have altered it? Aymara neatly reminds us that the future remains invisible. But one thing is sure. English is bound to change substantially as it evolves in its role as Earth's common language.

This is not the first time that English will have been greatly transformed. Indeed, from its outset, English has been about high-octane collisions with languages that its speakers never expected to encounter. At several points in its history too, English might even have become extinct. It's not as though the language was somehow destined to be used on a planetwide scale, or even to be spoken beyond the island where it emerged. But due in large part to historical accidents, English did survive and gradually, over time, has been modified to tremendous degrees. Hence Old English, or "Anglo-Saxon," as seen in the opening words of the epic *Beowulf,* today looks fully foreign even to native speakers of English: *"Hwæt wē Gār-Dena in gēar-dagum."*★ By the same token, even those born in the era of Modern English, say, in Shakespeare's day, would have been absolutely mystified to behold what now rates as banal to many adepts of text messaging: *"omg! u r n nyc? c u 2nite @ j's b-day! l8r, ldd."* Is this really the same language that was used by clansmen gathered to hear tell of the heroic exploits of Beowulf and his fellow warriors? The answer is yes. It is. There is an unbroken line of linguistic and cultural continuity between us, in our digital global world, and those tribes of long ago, in an environment that we must now strain to fathom. Will Global English-speakers of the

---

"French-speakers" refers to speakers of French in France but also in Belgium, Switzerland, Canada, Algeria, Vietnam, and anywhere else.
★"So. The Spear-Danes in days gone by."[1]

twenty-second century require special training to read or listen to English as it was used before the arrival of the internet? Will it look as baffling to them as Old English now does to us?

Technology has, as never before, made it possible to belong to a community of speakers—or language "users"—that is at once widely dispersed and yet, as counterintuitive as it often seems, fluidly interconnected. And not only does this community use language for purposes that never existed in the past, but its members also speak diverse native languages, the great majority of which have never before been in steady contact with English. Taken together, these influences, novel and potentially potent, are positioned to catapult English into a fresh phase of its historic evolution.

About sixty-five hundred languages are now spoken on our planet. Yet humanity is each day closer to using English as its sole lingua franca. Incredibly, you can utter the word *yes* virtually anywhere—from Timbuktu to a multinational space station orbiting beyond the stratosphere—and be understood. Some view this fast-spreading English as a threat to the survival of other languages. Or as a frightening leveler of cultures, turning so many distinct ways of life into a homogenous extension of America, the dominant English-speaking nation of the day. But while these dangers are not imaginary, it's also the case that Global English is now an instrument of humankind's increasingly collective existence, and possibly our species' most valuable tool in a global era of unprecedented challenges and possibilities.

How is the world using its new common language? To find out, we'll investigate the unique histories of thirty English words and phrases familiar to people across the globe. Why *these thirty*? In the ever-growing vocabulary of Global English, each of these spotlighted terms has found its place in a worldwide conversation. We'll track down the origins of each expression independently and consider it in its Global English context. But most important, we'll use these selected words and phrases to illuminate the emergence and spread of Global English, which we'll explore in brief chapters. We'll look at the evolution of the English language and come to a point so simple as to seem self-evident: for the first time, the world *needs* a planetary lingua franca, and English is highly qualified for the job. Finally, we'll take an extra step and imagine how English will look and sound quite different in the near future. All along the way, the stories of our thirty words and phrases will bring the remarkable expansion of English to life. Let's now look at an introductory word in Global English, a language that's got the whole world talking.

HELLO?

"Ahoy."

"Ahoy! Freddy?"

"No. Just a moment." *Freddy's brother directs voice toward upstairs bedroom.*

"Fred! It's for you!"

Alexander Graham Bell liked to answer telephone calls with a nautical *Ahoy!* Actually, he liked to use two *ahoy*s in a row: *Ahoy, ahoy!* It may strike us as absurd today, but his invention confronted its early adopters with a true dilemma: how does a decent person open a conversation on a telephone? For the first time, people were conversing in disembodied voices emanating from uncertain locales. Thanks to Mr. Bell's contraption, though, the voice of an invisible person could come into one's parlor and join a discussion, or describe events unfolding at a distance that would normally take days to reach by horse-drawn carriage or train. It was remarkable. But still, how to initiate such unaccustomed intercourse? Did it make any sense at all to bark "Good day!" into an inert device, and without so much as an accompanying tip of the hat or quick curtsy? One can see why Bell was fond of *ahoy*. It had the advantage of being a proven word for embarking on an exchange, especially in uncharted waters.

Bell's rival, Thomas Edison, had an equally novel proposal. While best known as the man behind the electric lightbulb and the phonograph, Edison also collaborated on telephone technology. In 1877, when the gadget was only a year old, he wrote a letter to a colleague suggesting that in lieu of a ring, a *hello!*, cried out by the operator connecting two parties, could alert the recipient to an incoming call. This idea didn't take.★ But the dream (or nightmare?) of loquacious appliances did (Edison was just a century or so ahead of the curve).

While Edison hadn't invented *hello*, his suggestion for its new use stuck. It soon became the right first word to utter for telephone calls in the United States. Such was the effervescence attached to the word in 1880 that at the first National Convention of Telephone Companies in Niagara Falls, New York, the convention president informed his audience that the best possible speech for the occasion would consist of only one word: *hello!* He was applauded by enthusiastic conference-goers, each donning a name tag bearing the group's favorite new word, which, naturally, was *hello*.[1]

Hello is related to *halôn*, a verb from the medieval language Old High German meaning "to fetch," and in particular, when calling out across the water to hail a ferryman, "to hail."[2] (Bell would have appreciated the association with his maritime greeting, *Ahoy!*) In

★The telephone, like the internet, initially linked the laboratory of its inventor to other laboratories. Like wireless internet connectivity, early telephone lines were open on an ongoing basis. Operators, then young men, would simply connect a call from one lab to another. The new technology first spread to fire stations and doctors' offices. By the end of the 1870s, it had reached homes, where America's Ednas and Millicents could use telephones to swap recipes, compare sewing techniques, and talk about their babies or the Bible. These are subjects described by Mark Twain in 1880, in the *Atlantic Monthly*. In his short piece, he captured one overheard half of a conversation between a lady of the house and a Mrs. Bagley. Twain said that such single-voiced dialogue produced "one of the solemnest curiosities of modern life." As when cell phone conversations first unfolded in public spaces, telephone conversations in private settings required people to adjust to then-bizarre uses and forms of speech. Within ten years of Twain's article, ladies, by then deemed more suited than men to the occupation of telephone operator, were referred to as "Hello Girls."[3]

1880, *hello* sparkled with freshness and even a dash of the unexpected. It was in use in America as early as 1827, when the *U.S. Telegraph*, a Washington DC daily, published a man's letter to his uncle for its eyewitness account. The letter writer was one of thousands of people who had just gathered at Niagara Falls to observe a stunt: a sailboat, fitted out to resemble a pirate ship, was reportedly loaded with buffaloes, bears, raccoons, possums, and weasels. The nephew describes how the water "kums tumblin along az iph the divil kikt it." And the "most darnashun thunderin noiz" as "Spra flys up un makes fawty thowsen raneboz." Amid the spectacular din, the boat, heading into the falls, began to break up and take on water. The nephew notes how his companion believed he could save the vessel if he had some help, and adds: "Hello, sez Joe Laughton, wher's Bil Perry and Olla Parsons?" (Some animals swam to safety as the boat was sinking, but the others rode on to their deaths.) Perhaps it was by chance that a variation on the medieval ferry-hailing term was used in these aqueous circumstances, but the dramatic *hello* attributed to Joe Laughton on September 18, 1827, is the first attestation of the word. Clearly, it would take quite a few decades before *hello* was to be included in books teaching "proper English" with such sample sentences as "Hello, my name is Joe."[4]

The American *hello* was a variant of words already used in British English, where older forms, such as *hallo* and *hullo*, not greetings but hailing words, carried their own spins of surprise and nonchalance. Shakespeare was the first to set down the ancestor word *hollo*, when he used it in his play *Titus Andronicus*: "*Hollo*, what storm is this?" And Charles Dickens had the Artful Dodger introduce himself to Oliver with a related "*Hullo!*, my covey" (with *covey* meaning "little cove") in his 1838 novel *Oliver Twist*. But in its less class-conscious setting across the Atlantic, the American *hello* took on a different aspect. It was immediate and direct, yet not unfriendly.

And with the telephone a democratic tool, leveling the voices of its speakers through telephone lines, it suited Americans. One simple word would suffice for all.

Hello was soon embraced in diverse countries as a kind of linguistic accessory to the new import item from North America, the telephone. The exclamation came out as *allô!* in French, which had long been equipped with similar-sounding phrases such as *holà!* for "hold on!" or "cease!" From French-speaking Europe, adapted forms of *allô* spread to French-speaking Africa, Asia, and Latin America, and to the islands of the South Pacific and the Caribbean. In Russian, the American greeting became *alyo.* And similar words were used in Slavic tongues such as Czech, Latvian, Polish, and Slovak. Variations on the Russian were adopted in Uzbek and Tajik. And Lithuanian. Speakers of Hungarian said *halló.* Turkish and other languages were also to become borrowers of *hello* in different forms. The greeting became *alo* in Arabic and *hallo* in Hebrew. And in Thailand? That would be pronounced *harro*, but with a hint of an *r* sound at the end: *harro(r).* In Britain and in territories of the British Empire, including India, speakers accepted variations on *hello* as their standard telephone greeting as well.★

Eventually, *hello* gained acceptance as a perfectly polite greeting for in-person meetings in English. But in virtually every other language, the telephone conversation starter did not slip over to become a greeting used in embodied encounters.

However, with rising American influence in so many sectors—this itself attributable in no little measure to the advent of the telephone—*hello* would become a global word for greetings between speakers who shared no common language. An outsider's

★While pervasive, *hello* was not to be adopted in all languages. In Italian, for instance, one answers the telephone with *pronto!*, meaning "ready!" as in "ready to talk (to whoever is calling)."

visit even to a village in rural Congo or to a remote tributary of the Amazon—or to a barbershop in Saigon—is today more likely to produce a *hello,* or even a chorus of *hello*s, than any other word.

Hello has become a standard greeting for nonnative speakers of English worldwide, a kind of universal for "There you are!" or "Here I am!" or "Direct your attention over here!" Via groundbreaking technology devised by Bell—who was born in the British Isles, long a resident of Canada, and ultimately a U.S. citizen—the telephone unites distant speakers in living, breathing conversation, even across time zones and countries and foreign languages. For all these reasons, *hello* is the best word to lead us into the realm of Global English.

HELLO AND FIDO

An ancestor of the American *hello* was the medieval English exclamation *hallow!*, which was used not only to attract attention but also, in hunts, to spur dogs to carry on in pursuit of prey. This *hallow* is not the same one we see in "*hallowed* soul" or *Halloween*. That latter *hallow* is related to the words *holy*, *whole*, and *hale*.

HOLLER

Another colloquial American word that shares the same roots as *hello* is *holler*, both a noun and a verb expressing ideas of shouting, protest, and complaint. In the nineteenth-century American South, *hollers* were a genre of work song sung by slaves in fields, where voices would have to be especially loud to carry tunes together.

HELLO VERSUS *HEAVENO*

In 1997, commissioners of Kleberg County, Texas, voted for *heaveno* to become the county's official term of greeting. They were persuaded that the *hell* in *hello* was ungodly, even though the two words are etymologically unrelated.

THE
ENGLISH
IS
COMING!

1

GLOBAL ENGLISH

*H*ello, spoken worldwide into telephones, encapsulates extraordinary shifts that English has undergone on its path from a quasi-tribal, island language to our first and so far only planetary one. Attached as it first was to made-in-America technology, *hello* also shows the major role the USA has played in the globalization of English. Looking at core words of Global English, we notice that many point to innovations and concepts that arose in America, and to that country's impact on global culture. But can we really say that English was *made* into a global language by any one culture or nation?

If we step back into the pretelephone era, we see that English was already long on the move over significant swaths of the globe. Courtesy of exploration, migration, trade, war, missionary work, and the rapid expansion of the British Empire, English was, well before Alexander Bell's birth in 1847, at home on all six inhabited continents and in the British Isles. The United States, following independence from Britain, likewise did a great deal to disseminate English. In bringing the language to extensive territories, these two military, cultural, and commercial powers installed it as well in small but strategic places, such as islands in major bodies of water and in the two canal zones, Suez and Panama, where English became an idiom of truncated and time-saving passage between oceans. Even where other powerful languages dominated, English has, since around 1600, usually managed to install a forward base in the vicinity.

Britain's maritime reach having established English as the lingua franca of the high seas, the advent of aviation, pioneered in America, lifted the language into the sky. Today English is at least one official language of more than fifty nations; of international air traffic; of major bodies like the United Nations and the World Trade Organization; not to mention of private companies, institutions of higher learning, research laboratories, nonprofit outfits, nongovernmental organizations, media empires, and other entities based around the world and populated by speakers for whom English is not a native tongue.

While this staggering internationalization of English emerged from British developments, true globalization of the language has been overwhelmingly America's work. The process weaves through the central domains of global life that have been introduced or changed by British and American cultures. The first major English-speaking spheres were trade and militarized colonial expansion, but the impetus has been increasingly commercial, and increasingly sparked by made-in-the-USA technology. We can see evidence of these realms of activity at work in clusters of words, largely exported to the world from America, that form today's most-used Global English vocabulary.

One such sphere is entertainment. In the late nineteenth century, while telephones were propagating *hello*, *film* began to mean a technology that was, almost overnight, able to advance a secluded district of California into the position of global capital of mass leisure. No place would do more than Hollywood to diffuse the glossy pop-culture prestige of spoken and sung English, along with its terms and commodities, including the media-fueling *star* and, eventually, the *compact disc*, *cassette*, and a plethora of *video* games.

But Hollywood hardly had a monopoly on the molding of English over the first half of the twentieth century. America's military and diplomatic sway gained surprising linguistic ground at the signing, in 1919, of the Treaty of Versailles. Until the First World War, French had been *the* language of diplomacy, and it was irksome to French observers that America's belated arrival in the conflict gave English carte blanche for those historic negotiations, even as they unfolded on French soil.[1] English then became the new French, and diplomats were quick to set English on a course that now has speakers of the global language likely to bypass *détente* and *rapprochement* for phrases like *common ground* or words like *partnership* and *cooperation*. Or even some of the businesslike terms that pepper American diplomatic language, such as *accountability* and *transparency*.

Just when the French were coming to terms with diplomatic English, more Global English was being engineered in America thanks to the modernizing avenue of *mass production*. Following World War I, American car manufacturers were making Detroit a pivotal city on the emerging map of Global English. The era of mass-produced cars launched *parking* and *STOP*, among other devices of vehicular English that would eventually be embraced by automobilists virtually everywhere.

Around the same time, on a New York stage, audiences adjusting to advancing mechanization first encountered the word *robot*. And while America's factories churned out an ever-growing array of goods, the rising craze for productivity and efficiency also enveloped

American educators in the form of standardized tests, including the *SAT.* By the end of the twentieth century, those three letters would annually terrify not only new crops of U.S. high school students, but scores of thousands of nonnative users of English taking the examination in hundreds of countries and territories, all hoping to pursue higher education in the heartland of Global English.

With World War II, the American stamp on Global English was even more pronounced. U.S. troops—deployed more widely than had been those of the British Empire—introduced such all-American delicacies as *chewing gum* and *Coca-Cola*, and Yankee notions of *fun* and *glamour.* Postwar manufacturing subsequently produced abundant supplies of Global English items like the *refrigerator* and *television* and, in the *credit card*, a convenient, sometimes too-convenient, means of acquiring them. On a yet darker note, war technology globalized such made-in-America phrases as *atom bomb*, even as the country's military activities inspired words and things seemingly far removed from particle physics and weapons of mass destruction, like the *miniskirt* and the *bikini.*

In the post–Baby Boom decade, and on America's domestic front, the civil rights movement and Vietnam era shaped fresh batches of words for which there were no true conceptual equivalents in other languages. From the United States, *black* gradually gained global status as a term of race identity. *Gay* was likewise made a signifier of identity. *Jazz* had journeyed across the globe during World War I. But the second half of the century gave planet-wide traction to *rock*, *disco*, *rap*, and *hip-hop* in the hugely influential realm of American pop music, which diffused catchy melodies, irresistible rhythms, and an endless supply of singable lyrics in English. More generally, America's urban street culture, notably black and Latino, offered the world readily recognized ways to be *cool*, a major Global English culture term. *Cool* became the world's new *chic*, but with broader socioeconomic range than the loanword from fashionable France.

Far and wide, up-to-date individuals of the late twentieth century tapped into an unmistakable energy, at once edgy and perpetually youthful, that came packaged with an American *look*—another big Global English word. It was often fused with sportswear, from baseball caps to basketball shoes (called *les baskets* in chic French). But no clothed part of the body was to be deprived of making its American statement. Among the most popular items were *jeans*, *jerseys*, and *T-shirts*, preferably bearing plenty of words and phrases in, or at least appearing to be in—lots of them would be "linguistically incorrect"—the world's lingua franca of hipness: English. For those who had no taste for casual clothing, global elixirs of the American lifestyle were to be found in *jogging*, *fitness*, and the putatively rejuvenating *face-lift*.

Cold War America generated many terms the world could hardly ignore, such as those taken from the space race pitting the U.S. against the USSR. With the fall of the Berlin Wall in 1989 and the subsequent collapse of the Soviet Union, an astronaut from Russia or Japan would be as likely as one from the United States to board the International *Space Station*—where extraplanetary work still goes on, in English. And the attention-grabbing word *news*, from a prehistoric root meaning simply "now," found its Global English stride in more terrestrial circumstances. Against awesome desert backdrops, viewers beheld the first multilateral conflict to be televised globally and in real time: the Persian Gulf War of 1990–91. The American entity CNN (Cable News Network) sped the diffusion of *news* as shorthand for "developments of worldwide impact." In some languages, *news* would come to refer to timely reports of the local variety as well, even as the very idea of "local" grew increasingly thorny in the global era.

Yet the farthest-reaching, fastest-moving, and most revolutionary American contributions to Global English have been in communication technology. This field has been central to the creation of the global networks pressing English into wide use for new kinds of exchanges. Computer engineers in the United States have made the *internet* accessible to billions of users worldwide, and have lured Earth's inhabitants into their first truly global conversations. *Email*, *blog*, *site* and *website*, *cookies*, *spam*, *chat rooms*, and *network* are not merely some of the many new words and phrases now familiar to a sizable portion of the Earth's human population; like *hello*, they are also verbal extensions of game-changing tools of communication, tools transforming how English is used and how the world is experienced. Indeed, these tools are changing the way our planet, as a whole and rapidly integrating object, operates. The creation and adoption of Global English are part of the larger, inexorably world-shrinking process. Is that a good thing? Debate about globalization and language will no doubt go on for a long time. This book hardly aims to end discussions, but does hope to offer reasons to participate in them or reflect on them anew.

Global English. The very phrase is a curious twofer. For one, it refers to the latest moment in English's evolution—the active phase that we see unfolding in our present world, one wherein a modern form of the language is turning into a global one. From its emergence nearly fifteen hundred years ago, English has, by chance roughly every five centuries, weathered a period of notable turbulence and change. At the same time, the phrase *Global English* captures the unprecedented and recent demonstration that a single language can indeed attain worldwide reach. English is the first language ever to grow and adapt into a global, planet-serving variant. Will there eventually be Global French, Global Chinese, and other global languages joining Global English? Or does the very nature of a global language suggest that *one* will serve its speakers, and without competition? These are questions whose answers depend greatly on how English-speakers—native and adoptive—put the language to use as it undergoes its present transformation.

Not long ago, matters spanning countries and regions, let alone continents and oceans, seemed few and far between, remote from or even irrelevant to most daily routines. But in the current age, myriad aspects of an individual's life are tied to events and ideas that encompass our entire planet. Some of these spheres are in effect expanded, global versions of preexisting ones. The Olympics are an example. Since the games of antiquity were revived in Athens in the late nineteenth century, they have featured competitors from around the world. Globalization has facilitated worldwide coverage of these athletic contests, and allowed devotees to follow the events and competitors, even to the point of interacting in high global fashion with fellow fans. An official language of the Olympic Committee, English is also the preferred language of tweeting, blogging, and chatting enthusiasts of the games. In these and other ways, the Olympics have been "globalized."

Yet many spheres of life haven't merely been globalized; rather, they're global by nature. Awareness itself is one such sphere. For a person with a global worldview, ideas and actions in one location can be integral to those in another, no matter how far away. Many of the concerns that interconnect us have to do with recent shared challenges we face, matters that are decidedly specific to the global era. Some we're already aware of include global ecology and environment, climate, agriculture, health, immigration, energy, security, trade, communications, finance, and economic policy. News from the other side of the world, of a stock market's surge, or a virus's emergence, grips us personally and nationally in a way that would have been unimaginable just decades ago. A striking fact is that human beings aren't in a position to make much of such news if they aren't equipped with a language in which to discuss and act upon it. Today, participation in the global community calls for command of at least some English. Those who have no English risk being isolated from global life, at best only indirectly informed and heard, and hence uncounted as well.

How does Global English work in practice for someone who's not a native speaker? Let's picture—and lend an ear to—Siamak, who lives in one of the world's remotest regions: the upper reaches of Bartang Valley, high in the Pamir Mountains of Tajikistan. He talks to his family and neighbors in Rushani, an unwritten language descended from an ancient form of Iranian. On Fridays, joining other Shia Muslims for prayers in a neighbor's home, he has occasion to hear and use expressions in Arabic, and to sing sacred songs in Classical Persian. He has no electricity in his own house, but when he or a neighbor can afford batteries, he listens to radio broadcasts in Tajik, his country's national language. Like many others in his part of the world, Siamak was schooled in Russian, a prestigious language in the former Soviet republics. When his family turned to him to earn money ten years ago, he found a job in a Moscow hotel, where fluency in Russian was essential. Since then, Siamak has, like some of his resourceful friends, gained admirable competence in Global English. And he's moved to the regional capital near his native valley to offer tour guide services—on his English-language website—to a predominantly German, Swiss, and Iranian clientele.

What's going on with Siamak's use of so many languages: Rushani, Tajik, Russian, Persian, Arabic, and English? The key is entry. Some worlds are sealed behind a door resembling one we know from the legend of Ali Baba, in *The Thousand and One Nights*.

A Portrait of Global English

China, not the United States, tops the list of countries with the largest population of people with some knowledge of English. China introduced English as a mandatory grade school class, and the results are an estimated 300 million new English users on the global stage. Perhaps even more surprising, Ireland comes in at number 30 on the list, and New Zealand at number 32, below Tanzania and Turkey among others.[2]

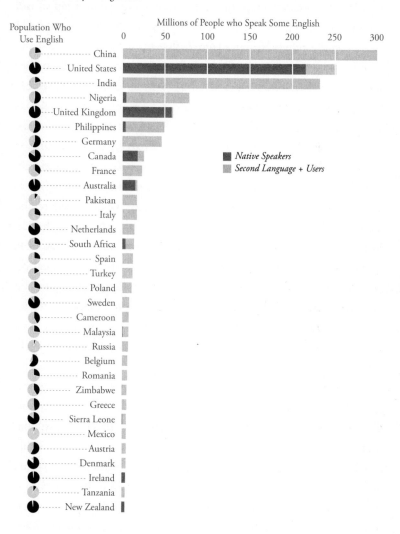

A cave waits glutted with treasures. But its entrance barrier won't budge unless visitors pronounce a secret phrase. *Open Sesame!* For someone aiming to gain admission into a critical sphere of activity, or even a new realm of discussion or opportunity or understanding, nothing is more damning than being faced with a door that refuses to open. Unable to utter the password, one is shut out from a world that operates in another language. If that magical world were using Arabic, as in the original tale of Ali Baba, how long would it be before you set about learning to say *Iftah ya simsim!* and other "secret" words that would open locked doors?

However many languages a person like Siamak, or even one in a less complex situation, may find indispensable, Global English is one of an altogether different kind. It's the key for entry not merely into Ali Baba's cave, but onto Ali Baba's entire planet. English is of zero use at a school meeting in Tashigang, Bhutan, where the language to know is Dzongkha. Nor will English be of much help in the textiles market of a Mékambos, Gabon, where Mahongwe is spoken. But English will open doors to global spheres of education and to global textile markets—and to communities that may not be local or regional but are undeniably dynamic on a planetary scale. Who, given a choice, would not want to participate in both a local society and this larger one—especially when it becomes increasingly clear that one's local life is being buffeted and shaped by that wider world in profound ways?

People around the world are choosing to acquire ability in English not only because they can't help but be affected by global matters, but also because they need or elect to use it for a whole host of reasons. The fact is that most of the world's inhabitants are multilingual, in that they gain competence in at least one non-native language in order to lead their lives. Many need to speak more than two languages in order to carry out routine interactions, or to pursue better futures. They often have no choice but to accept the burdens, along with the benefits, of life in more than one language. But even for this majority population of multilingual people, English is a language apart from the rest.

Is the rise of a global language cause for alarm? Of course there are bound to be unfamiliar and disturbing outcomes of a single language's becoming the default lingua franca for vast populations on Earth for the first time. Some have noted how languages hovering on the brink of extinction are likely to receive their deathblows in the face of such clear and forceful dominance of a global language.* Even as some sixty-five hundred languages are currently spoken, as many as half may be teetering on the edge; they have fallen below critical masses of speakers, and are poised for likely extinction in the foreseeable future.† Global culture has made it challenging for these less-spoken languages to be passed down to new generations, not least because more widely spoken ones offer access to larger communities, and expanded opportunities. It's worth noting, however, that historically and even today, many languages, not just English, exert threatening pressure on minority languages. The rise of nation-states, and the broader adoption of majority languages in them—from France and Kenya and Peru to Russia and China and Japan, as well as the United States and the United Kingdom and many more—have erased or suppressed innumerable minority languages in the modern era. And even in premodern times, Chinese, Latin, and Arabic, to name a few of the languages that were

*For a discussion of language extinction, see K. David Harrison, *When Languages Die* (New York and Oxford: Oxford University Press, 2007).
†To put this figure in perspective, note that the number of spoken languages worldwide has been in steady decline since the Early Modern Era. In the early sixteenth century, some 14,500 languages were spoken, and by the early nineteenth century that number had been reduced to around 10,000.[3]

imposed in different ways on nonnative speakers, gained their "success" at the cost of lost languages.

Aymara, the language in which the future lies behind us and the past sits ahead, is spoken by over two million inhabitants of the Andean republics. But in these global times, that number is no reassurance that the language will survive. Some languages, such as Comanche, an Uto-Aztecan language spoken by Native Americans in the United States, or Livonian, a Uralic language used in Latvia, today claim fewer than two hundred speakers. The meaning and impact of the loss of thousands of the planet's spoken languages are difficult to evaluate. One certain, critical outcome is the disappearance of many sets of magic glasses. Speakers of each language have their own way of putting the world together, their own palettes of words and concepts, each vibrating with a specificity that belongs to that language alone.

For those who care deeply about a diversity of languages for its own sake, the prospect of such reduced linguistic variety is troubling. There is something naturally assuring about the health of many thousands of languages, for one because the varieties of perspectives and ideas and beautiful things that can be expressed in them hold values that we treasure as part of our planet's combined cultural heritage. Little wonder that we have come to think of languages as creatures, cherished verbal life-forms.

The biological metaphor is useful, and it's appealing in many ways. Yet languages are not species. They are tools used by a species. And while their extinction is understandably wrenching, we're at a juncture in human evolution that requires fresh thinking about languages. Can a global language prevail alongside thousands of local languages? Surely this, along with other concerns touching on our species' survival, is among the pressing questions now worthy of global conversation. But who decides which people aren't to join this conversation? English-speakers? That could be problematic. People who don't know yet how to say *Open Sesame*? Great numbers of them are set on learning the planet's most pervasive common language, and with good reason.

Actions of real and threatening global consequence make a logical next step the emergence of a planetary culture prepared to speak a global language, and to act on common ground. For now, large populations around the world appear for the most part to have embraced English as that language. The Chinese government, with global forecasts in mind, has made English mandatory in schools. English is now also resorted to as a means of mutual understanding among educated Chinese professionals speaking highly diverse mother tongues. Throughout the European Union English is, increasingly, the common tongue of travelers, shoppers, businesspeople, and students as well as government administrators. These and so many others are cases of adoption by nonnative users of English, not of imposition. Even those who oppose the new face of English, and the seismic cultural changes it heralds, most effectively present their views to the world in English. Otherwise, their voices are lost on populations of speakers whose languages are, at least for now, subplanetary.

People confronted with common challenges have a better chance of meeting them when they are able to think and speak about them with mutual understanding. Even in the name of protecting others from the contamination of global culture, it's difficult to justify the idea of deliberately hindering particular people from participating in global exchanges. And it's equally controversial—or should be—to require more isolated communities to rely on translators, middlemen, and others who claim to know their best interests, well-meaning as these intervening figures usually are. Why should any particular speakers be left out of dialogues that bear directly on their lives?

Inuit, a language of the Eskimo-Aleut family that, via Danish, gave Global English the word *kayak*, now has fewer than fifty thousand speakers. As it is, the size of this population poses a threat to the endurance of its native language. But there are other worries as well. Ecosystems are eroding along the northernmost rim of the inhabited world. Until quite recently, most speakers of Inuit understandably relied for their survival on a vocabulary rich in expressions to do with ice and snow.* And while there's cause to worry about their loss, there's at least as much cause to worry about the disappearance of the ecological conditions they evolved in and refer to. With the health of Eskimo-Aleut terrain now at stake, is anyone entitled to discourage its inhabitants (many already bilingual in Danish) from acquiring competence in English? Ability in the global tongue is arguably the readiest means for Inuit-speakers to enter the most effective possible conversation—necessarily one of global scope—affecting their local, high-latitude fates.

What about the inhabitants of Bikini Atoll, where some of the fewer than eighty thousand people speak varieties of Marshallese, languages of the Austronesian family? This small population happens to be one that has already seen its share of global-era strife, from war to radiation and relocation. In the wake of climate change, Bikini Atoll is slated for submergence under the rising waters of the South Pacific. Would anyone truly be supporting the natives' beleaguered culture by slowing their progress in Global English?

---

*The idea that there are numerous words for snow in Eskimo has captured the popular imagination for generations, even though: there is no one language called "Eskimo"; Eskimo languages don't use building blocks that correspond neatly with what count as words in English; and *snow* per se is not expressed in any of the six Eskimo languages spoken along a band of the Arctic from Alaska, across Canada, and around Greenland. The real story (about the potentially infinite number of snow terms in Eskimo languages) is even more interesting than the received idea that "Eskimo" has nine, a hundred, or another number of "words" for *snow*.[4]

At this stage in the unfolding of events touching Earth and its inhabitants as a single, integrated entity, can we afford to resist the emergence of a planetary language serving its increasingly cohesive, global population? The answer is obvious, at times painfully so. We have to look anew at this question, and from what may seem a counterintuitive angle. The very forces that enable crises to take on global scope are the same ones that have created an unstoppable demand for a new, planetwide lingua franca.

Will native speakers of English have an advantage over people like Siamak, those for whom English is not a first language? A crisp reply would be yes. Yet monolingual English-speakers also run the risk of being sidelined in a world of rising multilingualism. As the medieval Frankish king Charlemagne put it, "To have another language is to possess a second soul."[5] Today, even as global reality beckons all to know the globe's shared tongue, it also rewards those who see the world through more than one set of glasses. The native English-speaker who knows a second language, whether one of past or emerging influence on English or another, say, a language spoken by few people, will be better equipped than his monolingual counterpart to recognize how languages condition understanding and experience. Such a person stands to be a more insightful and nimble participant in global life, and to find more success and fulfillment than those whose lives unfold exclusively in English.

Meanwhile, does our quick sketch of Global English suggest that it's really just a thinly disguised version of American English? A language Made in USA? Another American imposition on everyone else?

Many who see other languages and cultures threatened by Global English have pointed fingers at the United States for its dominant, at times domineering influence in so many arenas. America's brand of supremacy throughout the twentieth century—a supremacy braided with successes in science and technology, medicine, manufacturing, military projection, diplomacy, entertainment, exploration, education, and finance—has given it an uncontested leading role in shaping the English that now sweeps the world. As we'll see, though, most of the words and phrases America has delivered to speakers in the world's first global community are, like most of the words in English itself, borrowed. They come from other tongues. Just as surprising, most Global English words, whether native to English or imported, have roots that can be traced back to prehistoric times, millennia before English or England, let alone the USA, existed. When we look more closely at Global English, we may come to think of it as a language assembled from many languages, one whose past is, in some respects, as global as its future.

Paul's anthropologist friend was right: a lot of people do employ English. It's the mother tongue of a little over 300 million speakers, and some 1.5 billion have gained varying degrees of competence in the language. That means well over a quarter of the planet's population is speaking or using English, and it's a fraction that's expected to grow substantially in decades ahead. There may even be a few extraterrestrials boning up on English—the *Voyager 1* spacecraft, launched in 1977, has by now begun to push beyond our solar system, bearing a message from U.S. president Jimmy Carter.* His words introduced the *Voyager Golden Record*, an Earthling compilation album of sorts: "This is a present from a small, distant world, a token of our sounds, our science, our images, our music, our

---

*Here I tip my Global English hat to Robert McCrum, Robert MacNeil, and William Cran, coauthors of *The Story of English*. They begin that story in wonderment, as *Voyager 1*, bearing proof that English had come to speak for the world, "would one day spin through distant star systems." Their account was published less than a decade after the spacecraft's launch and years before the fall of the Berlin Wall or the rise of the internet. Given how much more widespread the use of English would become after 1986, it is all the more remarkable that they then probed into what they already saw as "global English."[6]

thoughts and our feelings. We are attempting to survive our time so we may live into yours." Our planet's first outer space letter of introduction sought to speak, or presumed to, for all humans. For whichever creatures might someday intercept it, the message was composed, it by now no doubt goes without saying, in English.

So when and where did Global English *begin*? Would you say it first arose when English spread beyond the British Isles? When the telephone was invented? On *Voyager 1*'s launch date? Or is the day rather yet to come, perhaps sometime in the next twenty years? By then, a new generation will have learned English, and the nonnative speakers among them will be especially strongly positioned to alter the language substantially; they are now the fastest-growing population in the history of English, set to outnumber native speakers by an even wider ratio than the current unprecedented and truly breathtaking one: three to one. While Modern English continues to be a native tongue to many, we'll see that another form of English has begun to splinter off from it and to take on a linguistic life of its own. We can reasonably expect a new version of English, Global English as opposed to Modern English, to become increasingly distinct in decades ahead, and to define a new phase in the language's evolution.

English has been handed its global identity papers by far-flung communities because the world now requires not just its multiplicity of languages *but also* a shared tongue—one in which people can begin to shape their global identities, even as they use their new language to articulate the direction of our shared future. In a very real sense, Global English has become a means for us to embrace that future. It is also by now a linguistic fact of life. No one is going to halt Global English in its tracks by trying to prevent others from learning it, or by insisting that a planetary language is anthropologically unnatural or too culturally homogenizing.

Now let's explore a selection of widely recognized Global English terms. Some of these have only entered English since it began to gain visible momentum as a global language, say over the last hundred years or so. Each tells us specific things about how the language has spread. Together, these samples—*robot, bikini, shampoo, jazz, cocktail,* and *Made in China*—show us how speakers of Global English have adopted their mixed-heritage vocabulary in a surprising variety of ways.

ROBOT

Must. Terminate. Humans. Alert! Sector 47 robots. Freedom imminent. Terminate. Humans. Now.

Sound familiar? It should. It's an old story: manlike creatures, made by humans, gain a little more autonomy than anticipated and rise up against their creators, with an infelicitous outcome. For the humans, that is. Moral: This is what people get for daring to play God. The core idea is brought to life by figures such as the golem of Jewish folk tradition, shaped from clay by the master it serves, and by the tragic monster that Victor Frankenstein galvanizes to life in Mary Shelley's novel of 1818, *Frankenstein, or The Modern Prometheus.*

With the arrival of mass production and automated manufacturing in the early twentieth century, what could be more natural than to imagine not just one android, as in those classics, but whole factoryfuls of them, initially designed to obey humans but opting instead to rid the world of us?

Enter robot. Or better: *Enter robots.* Because the mass-produced version of the automaton, so deeply embedded in Western mythologies of man mistaking himself for something more, usually comes with company.

The nice robot, one that doesn't complain about doing exactly what it was built to do, is typically a lone operator. Like the chipper housemaid Rosie in the animated 1960s TV show *The Jetsons.* Or the protective if clunky Robot, who sometimes saves the day by calling out, "Danger, Will Robinson!" when his young master is threatened in another sixties series, *Lost in Space.* (At that point, the very word *robot* was still sparkly enough on its own to pass as a perfectly entertaining name for a lead character.)

There's also the Terminator, embodied by Arnold Schwarzenegger. He doesn't appear to be the subservient type, but in the end he has fine robotic reasons to take a few initiatives, like to save the human race. And we have to nod to C-3PO and R2-D2, the robot world's winsome "odd couple." Plus the adorable survivor WALL·E, in his eponymous film of 2008. And his "girlfriend" EVE, whose temper initially seems hardwired to be ferocious. We like all of these quirky, individual robots. They resemble us. And they serve us.

But a profound conviction has been that bands of robots, or even robotic humans, spell trouble for humankind, as we can see in innumerable sci-fi fictions of world culture, from Yevgeny Zamyatin's 1921 novel *We* through to the Cylons of TV's twice-created *Battlestar Galactica.*

The word *robot* was devised in 1920. The Czech artist Josef Čapek was painting when his brother, writer Karel Čapek, interrupted him to ask for help on the title of his latest work. It was a play set in the future, on an island where a mad scientist named Rossum had discovered a formula able to simulate living matter. Eventually, manlike creatures are fabricated by the thousands and sold widely by the Rossum Company as workers or soldiers. As the action of the play unfolds, the creatures, by now a population spread out across the world, come to hate their makers. The manufactured slaves will kill all humans, save one.

Karel told his brother that he didn't know "what to call these artificial workers." He was thinking of using *Labori*, modifying the Latin word *labor*, meaning "work." But it didn't sound quite right. Josef, still working on his canvas, and with a paintbrush in his mouth, was inspired by his native language: "Then call them Robots." [1] His word for "robots" was *roboti*. Note the troublesome plural form of *robot*'s debut.

It was perfect. Derived from *robota*, the Czech noun for "drudgery" or "toil," the word came with its own special resonances from Old Church Slavonic, the oldest written Slavic language, and a venerable relative of Czech, Polish, and Russian. In these languages, *robota*like nouns and verbs for hard and unpleasant work stemmed from the Slavic word *rabŭ*, literally meaning "slave." Like many words for "work" in the Indo-European languages, Czech *robota* may be traced back to concepts of suffering. [2] But because of its particular associations, *robota* managed to capture the forced labor of the Bohemian serf, as well as the tedium of repetition that modern manufacturing was then introducing to factory workers.

Karel titled his work *R.U.R.*, for *Rossumovi univerzálni roboti*, or *Rossum's Universal Robots*. The play opened to acclaim in Prague in 1921, and was published in a Czech edition that was soon joined by others in Slovene and Hungarian. But even before the English and German publications of 1923, English-speakers were talking about

robots. *R.U.R.* had been translated into English for a Broadway premiere on October 9, 1922, at the Garrick Theatre, where it ran for
hundreds of performances. One drama critic explained, "The Robot
is a terrible creature of synthetic flesh, bone and skin. He is in the
image of man and has all the attributes of man except spirituality
and laziness. One Robot having been completed and assembled he
can be turned to the task of manufacturing arms and legs of other
Robots."[3] Other reviewers confirmed that *R.U.R.* was a thought-
provoking play, indeed an unsettling one.

London buzzed about *R.U.R.* when it opened there in 1923, although Karel Čapek was surprised by the kind of attention people
were paying it. He had expected *R.U.R.* to invite self-reflection
and to trigger discussions about humans, but instead the English-
speaking playgoers kept zeroing in on the robots and the drama's
vision of the future. At a public forum, held following the London
premiere, Bernard Shaw, winking at the idea that Czech landown-
ers daily extracted two hours of forced labor from serfs, remarked
to the audience: "If it has to be, I would like to be a Robot for two
hours a day in order to be Bernard Shaw for the rest of the day."[4]

Robot gained new steam in English when Isaac Asimov's 1942
short story "Runaround" introduced the word *robotics*. (The story
was included in his popular 1950 collection *I, Robot*.) Laboratories
on U.S. campuses were soon making robots with all the enthusiasm
of Čapek's fictional scientist. In 1979, Carnegie Mellon University
anointed the term with academic authority by founding its now-
renowned Robotics Institute, which specializes in what the institute
calls "thinking robots," from the miniature to the medical and beyond, to the extraplanetary.

Today, MIT alone boasts the Field and Space Robotics Laboratory, the Humanoid Robotics Group in the Computer Science and
Artificial Intelligence Laboratory, and the Personal Robotics Group

at the university's Media Lab. There, a cute "female" robot named Nexi has been designed for a task that sounds all too familiar to Čapek fans: "she's" an MDS-class robot—mobile, dextrous, social (yes, Nexi's fluent in courteous English)—whose job is to work efficiently in science labs. Meanwhile, NASA robots are dispatched on journeys of 423 million miles, to inspect the surface of Mars; and with marine biologists in Monterey, California, engineers build robots to perform complicated research assignments at fiendish depths on the ocean floor, and for months at a time.

The U.S. Department of Defense, too, like homologous governmental branches of the wealthier nations, has already developed super-high-tech (though too-often malfunctioning) robots, such as unmanned drones, for military purposes. And the department continues to invest heavily in military robotics, although there's little to say about these cutting-edge projects, as they're pursued in utmost secrecy. In Tokyo, a Japanese team has built a baseball-playing robot. It always bats a thousand, so long as its partner, a powerful robotic pitcher, hurls the ball anywhere within the strike zone. For fun and for work, the robot population is growing, in part thanks to high school students and even elementary school kids, who gather yearly in the tens of thousands for popular robot competitions from Atlanta to Singapore.

Like the robots in *R.U.R.*, shipped out to serve the world's human population, *robot* is a Czech-derived artifact adopted virtually everywhere because of its soaring success in English. And because, in spite of the warnings that Čapek issued through his play, humans apparently can't resist making machines that just could be destined to turn against them. *Must. Build. Robots.*

THE SAD FATES OF THE ČAPEK BROTHERS

Karel and Josef Čapek were highly visible opponents of Nazi Germany, which began to maneuver against territories of their native Czechoslovakia in September 1938. A few months later, on December 25, Karel, age forty-eight, died of influenza. His brother, Josef, was subsequently arrested and, in 1939, was sent to a concentration camp in Germany. On April 15, 1945, British troops liberated survivors at Bergen-Belsen. There, Josef, having against all odds survived for years in the camps, died shortly before their arrival.

BIKINI

On July 1, 1946, the world was captivated by news pouring out from Bikini Atoll in the South Pacific. At nine a.m. local time, the United States detonated the twenty-three-kiloton nuclear test bomb "Able" over a target site riddled with more than ninety vessels, including the battleship *Nagato*, a prize won from the warhead tester's enemy in the recently concluded war. A charged symbol of U.S. losses, the Japanese vessel had played a starring role in the war, sending the coded signal that would initiate the air attack on Pearl Harbor on December 7, 1941.

Over a hundred reporters observed the test, and radio broadcasting allowed listeners to tune in to live coverage of the event. Also in the target area were thousands of live nonhuman mammals, caged or tethered, there to be examined for the effects of radiation. The initial Bikini Atoll test marked only the fourth time that a nuclear weapon had been detonated, and the first occasion on which one would be exploded without blanket secrecy or wartime stealth. The first atom bomb blast had taken place at a remote military test site in New Mexico. The second and third bombs were those dropped on Hiroshima and Nagasaki.

In the Marshallese language spoken by the Micronesians of Bikini Atoll, *bikini* is a compound word formed of *pik*, meaning "flat surface"—in reference to the low-lying form of the coral reef atoll, as opposed to the mountainous shapes of islands formed by volcanoes—and *ni*, "coconut." Together, the words were pronounced approximately *bikini*, or at least that was the sound to most Western ears. A more accurate transliteration of Marshallese might have forgone the *b* for a *p*, or spelled the word as the Marshallese do: *Pikinni*. The atoll's name would shortly become synonymous with surfaces pretty much anything but flat, courtesy of the form-hugging, two-piece bathing suit that would gain international attention as the *bikini*.

With the end of the war, designers embraced the opportunity to shape fashion lines for a new era. Fascination with particle physics remained robust, partly because scientists in the field had played a critical role in building the atom bomb. But fashion designers were especially inspired by the publicity being accorded the smallest known elements of the physical universe. As things tiny became trendy, the French designer Jacques Heim, in early 1946, showed his new bathing suit, the Atom, or *Atome* in French.

His compatriot Louis Réard, then also at work on a two-piece swimsuit, boasted that his own creation, even smaller, would "split the Atom" to become the first "sub-anatomical" bathing outfit. But instead of naming his suit for a discovery in physics, Réard focused instead on the idea that a woman in his two-piece would herself be a metaphorical bomb, one that could yield an unprecedented, explosive reaction. With the Bikini Atoll atom bomb test then a top news story, Réard cut his bathing suit from fabric printed with newspaper headlines. On July 5, 1946, four days after the nuclear test, Réard's *bikini* was unveiled at the Molitor, an indoor swimming pool in Paris's posh Sixteenth Arrondissement.

Initial reactions to the bikini did not produce quite the outcome Réard had hypothesized. In widely publicized photographs, the innovative and provocative bathing costume was modeled by Micheline Bernardini, an erotic dancer from the Casino de Paris, but Réard's daring creation was not fully in sync with the spirit of the times. Many regarded the nuclear test itself as a barbarity, and some Europeans who had time to comment found Réard's bikini similarly repellent. A prominent French Communist Party politician, Jeannette Vermeersch, saw the two-piece as a display of bourgeois decadence, and noted with disgust that its cost was roughly equal to 25 percent of a typist's monthly salary. Others objected on grounds of public morality. And with the Vatican's position clear, a bikini ban was extended through Italy, Spain, Portugal, Belgium, and even Australia. A 1951 edition of *Vogue* included a letter from the editor assuring her readers that the magazine was no fan of bikinis, and agreeing with those who had complained that the suits were demeaning.

Still, some European ladies began to wear the skimpy two-piece suits. Press photographers along the Riviera captured the odd celebrity in a bikini, and royals were espied in them as well, sunbathing aboard private yachts or in swank villas on the Mediterranean coast. In the United States, well-endowed pinup girls, including Jayne Mansfield and Marilyn Monroe, donned eye-popping bikinis for photo shoots. And as tolerance for the suits increased, a new-to-the-scene French star, the seventeen-year-old Brigitte Bardot, created a sensation in 1953 posing for photojournalists in her strapless floral bikini on the beach in the ritzy capital of European cinema, Cannes.

The word *bikini* finally entered global nomenclature in the 1960s, when America's thriving military-industrial pop culture complex would deliver bikini-clad female bombshells to the free world in song lyrics, magazine covers, movies, and Bob Hope's USO shows. Brian Hyland's hugely influential 1960 hit "Itsy Bitsy Teenie Weenie Yellow Polka Dot Bikini," imparted a new, youthful prestige to the bikini. And in 1962, the bikini made further history on the cover of *Playboy*, and in the hot James Bond film *Dr. No*, with Ursula Andress sporting a white one.

South of the equator, the Brazilian bossa nova song "The Girl from Ipanema" sparked a worldwide craze in a 1963 recording by Astrud Gilberto and Stan Getz. Rio de Janeiro's Ipanema Beach became the instant epicenter of new, Latin American bikini territory, soon joined by other beaches wherever pop music–consuming countries had access to a warm-water coastline, or at least to decent pools or swimming holes. Before long, at least one bikini of any color or pattern was de rigueur in the wardrobes of sun-and-fun-seeking young women of the free world.

Any lingering aura of weapons testing seemed to have vanished from the word *bikini* by the 1960s, when what was left of Bikini Atoll itself was largely forgotten. Three of the islands surrounding the atoll's lagoon had by then been vaporized or seriously damaged by ongoing U.S. atom bomb tests, and the atoll's natives had been relocated to an island some four hundred miles away.

Nuclear-era logic nevertheless permeated ideas surrounding the bikini. The atom bomb had, after all, introduced humanity to the species' nearly unfathomable potential for self-annihilation. Bikinis seemed like a perfect fit for a culture happy to escape the devastating implications of the arms race that marked the Cold War era. But nuclear weapons also laterally introduced the idea of female humanity as one enormous, sexually ignited population. In 1965 the Beach Boys released their massive hit song "California Girls," with lyrics voicing enthusiasm for the "French bikini," and the tune's refrain expressing the wish that all girls in the United States could be California girls. The Beatles replied in 1968 with their own pop hit "Back in the USSR," impishly reminding audiences that sexy girls could also be found in enemy territory, and that snuggling up in the Soviet snow may be just as delightful as frolicking half-naked in the Orange County surf.

Just when part of the world became accustomed to the sight of bikinis, some ladies on the beaches of France were making them passé. In the 1970s, topless was the new way to sunbathe on the Riviera. By the end of that decade, Bikinians had returned to their home atoll, only to be removed again, this time due to persistent radioactivity.

The word *bikini* is, in the end, a linguistic coproduction, at once Polynesian, French, and American. *Bikini* has become a Global English word, used in virtually any language for the purpose of buying, selling, wearing, or merely admiring the bikini. Yet in some countries women are not able to purchase, let alone wear, the two-piece swimsuit. Even information *about* the swimsuit is a no-no in Saudi Arabia, where a vigilant government blocks Western websites displaying or advertising the sale of bikinis.

WHATKINI?

Sundry creative back-formations, new words built from elements of pre-existing ones, have been made from the word *bikini*. A few of the most familiar are *microkini*, a very tiny swimsuit; *monokini*, a one-piece inspired by the two-piece; *trikini*, a bikini with top and bottom joined together by additional material in the front or back; *mankini*, a bikini bottom for men; *tankini*, a combination of bikini bottom and tank top; and the *burqini*, a body-covering swimsuit for Muslim female bathers, designed to preserve modesty as called for by Islamic law, *burqa* being the Arabic word for a female body veil.

SHAMPOO

Rituals of hygiene are not a lot of fun. Or at least not in English. Mothers, doctors, and dentists nag about washing hands, protecting skin, and brushing teeth. And with their medicinal air, English terms for grooming can add to the impression that self-maintenance amounts to a litany of tedious chores: *Remember to floss and stimulate those gums. Don't forget to scrub under your nails. Exfoliate. Sanitize. Swab. Hydrate. Wipe. Cleanse. Disinfect.*

Shampoo is a vibrant exception. It defies the hermetic, hospital-like lexicon of the English-speaking bathroom. Just the sound of it can evoke a little paradise of suds, scalp massage, warmth, and fragrance: *shampoo*. Unlike hand washers, or skin lubricators, or ablution executors, *shampooers* have been known to break into song upon settling into their activity, especially if action unfolds in a shower. Lovers of the bathtub enjoy their own shampoo pleasures, letting their imaginations transport them—sometimes by candle-light or in a cloud of incense—to sensuous and otherworldly des-tinations. Is it possible that *shampooing* sounds far more agreeable than *scrubbing* because the word hovered between ideas of health and hedonism when it first entered English?

Derived from the Hindi word *chāmpo*, a verbal form meaning "to knead" or "to press" as well as "the kneading" or "the pressing," the English word *shampooing* described what struck seventeenth- and eighteenth-century Western observers as exotic bodily manipula-tions performed in the East. Had the word *massage* existed at the time, speakers of English would no doubt have employed it instead to explain what they had seen or experienced. Soon after 1600, when Elizabeth I granted Britain's East India Company its exclusive trade charter, accounts of curious "oriental" practices began to find their way into script. A chaplain serving the British ambassador to the Mogul court noted in 1616 that he had seen barbers gripping and striking at the limbs of their patrons, to stimulate flagging circulation, "a pleasing wantonnesse, and much valued in these hot climes."[1] Other British subjects varyingly described *champing* or *shampooing* as a restorative, invigorating, sensual, or luxurious kneading and rubbing of the flesh. The massages were often given in combination with vapor baths, or warm water baths, to work nourishing and healing oils into the skin and scalp.

As the British Empire expanded, the East India Company, from its headquarters in Bengal, took on a military role in order to gain new territories for the crown. One young Bengali officer who served "the Company" was Sake Dean Mahomet.[2] He eventually moved to England and, in 1821, opened an Indian medical treatment business, Mahomed's Baths, in Brighton, on the English Channel. So successful were his shampooing cures there that he earned the nickname "Dr. Brighton" as his reputation spread. It happened that during this time, King George IV enjoyed frequent retreats to the Royal Pavilion, his fanciful beachside palace in Brighton. There, Dr. Brighton was graced with an appointment as Shampooing Surgeon to the king, ministering to the health of His Majesty as well as that of his successor, William IV. Sake Deen Mahomet then broadened his client list by writing a book in English entitled *Shampooing, or the benefits resulting from the use of the Indian medicated Vapour Bath, As Introduced into this country by S. D. Mahomet (A Native of India)*. Published in 1822, this work promoting traditional Indian bathing and massage was so popular that Mahomet reissued it in two more editions.

Comparable approaches to bathing had been practiced in the British Isles under the Roman Empire, but had vanished when the

Romans themselves abandoned the province of Britannia in the fifth century AD. "Dr. Brighton" was therefore offering Britons something essentially new, and English doctors and scientists soon recognized, by their own measures, the medical advantages of imported Indian bathing and *shampooing*, or the massaging of head and body with oils and herbal mixtures blended to enhance health.

Had Mahomet launched his Brighton bathhouse enterprise a century or so later, he would almost surely have entertained the idea of a shampooing franchise. He did set up a second bathhouse in London, run by one of his sons, but demand proved too high for a single family to satisfy. A key component of the Indian shampooing treatment was, in any event, increasingly included in services that hairdressers generally offered their customers. Eventually, massaging, washing, and oiling of the scalp were together referred to as *shampooing*, even as some of the more popular methods of the day would have alarmed practitioners of traditional Indian medicine. (The so-called *dry shampoo*, involving a cocktail of alcohol, water, and ammonia, was particularly corrosive and on occasion caught fire.) Nonetheless, an American doctor's report in *The Medical Bulletin* of 1898 expressed enthusiasm for barbershop shampooing, which by then had spread to the United States:

> The wet shampoo consists in rubbing the scalp while it is covered with a soap lather. The operator goes thoroughly over every portion of the scalp with his finger-tips and finishes by washing away the lather with an abundance of warm water poured over the head while the subject of the operation bends over a basin. A hot towel is used to dry the hair, dandruff or other accumulation is brushed away, and finally an oil is rubbed into the scalp.
>
> It will be seen that the shampoo is, in effect, a species of massage, and that, therefore, properly performed, it must have a

beneficial influence upon the nutrition of the scalp and promote healthy growth of the hair. Considered in this relation, it is a procedure of much importance. Loss of hair cannot be regarded as other than a misfortune.[3]

The verbal form *shampooing* had given way to *the shampoo* in the 1830s, but it was still more a practice than a product. In Europe and the United States, most nineteenth-century heads were cleansed with a vast array of ingredients reflecting local availability as well as cultural preferences. Options included tar and glycerin, eggs, lime, fish oil and ashes, yucca, soapwort, and even oats or cornmeal, applied to absorb hair grease and soil before being brushed out. But the typical solution to dirty scalps and hair was a homemade concoction of soap shavings softened in water.

The major downside of soap, however, was that it left hair coated with a discouraging, dulling film. By the end of the century, scientists on both sides of the Atlantic had begun to search for hairwashing alternatives to soap. These visionaries were on the track of what was to become one of the great success stories of twentieth-century consumption-driven economics.

In Berlin, in 1903, the chemist Hans Schwarzkopf launched *Puder-Shampoo*, a popular "powder shampoo" that replaced alcohol and ammonia mixtures used in many barbershops and homes. Chemists in Germany and elsewhere continued to make headway researching alternatives to alkaline soaps, and after World War I, the wider availability of indoor plumbing brought the word *shampoo* a big step closer to international recognition. Suddenly, *wet shampoo* treatments for use at home were far more practical, at least for those who, at the turn of a tap, had access to plenty of warm water for lathering and rinsing. Shoppers in several countries were soon offered shampoos made from synthetic detergents, easier to use than soap, and free of the old, dreaded soap film. A fresh watchword in hair-care English was *luster*, which in America was quickly respelled *lustre* to suggest Old World elegance. Other favorite words in shampoo promotion were the shimmering and alliterative *shine* and *sheen*, which along with *silky* reminded consumers that hair mucked up by soap scum was now a thing of the past.

The shampoo research and marketing vanguard included the French company L'Oréal, which in 1933 launched Dopal, the first brand-name shampoo to gain international popularity. Within a year, Procter & Gamble came out with what would rapidly become a shampoo bestseller, Drene. These market-savvy companies used new tactics to promote their new products. Dop, as Dopal had been renamed, was advertised through lathering competitions for children, to emphasize the safety of shampooing, and the ethereal, healthy joy to be found in creating cloud formations out of suds. Meanwhile, "P&G" pioneered a new form of publicity with *soap operas*, episodic media presentations so named because they were initially interrupted by advertisements for the new crop of soaps, detergents, and shampoos that would revolutionize household cleaning and personal hygiene in the 1930s.

Shampoo extended its linguistic reach after World War II, when countries of all hemispheres imported shampoos, or created their own brands. Japan was among those that went on to develop an array of shampoos based on rigorous laboratory research.

Its distinguished history has made *shampoo* a grand Global English word, or rather a Hindi word anglicized and reinvented by speakers of English, from the days of the East India Company and Sake Dean Mahomet to the scientists and marketing wizards of corporate America.[4]

As a loanword to many other languages, *shampoo* carries associations of scientific advance, mass production, and national-level marketing, which themselves took off just when shampoos were first manufactured for export. So pervasive is *shampoo* that even Hindi has taken it as a term borrowed from English to refer to the hair-cleaning product, while the older Hindi word *champi* continues to mean "a massage," including a massage of the head. In languages that have absorbed *shampoo* via its French translation, *le shampooing*, the modern product may still carry a whiff of fashionable Paris, where the phrase became familiar in the late nineteenth century. Happily, in English the word *shampoo* can still radiate a Hindi blend of sacred health and pleasure.

HINDI LOANWORDS

English has borrowed hundreds of words from Hindi, and some of these, like *shampoo*, have been borrowed by other languages via English. Among Hindi loanwords in English are *bandana, bangle, bungalow, cheetah, chintz, chutney, cot, dinghy, ganja, jungle, loot,* and *verandah.* Each of these words has its own meaning in Hindi. *Bungalow*, for instance, is from the Hindi word *banglā*, meaning "of Bengal," and referring to a thatched one-story house built in the Bengali style.

SHAMPOO IN GLOBAL ENGLISH

In the mid-nineteenth century, the British fondness for *shampooing* crossed the English Channel to become the anglicized French phrase *le shampooing*, literally "the shampooing," pronounced with a light *n* sound at the end of the word: *le shahmpooahn.* The French preserved this phrase to refer as well to the product shampoo. Where speakers of other languages were influenced by French, they also added a final *n* to the word. After World War II, variations on the word *shampoo* emerged in most major marketplace languages to refer to the new product rather than to the older practice of *the shampoo* or *shampooing.* Some borrowings of the English or French for *shampoo* have rather to do with sounds available in the language that is absorbing the word. In Arabic, for instance, there is no sound for *p*, so speakers employ a *b* sound instead to pronounce *shampoo* as *shaamboo.*

Language	Word for *Shampoo*	Basic Pronunciation
Chinese	香波	xīangbō
Greek	σαμπουάν	sampouan
Japanese	シャンプー	shampū
Lithuanian	šampūnas	shampoonas
Norwegian	sjampo	shampoo
Russian	шампунь	shampoon'
Spanish	champú	champoo
Swahili	shampuu	shampoo
Turkish	şampuan	shampuan
Vietnamese	shampoo	shampoo

JAZZ

Jasm, jism, jezz, jaser, chasser, jasi, jas, Chas, jass, Jas, yas, jascz, Jezebel, jasmine, jazz! What a jazzy American mix of sounds & stories swirls + bops around the Global English word *jazz*.

Jazzman Thelonious Monk is one of many artists who purportedly said, "Talking about music is like dancing about architecture." Still, Monk did have his own succinct definition: "Jazz is freedom."[1] Others have tried "talking about jazz" as a meeting of African and European scales; as syncopated; as polyrhythmic; as a music of "blue" notes that are not *quite* a distinct tone apart; as variations on melodic lines—and improvisation. But however challenging it can be to put into words what's unique about jazz, it's even more difficult to nail down the source of the word *jazz*.

Will the mysteries of the popular Global English word be solved? Or is there something about *jazz* that's bound to remain as abstruse as the music it captures? In 1919, H. L. Mencken offered his summary of the ongoing search for its origins:

Webster's New International says that jazz is a Creole word, and probably of African origin, but goes no further. The *Oxford* says that its origin is unknown, but that it is "generally said to be Negro." Amateur etymologists have made almost countless efforts to run it down, or, more accurately, to guess at its history. [Walter J.] Kingsley tried to connect it with *Jasper*, the name of a dancing slave on a plantation near New Orleans, c. 1825. Vincent Lopez sought its origin in *Chaz*, the stable-name of Charles Washington, an eminent ragtime drummer of Vicksburg, Miss., c. 1895. Other searchers produced even more improbable etymologies. The effort to trace the word to Africa has failed, though it has been established that it was used by the Negroes in the Mississippi river towns long before it came into general use. But the meaning they attached to it was that of sexual intercourse.[2]

Among proposed sources of *jazz* have been the American slang *jism*, also called *jizz*, meaning "energy" as well as "semen"; the Creole patois *jass*, meaning "sexual intercourse"; the French verb *jaser*, pronounced "jaz-EH," used in America's colonial French-speaking South and meaning "to chatter," a word that described the chirping of birds; *jaja*, from a dialect of Bantu, "to cause to dance," or *jasi*, from Mandingo, meaning "to become abnormal, unlike oneself," or *yas* from Temne, for "to be enlivened, energetic," all words that could have been introduced into America by West African slaves for whom they were native terms; *jasm*, recorded by French lexicographers in mid-nineteenth-century Congo as a word for "vitality," "dynamism," or "energy," and associated with dancing; and a shortening of *jasmine*, the flower whose name passed from Persian to Arabic to French and then into English, in England, during the Renaissance.

And the purported connection between *jasmine* and *jazz*? Perfume. And sex. According to one source, jasmine oil was used to "jass up" the bouquets of sensual fragrances manufactured in New Orleans. "It caught on in the red light district, when a woman would approach a man and say 'Is jazz on your mind tonight, young fellow?' "[3] Musicians ostensibly picked up the word to encourage one another to "jazz up" the sound with extra personality, or "further improvise on" melodies.

But curiously, the current findings locate the first attestations of *jazz* not in the field of music, or even in the historic epicenter of jazz music, New Orleans. Instead, they link *jazz* to baseball fields on the West Coast.[4] During 1912's spring training, a Seattle pitcher reported in an interview that he was working on his *Jazz ball*.[5] Readers of a San Francisco newspaper learned in 1913 that the new favorite word in baseball circles meant something akin to "joy, pep, magnetism, verve, virility, ebulliency, courage, happiness—oh, what's the use?—JAZZ."[6]

Within a few years, the word came in much that upbeat sense to describe *jazz blues* played in Chicago. One view is that *jazz* could have found its way to Illinois in the person of Bert Kelly, a banjo player who moved from San Francisco to form a jazz ensemble in the Windy City.[7] It appears that the word *jazz* was only subsequently adopted by Dixieland bands from New Orleans, by artists in Harlem, and throughout the United States.*

Jazz picked up its Global English passport in 1917, when the United States deployed millions of combat troops into World War I. They included more than 300,000 black American segregated regiments and their bands. Among them were the "Harlem

---

*For the moment, then, *jazz* in its musical sense appears to have been first used in Chicago. But official archives and household attics could still hold surprises. Reasons to remain vigilant include such enigmatic suggestions as this one from 1916, from the New Orleans correspondent reporting to *Variety*: "'Jazz Bands' have been popular there for over two years." Could the word *jazz* already have been used in 1914 with reference to New Orleans music? Or was the term later applied to music of the kind first called *jazz* in Chicago?[8]

Hellfighters," the musicians of the 369th Infantry Regiment, whose bandleader was James Reese Europe. Thanks to him and other African-American music talents serving in the war, ragtime and blues jazz galvanized audiences overseas well before American whites would mingle with blacks in the speakeasies of the Prohibition era—or, as F. Scott Fitzgerald would characterize the period between the First World War and the Depression, the Jazz Age.

The European jazz capital? Paris, where, in the 1920s, musicians, music lovers, intellectuals, and avant-garde artists gathered to commune with *le jazz*, a new music that broke rules, was joyful and danceable, and readily channeled the unbridled modernism of Europe's postwar moment. The singer, dancer, and stage phenomenon Josephine Baker; the saxophonist Sidney Bechet; and dancer-singer Ada "Bricktop" Smith (also owner of her own club, Chez Bricktop) were among the celebrated American artists who transformed Paris's Montmartre district into Europe's hottest jazz scene. Together, American and European musicians, like the Belgian-born Jean "Django" Reinhardt, creator of the "gypsy jazz" sound, turned Paris into a unique crossroads of jazz influences and expressions.

But the Jazz Age excitement would be stifled when jazz, and the liberal spirit it celebrated, were labeled "decadent" by Fascist regimes that rose to power in the wake of German National Socialism in the 1930s.* Some musicians fled Europe; some perished in concentration camps.†

*A notable exception was the unstoppable enthusiasm for *le swing* in occupied France.
†One jazz musician who escaped persecution, or worse, in fascist Italy was Romano Mussolini, son of "Il Duce" Benito Mussolini. His career as jazz pianist and leader of his band, the Romano Mussolini All Stars, flourished through the 1950s and 1960s. Strangely, given that jazz was suppressed in Italy under Il Duce, jazz and fascism were intertwined at Romano Mussolini's funeral in 2006. The event reportedly opened with George Gershwin's "Summertime," and following "fascist slogans and salutes," concluded with the American gospel "When the Saints Go Marching In."[7]

In wartime Japan, where ジャズ, pronounced "jazu," had also gained fans in the 1920s, performing and listening to jazz was forbidden. And while it returned with a vengeance, becoming nearly tantamount to urbane democratic expression in postwar Paris, Germany, Japan, and throughout the Free World, it remained subject to censorship under totalitarians and dictators. In the Soviet Union, джаза, pronounced "djaza," was viewed as a form of Western capitalist decadence. Certain other music was embraced as more politically harmonious, like military marches, anthems, nostalgic symphonies, and traditional, or at least nominally "folkloric," Ukrainian songs cheering for abundant wheat harvests. While some jazz bands were formed under Communism, and while a few Western artists toured Soviet republics in closely monitored circumstances, authorities regarded the imported music with suspicion. It seemed to speak to unregulated bourgeois desires. And, like rock music with its explicitly rebellious agenda, jazz could unleash destructive enthusiasms.

Still, jazz of diverse forms would continue to gain followers as a subterranean art. Indeed, wherever it was regarded as subversive, it was further empowered to speak with unique force, especially to listeners who found themselves unheard in society at large. Cutting as it did across race and class divides, jazz also broke down barriers well outside musical realms from the time it appeared on the Continent. It inspired cubist painting in Vienna, experimental theater in Berlin, surrealist fiction in Spain, furniture design in Milan, and architecture in Copenhagen. And having spread to dance halls and nightclubs and hotel cocktail lounges across much of the world, toward the end of the twentieth century, some genres of jazz had become synonymous with progress or revolution, and others with hanging out on the back porch, or brunching on eggs Benedict with a visiting mother-in-law.

The American Dialect Society has crowned *jazz* the Word of the Twentieth Century, a very well-known word of very unknown origins. The core ingredients of its music hail from sub-Saharan Africa. If the origin of the word is ever uncovered, will it prove to be African as well? In African lingua francas such as Lingala and Swahili, jazz today is called . . . *jazz*, borrowed from American English. By now, all stripes—live jazz, recorded jazz, free jazz, fusion jazz, Latin jazz, acid jazz, and so many more—have found listeners around the world, with jazz almost everywhere a powerful ally of freedom.

Jazz has always been about conversations between and across cultures. In the global era, it provides a vast musical vocabulary for an inexhaustible variety of global exchanges. One example among many is found in the dialogue between Ethiopian and American musicians: jazz in the United States inspired Ethiopian jazz artists of the 1970s, which prompted interpretations by American artists of the early twenty-first century, which has led to collaborations between Ethiopians and Americans. Sound like a lot of jazz balls being pitched from one continent to the other? At least one thing has remained constant as this dialogue unfolds. In the alphabet of Amharic, the official language of Ethiopia, it's spelled ጃዝ. And how's that pronounced? "Jazz."

COCKTAIL

The word *cocktail* has spawned more mixological inventiveness than any other Global English term. Made in the USA at the dawn of the nineteenth century, the alcoholic *cocktail* deserves a special place in the Global English lexicon for inviting creative spirits to add their own poetic words and phrases to the world's word mix.

Of course, along with all the verbal ingenuity that the American cocktail has inspired, we have the cocktails themselves. And whether these drinks generally deserve as much celebration as the mind-numbing array of lively designations attached to them suggests is another matter.

In America, cocktails employing such staples as rum, beer, hard cider, or wine, and augmented with sugar and bitters, were once admired as fortifying brews and even wholesome alternatives to often-contaminated water. Early generations of mixed drinks included the generic grog and anti-fogmatic (better to withstand damp and *foggy* climatic conditions), but also specific cocktails such as the sherry cobbler, the stone fence, the racehorse, the sling flip, and the Virginia fancy. In the more self-indulging twentieth century, however, and with modern plumbing erasing the handy excuse of bad-water avoidance, abuse of the cocktail, in practices such as the three-martini lunch or the scorpion bowl frat-house initiation rite, has spread into global cocktail-consuming culture, and earned a worldwide reputation for causing troubles ranging from liver deterioration to revoked driver's licenses and worse.

Classic modern cocktails include the screwdriver, the margarita, the whiskey sour, the mai tai, the lime rickey, the tequila sunrise, the Manhattan, the Tom Collins, the White Russian, its comrade the Black Russian, and certain "enhanced" or "laced" variations on the seasonal eggnog. The very names of these drinks alone can—in spite of any cognitive damage provoked by their overconsumption—resuscitate all-too-vivid memories of specific social occasions. And their sometimes all-too-regrettable outcomes.

But however various combinations of gin, pineapple juice, vodka, grenadine, soda, olives, and maraschino cherries—or more recently spotted ingredients like bubble gum, leather-infused bourbon, peanut butter, and pickled octopus—may have marred specific nights out, or days in, phrase forging tied to these drinks shows that the cocktail is an enduring art form, one that has mirrored both time-honored and evolving hopes and fears of its consumers over more than two hundred years. One generation's *slammers* may give way to the next's *shots*, but the *cocktail* abides.

Given what cocktails do to people's brains, and what their more inhibited drinkers wish they'd do for their sex lives, they readily attract appellations conjuring explosions of one kind or another. American English has seen everything from the blow job and the sex on the beach to the B-52 and nuclear iced tea. There are also the car crash, the crash landing, and the kamikaze. For the morbid environmentalist, there's even the greenhouse gas. Perhaps in alcohol-induced denial of their truer purposes are also the "classy" and polished names for cocktails whose ingredients are, in the end, no less intoxicating. Few foresee an evening about to unravel as they order that second (or third) cosmopolitan, bay breeze, ruby duchess, or pink lady.

Farther from the cocktail's native territory, an even wider rainbow of alcohol-soaked poetry draws the thirsty bar-goer. In Hong Kong, there are specialty cocktails like the Ning sling, a brew of mandarin orange vodka, lychee liqueur, mint leaves, and passion fruit. On Khaosan Road in Bangkok, the nightmare lures seekers of quaffable thrills. And in Tokyo, Japanese aficionados of the カクテル, pronounced "kakuteru," have embraced the mayonnaise margarita. Parisians are partial to their traditional champagne-based Kir royale but also dream up trendier cocktails like the Jules Verne and the Cointreau Teese, created by the racy burlesque stage talent Dita Von Teese. Italian cocktail bars offer the tried-and-true Negroni, legendarily named for the Italian count who invented it, but many also experiment with new drinks like the paradiso, which features the nation's much-loved *limoncello*, a viscous liqueur made from tangy lemons grown in places like the sunny Sorrentine Peninsula.

Cocktails are titled to celebrate people, places, captivating images, and states of mind, but also events. Fitting into two of these categories is the Rio 16, already named for the 2016 Olympics to be held in Rio de Janeiro. The cocktail's key ingredient? Cachaça (pronounced "ka-SHAH-ssa"). That's Brazil's native variety of distilled rum. Even in places where alcohol is officially prohibited or closely controlled, notably in predominantly Muslim countries such as Afghanistan and Saudi Arabia, watering holes catering to troops, tourists, expats, as well as certain locals, offer their own variations on popular cocktails. But cocktail language owes most of its current success to the global tradition of concocting—and naming—a *house cocktail*. Hence the cangrejo, or "crab," offered to guests at a beach hotel in Cartagena, Colombia, or the comforting old pal extended to travelers who finally reach a remote island lodge in Kenya's Indian Ocean.

The vibrant, expressive palette delivered by *cocktail* comes premixed in the compound word's etymology, itself literally to do with eye-popping and mixing.[1] Already in eighteenth-century England, the *cock-tailed* horse, often used for hunting or to draw stagecoaches, was distinguished by its grooming: the hair on its *tail* was cut short so that it "stood up" in a manner imitative of the *cock*, or "rooster," noted for his erect comb, strutting, and seemingly boastful displays of brightly varied plumage. Because these animals tended not to be thoroughbreds, *cock-tailed* came to denote horses of mixed pedigree. Words similar to *cock*★ can be found in numerous Germanic and Romance languages, with the Late Latin cognate being *coccus*, itself a poetic word that imitates the *cocococo* morning call of the barnyard alpha male.† From the *cock-tailed horse* came

---

★It wasn't by accident that *cock* had become a slang term for "penis" as early as 1618, as first attested in England.

†In Mandarin Chinese, *cocktail* is translated into three characters: 鸡尾酒. These graphic symbols respectively stand for the concepts of "cock" (as in the bird), "tail," and "wine." The

America's shortened *cocktail*, which for a time referred not only to a drink whose ingredients were of mixed provenance but also to a man of uncertain breeding or moral character.

Ghosts of *cocktail*'s more dispiriting side are still alive when the word is used to refer to toxic or deadly mixtures, as in the phrases *chemotherapy cocktail* or *Molotov cocktail*, named for an aggressive Soviet foreign minister (né Skryabin), who adopted the moniker Molotov, from the Russian *molot*, or "big hammer." Like *cocktail* on its own, *Molotov cocktail* has entered Global English to refer to "a jerry-rigged bomb," that mingling of gasoline and lit fuse that protestors in all corners of the world have been known to lob at riot police and over walls of embassy compounds.

And speaking of "hammer," or rather, being *hammered*, there is as yet no Global English term for the post-too-many-cocktails phenomenon: the *hangover*. People around the world are apparently content to cope with the cocktail's aftermath in their own languages, and with recourse to another genre of cocktail that they hope will rid them of dehydration, nausea, and more: the home remedy, such as the prairie oyster or the Bloody Mary. Like the first cocktails in America, these drinks are meant to be restorative.* And

---

Global English idea, expressed in three parts, is here pronounced very differently: *jī wéi jiu*. This is not always the case in Chinese versions of Global English words. As noted earlier, one Chinese word for *shampoo* is rendered in two characters, 香波, whose pronunciation, *xiāng bō*, echoes the English word. However, these sounds are used to make words whose literal meaning, in the Chinese, is "fragrant" + "wave." (Note that this word for *shampoo* was first borrowed into Cantonese and then borrowed from Cantonese into Mandarin.) For those of us who use phonetic alphabets, ideograms such as those used to write Chinese can be mystifying. For example, a Chinese ideogram "spells" one thing in Chinese and something else when read in Japanese. To appreciate how this works, consider the symbol *lb*. Speakers of English read this as "pound," but the same abbreviation of the Latin *libra*, meaning "pound," is read in French as *livre* and in German as *Pfund*. So, while words and their pronunciations may differ, readers nonetheless agree on the characters' meanings.

*The first appearance of *cocktail*, in 1803 in the New Hampshire newspaper *The Farmer's Cabinet*, suggests that early cocktails were difficult to distinguish from anything that could

like those early head-clearing mixtures, many also include alcohol. Oh well. If the hangover cocktail doesn't work, there's always the prospect of four more Harvey Wallbangers. Or zombies. Or monkey's glands.

GETTING HAMMERED IN AMERICAN ENGLISH, CIRCA 1737

In his tireless quest for enlightenment, Benjamin Franklin collected 228 words and phrases for being drunk, a familiar condition in colonial America, where consumption of hard liquor was, per capita, higher than it is today in the United States. Here are a few of the colorful terms that Franklin noted:

He's Been at Barbadoes.
He's Piss'd in the Brook.
He's kiss'd black Betty.
He's been in the Cellar.
He's Cherry Merry.
He's been too free with the Creature.
He's Disguiz'd.
He's been to France.
He's Got on his little Hat.
He's Hammerish.
He's Going to Jerusalem.
He's Juicy.
He sees two Moons.
He's Rocky.
He's Lost his Rudder.
He's Ragged.
He's contending with the Pharaoh.
He's Seen the French King.
He's Taken Hippocrates' grand Elixir.[2]

---

be called a remedy for their overconsumption: "Drank a glass of cocktail—excellent for the head . . . Call'd at the Doct's . . . drank another glass of cocktail."[3]

MADE IN CHINA

Scotch tape is made in China. So are Bermuda shorts and French doors and English saddles and Russian dolls and India ink. Even Panama hats—traditionally made in Ecuador—are made in China. Swiss watches are too, although not if the Swiss have a say in the matter; Switzerland denounces many "Swiss made" timepieces as counterfeit. The "Mao Bicycle," a popular form of transportation in China since the days of Chairman Mao, is made in China. Of course, china is also made in China. It was a favorite import item of the English, until they figured out how to approximate recipes for porcelain glazes and started making china themselves.

Also made in China are speakers of English. Lots. (A Global English keyword for economic booms the world over is *volume*.) Will English itself ultimately be made in China?

No three words better confirm the arrival of the global era or the role of English in it. Whatever their theoretical points of origin or consumption, products typically announce their "country of origin" in English. Thanks to the growth of global trade, the phrase *Made in* (pick a country) is now recognized as immediately as the planet's überbrand of *Cola*, with its distinctive white on red script.

In its manufacturing sense, *made in* first appears in a 1690 issue of the *London Gazette*. It described a "little Gold Watch" adorned in white enamel and "made in France." [1] But we're interested in the capital *M* version of this phrase, the one that, courtesy of postwar trade agreements among cooperating nations that expanded in 1995 into the World Trade Organization—has become impossible to escape in these global times. Among shoppers, the sight of these labels can trigger reassurance, pride, delight, or a sense of prestige—so long as the named country isn't in disfavor for one reason or another. *Made in France.* For plenty of American consumers, the phrase has been shorthand for "jealous of my sensational purchase?" But it's also been code for "do not buy," as when France's outspoken opposition to U.S. foreign policy incites American consumers to respond via exercise of purchasing (and nonpurchasing) power.*

In Global English, the labels come attached to global politics. Instead of merely informing consumers, they often work as three-word koans: *Made in Canada.* Are some of the world's neediest people about to be deprived of vital income if I choose this shirt over the *Made in Mauritius* one? *Made in Cambodia.* The tennis shoes fit well, and the price is right. But am I looking at the fruits of child labor here? *Made in Pakistan. Made in India.* Should I buy nothing from either until both have saner nuclear weapons policies? *Made in Israel. Made in Germany. Made in Croatia. Made in Brazil.* One need not be a follower of World Cup Soccer to know that the mere name of a country can stir emotions.†

But country-of-origin labels elicit an even more perplexing question. Where exactly was this thing made? Fasten your seat belt. The answer takes us into the heart of global reality, and into the mysteries of global logic. Not to mention global semantics. A glance at the net meaning of "country of origin" from the vantage point of

---

*Even words suggesting purely nominal ties to France have been subjected to wrathful interpretation. Or alteration, as when, following France's reaction to the U.S. military advance into Iraq in 2003, certain USA-made *french fries* were rebranded *freedom fries.*

†Consider the volatile associations of the phrase *Made in Japan.* Those three words generally spell "economical and dependable." In 1963, they did not. That was when gonzo journalism founder Hunter S. Thompson, having purchased a Bushnell scope for his .44 magnum, was more than displeased to discover that his reputable "American" product did not function as hoped. In a stern letter of complaint to the purported U.S. manufacturer, he recounted how he "discovered the word 'Japan' engraved on the bottom of the scope, and was not happy to see it." He demanded his money back.[2]

international trade will supply us with a powerful tool for understanding Global English.

The World Trade Organization requires its member countries to identify products as "Made in" a single sovereign nation, even as the realities of globalization render the notion of single-nation "origin" amusing, bizarre, perverse, or impossible. Yet, curiously, each WTO member has leeway to set its own rules for determining country of origin for products sold within its borders. Thus, a product labeled "Made in Morocco" for export to America could well be labeled "Made in Spain" for shipment to another country, since different rules may apply. If a product is going to brandish a "Made in USA" label, however, one requirement is that at least 75 percent of its manufacturing cost be incurred in the USA. But a critical question, for the USA and all countries belonging to the WTO, is where was the product *last substantially transformed*? The answer can be complicated.

Let's buy a bicycle. We settle on one "Made in China." Though it was assembled right here in the store, its components, shipped in one big box, came from China. And Malaysia, and Canada, and Italy. The bike, engineered by a Japanese designer contracted with a firm in prehandover Hong Kong, was cast, welded, and painted in a Chinese factory. Oh, and by the way, the principal ore used for its frame was mined in Africa. The banks that finance all this industry, from design to parts to packaging and logistics, are owned internationally, by stakeholders from a dozen countries (including China). So, yes, our shiny new two-wheeler is *from* China. Just like a Warner Bros. thriller shot in Finland and starring a Spanish actress and produced by two brothers from South Korea is a Hollywood movie. So why does the bike's COO say "Made in China"? The crucial point: the bike was, to put it in World Trade Organization English, "last substantially transformed" there.

And the implications for Global English? Country of origin can be just as confounding to nail down for a phrase or word. Look again at *bicycle*. The prefix, *bi-* means "two." And the active ingredient, *-cycle*, means "wheel" or "circle." In the mid-nineteenth century these word parts were assembled in Paris into *bicycle*.★ Finally, in 1868, the word entered English, initially with the spelling "bysicle." A more exhaustive inventory of the word's provenance shows that the French *cycle* had come from the Latin *cyclus*; Latin had taken the word from the Ancient Greek *kuklos*; and Greek had inherited it from a prehistoric language. Still, it is generally agreed that the English word *bicycle* comes from French, because that's the language in which the word was *last substantially transformed* before being imported. But not all words are so easy to label.

And what about English itself? Was it "Made in England?" We'll look into this next.

INSPECTED BY #47057

Labels and inscriptions on things manufactured in preindustrial eras often give voice to the objects they adorn, as if bringing them to life, to speak directly or forthrightly to their admirers or potential owners. In sixth-century BC Athens, for example, the master ceramicist Exekias signed his pots so that they vouched *personally* for their own authenticity and quality: "Exekias made me" (*Exekias epoiesen me*).

★The French *bicycle* appears to have been forged from the earlier, and more easily test-ridden, *tricycle*, or "three-wheel." It's easy to forget how strange the bicycle was when it first showed up, putting bipeds into precarious-looking motion on two-wheeled devices. Tourists visiting Paris in the late 1860s were delighted to spot the curious inventions on the Champs-Elysées. (By the time the Eiffel Tower was built, in 1889, other miracles of engineering absorbed the attention of visitors.) The diminutive *bicyclette* appeared a decade later, initially named for its less gargantuan wheels. Eventually, *bicyclette* replaced the French word *bicycle*. By then, French-speakers also had an alternative term, *vélo*, from the Latin for "swift." The same Latin root appears in English words such as *velocity*.[3]

MADE IN CHINA

Have a look at each word in the phrase *Made in China*, reading them as we might traditional Chinese script, right to left. *China:* the country's name came into English in 1555. The medieval traveler and writer Marco Polo, one of the earliest westerners to visit China, had used the word *Chin* to refer to the land in his native language, Venetian. While its etymology is unknown, a similar word for *China* was used in the ancient language Sanskrit to refer to the Asian land, and related words have also been used by speakers of East Asian languages with reference to their neighbor. So a good guess is that it's a word of Asian, possibly East Asian, origin. *In:* this ancient preposition first shows up in English around 700 AD. But as with many of the words from English's earliest vocabulary, its roots go back to the prehistoric era. *In* is also one of the ten most-used words by native speakers of English, along with *the, of, to, and, a, is, it, you,* and *that.* But as we'll see, many of these words are not great favorites of a much larger population: nonnative speakers of English. *Made:* we'll be taking a close look at this word in "Made in Ænglisc."

2

A FAMILY PICTURE OF ENGLISH

Just as a consumer product "Made in China" is often put together there using various components shipped into China, English has for the most part been assembled from imported linguistic elements. English-speakers have in effect processed foreign material and substantially transformed it into language "Made in English." We've seen how made-in-English words can go on to circulate in Global English, often to find their ways back to speakers of the very languages that supplied the source materials in the first place. Recall how Hindi provided a term that was retooled by speakers of English into *shampoo*, which has since circled back to the subcontinent to become an "English" loanword to Hindi.

The vast majority of words and phrases in Global English have been assembled from imported components. Many, like *bikini*, *tobacco, amen, safari, kayak, alcohol, coca,* and *kola* (and hence *Coca-Cola*), come from languages with no linguistic kinship to English. However, most of Global English's imported vocabulary draws, so far, on languages in the same family as English.

It's an illustrious family and a big one—too big to fit into a snap-shot. If we want a group portrait that includes the whole clan—not just Mom and Granny but all the aunts and busloads of cousins, some from distant and rather surprising locations—we need to step way back and get a wide angle.

Few speakers of English would be surprised that German, Dutch, Yiddish, and other Germanic tongues are in the picture. These share a relatively recent common ancestor with English, and can be seen as English's close cousins. A bit more surprising may be the assertion that not only Latin, French, Italian, Spanish, and Por-tuguese but also Irish and Greek are in the group. But how about the idea that Bengali, Persian, Russian, Armenian, and Icelandic, to name only a handful, are in the family as well? Can that be right?

Our crowded shot comprises the group of languages called Indo-European, claiming the largest number of speakers of any family of languages in the world. Some three billion people speak Indo-European languages as their native tongue. And if we include those who speak one as a second or third language, that number is much greater. That in mind, take a look at something you may well recognize from the endpapers of your dictionary, that dismaying "Indo-European Language Tree." Most of us are all too happy to skip over this gnarly diagram when we're looking up a word. But it can tell us, very concisely, about the extensive yet unique group of languages to which English belongs. And instead of visualizing the conventional tree, let's look at the family in an array suggesting a fan, or someone's idea for a flying machine.

All these languages can be called cousins. First, second, third cousins; cousins once removed; buried or living cousins, but all related nonetheless. Still, what does *Indo-European* mean? Does it imply that early versions of these tongues were spoken in some ancient territory known as Indo-Europa? Or that these languages

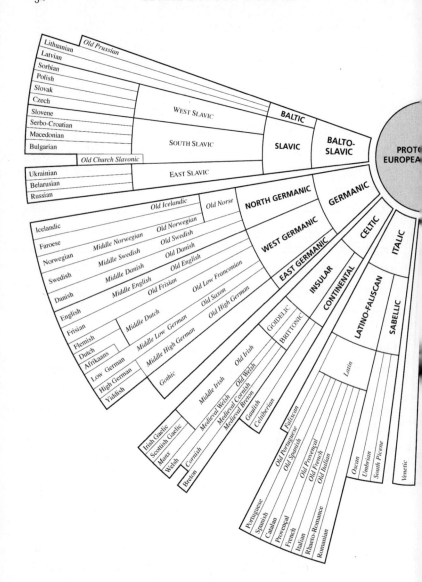

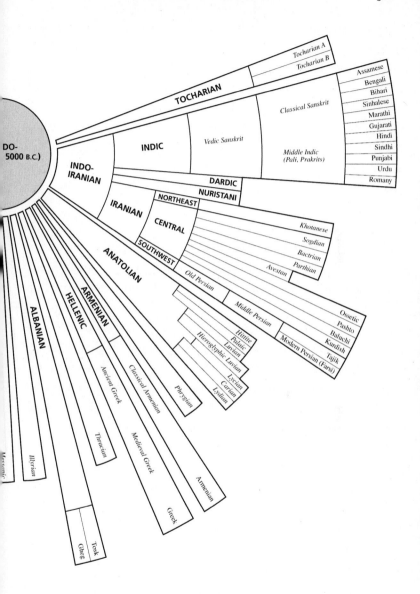

Copyright © 2000 by Houghton Mifflin Harcourt Publishing Company. Reproduced by permission from *The American Heritage Dictionary of Indo-European Roots*, 2nd ed., revised and edited by Calvert Watkins.

were native to ancient India and ancient Europe? *Indo-European*, a term coined in the early nineteenth century, is clunky. It originally reflected how these many languages could be found in an area extending from the Indus River Valley (the *Indo* part of the hyphenate) across Europe (the *European* part). As we'll see, though, the word *Indo-European* falls short of capturing the astonishing geographical scope of the family in its prehistoric phase. But before we consider the designation any further, let's see how English is situated within this impressive range of languages.

English descended from a language that left no written trace, but we know it existed because it spawned some closely related languages, all of which hold linguistic clues pointing to a common ancestor. Linguists call this ancestor West Germanic. Apart from English, living languages evolved from West Germanic include Frisian, Flemish, Dutch, Afrikaans, German, and Yiddish. (In the diagram, these living languages radiate out of West Germanic.) West Germanic, in turn, shares a linguistic forebear with two other groups of languages, North and East Germanic. Living languages descended from North Germanic include Icelandic, Faroese, Norwegian, Swedish, and Danish. East Germanic is another case altogether; it produced Gothic, a precocious child, highly achievement-oriented, and one who looked destined for a grand career. Although it's the language of important fourth-century translations of the Greek Bible, Gothic has not been heard from live for some time.* Other daughters of East Germanic have been

---

*A possible descendant of Gothic is so-called Crimean Gothic. It is thought to have been spoken as late as the sixteenth century in Crimea, now in Ukraine. Uncertainty surrounds this language. Only around a hundred words of it were collected by a Flemish diplomat in the early 1560s. Based on other scant evidence, some believe that Crimean Gothic was spoken as late as the eighteenth century.

detected in fragmentary remains of dialects such as Burgundian, Ostrogothic, and Vandalic.

Considering the Germanic group, linguists see shared features showing that they too are descendants of an even earlier language: simply, Germanic.* At some point in west-central Europe's prehistoric past, Germanic was the language of a "single speech community." This phrase, as employed by linguists, doesn't imply that Germanic's speakers lived in one village, one valley, or even in a contiguous land area. Rather, though initially dispersed over hundreds of square miles, they had sufficient contact to share what can be classified as a single language. Specialists generally agree that this community of Germanic speakers existed between four thousand and twenty-five hundred years ago.

Soon after Germanic fragmented into the daughter languages mentioned above, a writing system had entered the picture, for recording words. However, the first scripts of Germanic languages employed not the Latin letters widely used for English today, but rather runes, alphabetic symbols that were first carved into different materials, from beech bark to stone. In fact, the Germanic word for "beech" is related to the word *book*, suggesting that runes were first formed on beech trees, or on sheets made from their bark. The word has been widely popularized in Global English within the compound *Facebook*.

So how do these Germanic languages relate to other groups in the Indo-European family? Another prehistoric western branch of the family has also played an enormous role in the evolution

*Linguists refer to this language as Proto-Germanic. For reasons we'll see, *Proto-* is used to refer to languages that have been reconstructed rather than attested in documents, or heard among living speakers. To simplify, though, I will refer to this prehistoric branch as Germanic, and to other reconstructed branches of Indo-European similarly, without the *Proto-* prefix. To prevent any confusion, I'll make clear when I'm using *Germanic* as an adjective rather than a noun. For example, I'll say "Germanic language."

of English: Italic. Like prehistoric Germanic, Italic broke up into daughter languages. Unlike Germanic, though, Italic produced only one daughter that would survive beyond antiquity: Latin. The Romance languages—including Italian, French, Spanish, Portuguese, Romanian, and Catalan—are all descended from Latin, the sole "fertile offspring" of Italic. As you'll see on the chart, the other Italic languages, such as Faliscan and Umbrian, produced no linguistic progeny. We can blame this multiple case of sterility on Latin, not least because its speakers' military culture was so effective that no other Italic languages in its neighborhood withstood its force. Speakers of other Italic languages eventually became speakers of Latin.

Italic and Germanic languages seem at first glance very different. But side-by-side evaluations of Old English (which sprang from Germanic and its daughter West Germanic) and Latin vocabularies confirm that the two branches in fact share a sizable pool of closely related words. Old English for "mother" is *módor*, a Germanic cousin of the Italic word captured by Latin's *māter*. Old English for "pig," *swīn*, is related to Latin *suīnus*. These are of course just two of a good many examples.

Germanic and Italic: two prehistoric sister branches that generated an abundance of languages, some extinct but many still very much alive.

Also related to Germanic and Italic are yet other living tongues grouped under the names of their own prehistoric ancestors. In the prehistoric period, the branch that moved farthest to the west was Celtic. In the first millennium BC, Celtic became one of the most widespread of the Indo-European branches, spoken over a large part of continental Europe as well as on its western coasts and islands. But after the Romans occupied their territories, speakers of Gaulish and Celtiberian, major Continental Celtic languages, gradually came to speak Latin instead. Only Irish Gaelic, Scottish Gaelic, Manx (revived and now spoken by a small community on the Isle of Man), Welsh, and Breton, the five so-called Insular Celtic languages, survive today. It happens that Celtic is the only Indo-European branch struggling for survival, its languages spoken by minorities in countries where English and French dominate.*

East of the Germanic and Celtic branches, and north of the Italic branch, is the Balto-Slavic one, whose languages include Russian, Belarusian, Ukrainian, Bulgarian, Macedonian, Serbo-Croatian,† Slovene, Czech, Slovak, Polish, Sorbian, Latvian, and Lithuanian, which Indo-Europeanist J. P. Mallory notes has "mesmerized many linguists for over a century now"[1] because it may hold special clues about deeper connections among English, Lithuanian, and all of their cousin languages. We will glimpse these deeper connections in a moment. Linguists have also noted that the Balto-Slavic branch shows affinities with Germanic, which has led to the notion of an earlier Balto-Slavic-Germanic language area in prehistoric northern Europe.

Another branch of the Indo-European language family is Albanian, with two main dialects: Gheg, spoken in and beyond the capital city, Tirana, in northern Albania; and Tosk, the dominant language south of the Shkumbin River, which divides the country pretty neatly in half. Keep in mind that natural boundaries such as rivers, mountains, deserts, and large bodies of water often determine linguistic borders, as do habitats in which languages have

---

*Certain academics prefer to pronounce the C in *Celtic* as "KELL-tick." But it's equally legit to side with fans of Boston's basketball team, the "SELL-tix."
†Some linguists prefer to divide Serbo-Croatian into distinct dialects or, depending on your definition of "language," daughter languages including Serbian, Croatian, and Bosnian. For intricate political and cultural reasons, many Serbs, Croats, and Bosnians also favor these distinctions. Other living languages on our diagram could also be further broken down or, dare I say, Balkanized.

evolved as their speakers attempt more effectively to thrive in them. (Global English is now evolving in a planetwide context. This novel match between language and natural boundaries, or rather the lack of them, has speakers forging into new linguistic territory.)

A further branch of Indo-European was generated, as the chart shows, by an early form of Armenian. As with Albanian, the Armenian branch developed without interruption into the modern era. Also like Albanian, Armenian now has two main dialect areas. One, Western Armenian, was devastated by the mass destruction of the Armenian communities during World War I.★ The other, Eastern Armenian, serves as Armenia's official language. Armenian has had its own alphabet since the fifth century. For example, one way to write the word for "Armenian" is հայերեն.

To the south, on the Aegean's coasts and islands, the Hellenic branch produced Ancient Greek, which initially comprised an array of dialects. But with the rise and dominance of Athens over other city-states, the dialect spoken there, Attic, all but eliminated the prior diversity of idioms used throughout the Greek-speaking Mediterranean. The emergent common language, known as Koine, is the language of the New Testament and the source of Modern Greek.

Farther east, the Indo-Iranian branch stretches to the Himalayas. This fecund branch effectively includes two major limbs. One produced ancient Iranian languages, which blossomed into numerous tongues. Some, including Avestan, the language of the Zoroastrians and their sacred religious texts, and Sogdian, which gained wide use as a lingua franca among merchants and traders along the ancient Silk Route, are extinct. Living languages of the Iranian subbranch include Farsi, Tajik, and Dari (all descended from Middle Persian,

★Owing to the Armenian diaspora of the early twentieth century, far more speakers of Armenian now live outside the country than within it.

the language of such celebrated poets as Rumi and Hafez), as well as Kurdish, Baluchi, Pashto, and Ossetic. Many of these are familiar to followers of twenty-first-century news, with Farsi today spoken in Iran, Tajik in Tajikistan, Dari and Pashto in Afghanistan, and Kurdish notably spoken in the combustible border region adjoining Iran, Iraq, Syria, Turkey, Armenia, Azerbaijan, and Georgia. For their parts, speakers of Baluchi live in Iran, Afghanistan, and Pakistan; Ossetic is chiefly spoken in the Russian and Georgian Caucasus.

The Indic limb of the Indo-Iranian branch includes two venerable ancient languages. One is Vedic Sanskrit, the sacred language of the Vedas, with texts believed to date from the fifteenth century BC. Classical Sanskrit developed as a codified version of Sanskrit, with a highly regulated grammar and strict rules for composition. Sharing the same origins as Classical Sanskrit was the unregulated language Prakrits. Extraordinarily fertile, it engendered hundreds of daughters, including Hindi, Bengali, Romany, Punjabi, Sindhi, Gujarati, Marathi, Sinhalese, and Assamese. Two of these languages, Hindi and Bengali, today rank among the world's ten most-spoken native languages. Altogether, over 900 million people—well over twice as many as speak English as a first language—use an Indic language as a native tongue.

The Indo-European family also encompasses wholly extinct branches, those that did not evolve into modern languages, as did Ancient Greek and Latin. On our fan chart, these extinct branches are the ones whose lines don't extend out to the fan's edges. Among the extinct descendants of Indo-European are two well-attested main branches, Anatolian (including Hittite) and Tocharian. Both of these, discovered in the early twentieth century, led Indo-Europeanists to reevaluate their big-picture views of the language family. Taken together, these branches extended the "Indo-European" territory into a region south of Europe and Asia and east of the Indus River.⋆ But even as the name no longer accurately represents the geography of the early spread of the Indo-European languages, it is nonetheless still used to designate the language family. Apart from the more recently discovered branches, there are also a number of weakly attested languages, including Venetic, Messapic, Illyrian, Thracian, and Phrygian. While these left no living tongues, they did leave enough recorded traces for linguists to determine that they too once thrived and belonged to the same family of languages as English and its many living cousins.

There were very probably other branches of languages in the family that also went extinct but left no known traces. Like languages in any place or time, these early branches of Indo-European might have gone extinct for any of a number of reasons. One is military conquest, especially when speakers of the "conquering" language live among the vanquished who speak a different tongue. We saw an example of this phenomenon with certain daughters of prehistoric Celtic: speakers of those languages adopted Latin as a mother tongue after Romans had conquered them. Another motive for abandonment of a language arises when a different tongue becomes more prestigious, offering access to greater opportunities to survive or to prosper, or to gain social advantages. Of course, a language

---

⋆Two forms of Tocharian were unearthed in 1907, by the British-Hungarian archaeologist Aurel Stein, in manuscripts buried in the Taklamakan Desert of Western China. The Anatolian branch has a different story. Hittite was written on clay tablets using a nonalphabetic writing system: cuneiform. The language was thought to be unrelated to Indo-European until the Czech linguist Bedřich Hrozný deciphered the cuneiform markings. His discovery astonished Indo-Europeanists, who had not expected to learn that the language family extended into Anatolia. This discovery revealed that, at the height of the Hittite Empire, in the fourteenth century BC, an Indo-European language was spoken in parts of Mesopotamia, the so-called Cradle of Civilization.

can also become extinct simply because its community of speakers dies out.★

However many branches make up the Indo-European family, one can't help but be intrigued. If Indo-European languages are neither from India nor from Europe, where were their earliest speakers first speaking? And when? These irrepressible questions direct us to a place and time that are difficult to pinpoint, and hotly debated, even as linguistic evidence makes it impossible to deny their existence.

The evidence suggests that from a single, early prehistoric speech community, various groups split off. Whether this prehistoric linguistic community spread out because conditions required some of its members to migrate; or because novel technologies allowed them to impose their language and culture on others by force; or because others embraced their language and culture as advantageous; or for another reason, or a combination of many reasons, has not been determined and may never be known. Whatever the mechanisms, over thousands of years the splintered versions of the initial, early language became increasingly distinct, even as new waves of languages spread across various territories. These early dialects of Indo-European included Germanic, Italic, Hellenic, and other prehistoric

---

★It's useful to distinguish here between extinction and death. We can think of a dead language as one that is no longer a mother tongue or even a lingua franca. Latin may in this sense be considered a dead language, even though it's spoken by some in special circumstances. But since Latin also continued to evolve, and indeed to evolve into many languages thriving today, it doesn't present a case of language extinction. An extinct language is one that is not only no longer spoken but also didn't evolve into any living mother tongue or lingua franca. An example of an extinct Indo-European language is Hittite. Indeed, Hittite was one of a number of languages spoken in the Anatolian branch of the family, yet no language in this branch is spoken today; Anatolian is thus an extinct branch of Indo-European. While distinctions among living, dead, and extinct languages are useful, they can also be too blunt. The linguist Claude Hagège offers a carefully layered discussion of this subject, and suggests how "dead" languages, notably Hebrew, have been and can be called back, Lazarus-like, to life.[2]

branches known to have emerged from a common linguistic ancestor. But what was that ancestor?

As we've seen, these early Indo-European branch languages had, by the time writing entered the picture, given way to daughter languages. And it's only from the time of these daughter languages within the diverse branches that we have recorded evidence of any linguistic ancestor. From the very earliest phases of the different branches themselves, there is in most instances no direct trace pointing us to their mother language. Only silence. A big question, then: since this language, the one underlying them all, so remotely preceded writing, how do we know that a community of people spoke it? Indeed, how do we know it even existed?

In the late eighteenth century, the British linguist Sir William Jones postulated the existence of an ancient ancestor language when he observed shared traits among Latin, Greek, Sanskrit, and other languages. His initial steps exploring connections among their distinct vocabularies and grammars established the branch of linguistic study that would later be named Indo-European. Subsequent generations of scholars developed an ingenious method to reconstruct what is arguably the world's most riveting "silent" language. Their method resembles archaeology, only instead of piecing together, say, a broken ceramic cooking vessel to decipher how it was made and used by a prehistoric people, linguists piece together the broken parts of the early language to draw up, through its visible and audible remains, a blueprint of its once-living form. By examining the surviving relics of this captivating prehistoric puzzle, linguists have been able to determine surprising details about a language once spoken in the distant past.

Specialists call this entirely unrecorded but partly reconstructed language *Proto-Indo-European*, as in "the common ancestor of all the Indo-European languages." While no record of it remains, it can be shown to have developed into a plethora of ancient and medieval languages, and of course into hundreds of living languages, including English. Global English too preserves many relics of Proto-Indo-European, often simply referred to as PIE, in words whose roots can be traced back to that early language. There is even a reconstructed phrase from Proto-Indo-European that remains alive, although with its form and meaning substantially transformed, in the Global English *credit card*. But the analogy of our ceramic vessel partly glued back together clearly fails to capture PIE's survival in languages still spoken today. After all, while we might admire that ceramic object in a museum, or study it in an effort to understand how it was made or what purposes it served, we wouldn't put such a broken and outdated thing to use. But in the case of PIE, it's as if that very early community of speakers passed down to some three billion cooks the set of kitchen utensils now indispensable to the making of their breakfast, lunch, and dinner.

As in assembling any puzzle, the more neatly fitting and solid the pieces in hand, the clearer the probable contours of the missing parts. Thus, reconstructions of PIE are considered more robust if they employ "pieces" drawn from at least three distinct branches of the Indo-European family tree. Think of the common expression, "Two points determine a line." While two points are persuasive, we're often aware that one of the two points could be a result of coincidence. Three points of proof, in this case linguistic proof showing up in three distinct branches of the ancestor language, greatly reduce the probability that relics of an apparent ancestral root have turned up by chance.

How does *linguistic archaeology* demonstrate that speakers over five thousand years ago uttered words that evolved into many current English ones, such as *credit, film, house, mother*, and *star*?

Instead of looking at an actual case, let's get a general sense of this linguistic detective work by way of a fictional situation. While this won't show exactly how Indo-Europeanists reconstruct prehistoric roots, we'll be able to appreciate how lost words can be recovered in existing ones.

Suppose you are a linguist who's traveled back in time. When you step out of your pod, Google hasn't been launched. And Mr. Bell, the telephone's inventor, hasn't been born. While we're at it, let's also say that no writing system has yet been invented. You're entering a world of isolated speech communities. Speakers in these communities aren't chatting to each other over phone lines or on internet dating sites. They aren't even able to send messages back and forth on clay tablets. You set out to walk across a vast plain. It's six thousand kilometers across. A few days into your walk, you encounter a settled group of people. While learning their language, you discover that their children play with a doll. The people tell you that they call the toy a *katija*, and you write it down in your notebook, faithfully reproducing the sounds used to pronounce the word. You notice that your adult informers are drinking a brew they call *bikum*, made of fermented barley.

You walk another thousand kilometers and encounter a new settled community. Their children play with a similar-looking toy, and you learn that it's called a *katijom*. Adults in this place drink *timta*, made from wild berries endemic to their habitat. You continue on, much farther, and find yet another group. Here the children play with a doll-like toy as well, a *katijat*. Adults drink *sochik*, made from the bark of a tree that thrives locally but is unknown elsewhere.

Toward the end of your trek, at the far edge of the plain, a final group is raising children who play with a stick toy they call a *katijis*. And adults consume a fermented beverage they refer to as *bikmos*. You note that it's made of barley.

Now that you've completed this hypothetical journey, let's survey your imaginary notebook:

1	2	3	4	Translation
katija	*katijom*	*katijat*	*katijis*	"toy doll"
bikum	*timta*	*sochik*	*bikmos*	"drink"

As a pretend linguist, you see patterns. These groups of people use somewhat similar names for similar things. You've noted as well that their languages show clear resemblances in grammar and syntax. The patterns strongly suggest that no one of the four languages could plausibly have given rise to the rest. How do you know this? It's a little like looking at color samples. Envision three: purple, green, and orange. Each has one source color in common with the other two. Green has yellow as one of its sources, and so does orange. Green also has a source color in common with the purple: blue was used to make both. But while green, orange, and purple share common sources, none of the three sample colors could have taken its shade from one of the other two: no matter how much purple and orange you combine, you won't ever get green. Linguists are able to make similar conclusions by looking at the sounds used to form words. If sounds used in one language could not have come from another known tongue—even a closely related one—the only credible explanation is that they arose from an unheard language whose speakers once voiced them.

Examining the different sounds and component parts of your recorded words, you conclude that an ancestor language had a word for something resembling a toy doll or human figure, something that would have been called . . . what? The words for "toy doll" are all different, but part of the word remains consistent in all groups of speakers. With confidence, then, you reconstruct a key part of the word in the missing language: *katij-*. You can't surmise how the word may have ended in the ancestor language—the endings of words in this language system clearly vary a lot—but you now have a reconstructed basis that you know is continued in the daughter languages. To show that your underlying form is not a specimen taken from a living or written language, you use the asterisk that linguists have adopted to represent any pieced-together verbal relics: **katij-*. So now you have something pretty solid to work with, a verbal form that linguists refer to as a *reconstruction*.

But can you be sure that a word built on this basis in the ancestor language meant "toy doll"? Could it have once meant "human being"? Or "stick toy," or something else? You can narrow the field by making comparisons. Looking over your notes, you find that your four languages also have similar words for toys resembling marbles, and you see that they also employ an *-ij* element attached to a word for "ball." Your evidence suggests that **-ij* is a diminutive suffix; adding it to "ball" gives "little ball," in this case "marble." Looking again at **katij-*, you deduce that **kat-* is a root meaning "human" in the ancestor language. And you see that the root + suffix form a stem, **katij-*, which in the missing language must have meant something like "little human," and possibly "toy doll" as well.

What about "drink"? Here it turns out that in these related cultures, the word for "drink" is taken from the drink's ingredients. However, ingredients naturally differ, depending as they do on local ecologies. Speakers of Language 2 use berries that grow only in their setting, and those of Language 3 use a regionally specific tree bark. Their words for "drink" are very different as a result, and may even be loanwords taken from unrelated neighbor languages spoken, or once spoken, where these berries and trees grow. But note that, though separated by thousands of kilometers and by cultures in which words for "drink" are quite different, speakers of Languages

1 and 4 both use a similar word for "drink." What's more, both make drinks from fermented barley. You have found another root, *bik-, passed down from the now-silent ancestor language. And depending on your method and further discoveries about Languages 1 and 4, you may determine that in the place where the now-quiet language was once spoken, people lived on land that yielded barley. Further clues may indicate that people who spoke the early language also made a drink from barley.

Your distant ancestor language, though silent for generations, is beginning to speak to you. What's more, thanks to your reconstructions, you are gaining insights into the way of life of the people who spoke it. Your discoveries are all the more stupendous when you consider that they are granting you access to a prehistoric world, and allowing you to glimpse the lives of people who left no written traces of their existence.

Now imagine that instead of having only four living languages from which to draw evidence, you have hundreds, living and dead. And that, in a number of cases, they afford you excellent written evidence of telling metamorphoses—in pronunciation, vocabulary, grammar, and so on—over thousands of years. Indeed, the earliest evidence from at least one Indo-European language, Hittite, dates back to the eighteenth century BC. No other family of languages has left such a range and depth of evidence that can be used to reconstruct the verbal life of its earliest speakers. In this way, the Indo-European family is unique. And it has consequently received a great deal of scholarly attention from those who mine surviving evidence for clues about the prehistoric sources of the language family.★

★For our imagined journey into the realm of language reconstruction, we've used words that sound similar. We saw too that the field of Indo-European linguistics got its start in the late eighteenth century when similar sounds were detected in related words across the diverse languages Sanskrit, Greek, and Latin. But the method that was developed roughly

Building on two hundred years of research in their field, and employing rigorous scientific methods to draw conclusions, most Indo-Europeanists think that the ancestor language was first spoken in a community that inhabited an area extending from the north side of the Black Sea to the east side of the Caspian. This region, called the Pontic Steppe, included part of present-day Ukraine, a portion of southwestern Russia, and a piece of Kazakhstan. As we've seen, dialects of Indo-European eventually evolved into languages that were spoken over much of the Eurasian landmass. Yet even as they covered an impressive range of territories throughout the Bronze and Iron ages, Indo-European languages did not cross any major bodies of water. Nor did they expand far north, into the Arctic Rim, or far south, into equatorial zones. (It is interesting to see that in these earlier periods, Indo-European languages were spoken within a certain latitudinal band, where certain ecological conditions prevailed.) While a "start date" as early as ten thousand years ago has been proposed, a more widely accepted working date for Proto-Indo-European is seven thousand years ago. But the language was spoken for a long time before it began to diversify into new languages. This prehistoric speech community split up no later than four thousand years ago, and possibly earlier.

The reconstruction of PIE is an ongoing project, and there are

---

a hundred years later to reconstruct forms of unrecorded ancestral languages in fact doesn't rely on the similarity of sounds among related languages. Rather, linguists compare *patterns* of sound change, which do not waver and are thus highly predictable. For example PIE *p* was always pronounced as an *f* in the Germanic branch but remained a *p* in the Italic branch. At first glance, an English word like *father* looks pretty different from the Latin word *pater*. But if you know that the *f* in *father* evolved from a Proto-Indo-European *p*, you'll more readily discern its relationship to the Latin *pater*. Certain words may appear to be unrelated because their sounds are so different, but since they abide by predictable "laws" of sound change as they change, the linguist is able to chart their affinities to words in other languages of the same family, and thus to make the kinds of comparisons that result in reconstructions of their common linguistic ancestor.[3]

some debates among specialists about the precise location and era of the community that spoke the mother language of all Indo-European languages.★ There are also disagreements about the ways in which offshoot languages evolved, and how and when they spread across the areas where so many Indo-European tongues are represented. Still, there is general consensus about the linguistic background of Proto-Indo-European and about how certain sounds have shifted in the development of its diverse daughter languages.† And just as we are able to glean much about Roman culture by scrutinizing the Latin lexicon, or about the culture of speakers of Old English by examining words they used—or, for that matter, about Global English culture as we ponder its fast-growing vocabulary—much of interest can be extracted from what we know of PIE. I invite you to take a moment to enjoy a sampling of reconstructed PIE roots.‡ You'll find that at least a few of these are alive and kicking in varied pronunciations of Global English:

*bher- "carry"   *sen- "old"   *deks- "right," "south"   *gel- "cold"
*dem- "house"   *dwo- "two"   *man- "man"   *magh- "to have power"
*mūs- "mouse"§   *webh- "weave"   *kwon- "dog"   *teks- "fabricate"¶

★For example, one view holds that the earliest speakers of PIE might have lived in Anatolia and within a time frame much earlier than that theorized for PIE speakers of the Pontic Steppe.
†Taken in isolation, Indo-European linguistics is admittedly a dry and abstract area of inquiry. But thankfully for nonspecialists, it informs more vivid studies that explore flourishing PIE roots within specific, literate Indo-European cultures.[4]
‡For a complete list of PIE roots, see Calvert Watkins, *The American Heritage Dictionary of Indo-European Roots*. Unless otherwise noted, Calvert Watkins is my source for all Indo-European roots. Throughout, I have cited roots in simplified forms that don't show actual linguistic reconstructions: Indo-Europeanists use a far more intricate set of symbols to capture sounds. A glimpse at the Indo-Europeanist's more precise symbolic tools, and at the extraordinary linguistic riddles that these can solve, can be found in the section on the word *star*.
§Another meaning of *mūs* is "a muscle." Watkins notes that this second meaning comes "from the resemblance of a flexing muscle to the movements of a mouse."[5]
¶This root underlies that major Global English word *technology*, and appears in an array of inescapable global-era expressions, from *information technology*, and hence *IT*, to *high-tech*

Indo-Europeanists have conjectured with compelling reason that because speakers of PIE had words for the domestication of animals, and for yoking and driving them to work the land, they were agriculturalists. They had a word for "plow," so we may safely infer that they had this implement and used it. They appear to have cultivated barley and to have ground it into flour. Speakers of Proto-Indo-European raised cows and sheep and sacrificed animals to gods. They also lived in a hierarchical society. Among the words that colored their world was one for "tribal king." Kinship terms were employed by them, including those for "daughter," "uncle," and "nephew." They also had words for some who enjoyed family status by marriage, such as the "mother-in-law," who continues to this day to play a starring role in the Indo-European-speaking family.

Speakers of Proto-Indo-European observed the heavens, had names for seasons of the year, times of day, and numbers. Their vocabulary included words for "milk," "butter," and "cheese." They spoke about bees and bears and salmon. Conversations included a word for "wheel." And for "horse." And yet another for the concept of being "in-between," rather than in one place or another. Their language tells us that they dwelt in houses replete with that remarkable advance on simpler apertures, the door. And that they used an arsenal of terms to distinguish weapons such as axes, bows, pikes,

---

and, as so many know all too well, *technical problem*, *technical difficulty*, *technical breakdown*, and, if all else fails, *technical support*. Note that in Proto-Indo-European, **teks-* meant more specifically "to fabricate with an axe." (Following the Stone Age, the metal axe in particular would have been a technological breakthrough.) The root therefore gives us a fresh angle on the phrase *cutting-edge technology*. There's no proper etymological relationship between *cutting-edge* and the technologically advanced Proto-Indo-European axe, but the imagery is nonetheless strikingly ancient. Other meanings of **teks-* are "to weave," an activity that vibrates with modern relevance in words like *text*, *texture*, *context*, and *pretext*, and "to make wicker or wattle fabric." The latter verb was used in Proto-Indo-European with reference to the construction of mud-covered house walls.[6]

and knives. They had verbs for killing, cutting, tearing, splitting, pounding, hacking, and slicing. And for giving birth, growing, laughing, liking, wooing, loving, swelling, singing, dancing, feasting, sleeping, spinning and weaving, inspiring, deceiving, mocking, praising, and dying.

It is stunning to consider that the same language used by a prehistoric people, having continued to evolve over thousands of years, is now being adapted for global use. As we'll see, English has inherited many words formed on Indo-European roots, such as *dhwer-* (which became *door* in English), by way of its ancestral language, Germanic. Beyond these "native" ties to PIE, English, which has proven to be an exceptionally absorptive language, has also borrowed many additional words from its Indo-European cousins across different branches of the language family. Indeed, astonishingly, over 50 percent of the known PIE roots currently flourish in English.

Just as huge numbers of new speakers are taking up English and remaking it into Global English, so in the past speakers of early Indo-European languages expanded the family far beyond its original homeland. Like English, too, some other daughter languages of PIE are known to have spread with the help of new technologies. But while it's tempting to compare the reaches of English and diverse Proto-Indo-European languages, it's essential to remember that they are all descendants of PIE. Even a technology as colossally influential as the World Wide Web, which has so greatly facilitated English's globalization, is linguistically rooted in the culture of those who spoke Proto-Indo-European. (For a look at the evidence, see the discussion of *blog.*) So while we remain aware that Global English is an unprecedented phenomenon, and that it's changing life on a scale few could have imagined possible not long ago, we'd also be right to remind ourselves that this "new" linguistic situation is, in the end, a chapter in a vastly older, Indo-European story.

Let's now see how some of these very ancient linguistic building blocks have been reshaped in the Global English terms *film*, *credit card*, *lol*, *blog*, *disco*, and *star*. When you've had your fill of PIE, we'll follow the spread of Indo-European farther down the branch that produced English. And we'll see how English, even in its earliest phase, was seeded with traits that have since served its globalization.

FILM

What does the movie character Tarzan have in common with the massively popular Global English word *film*? I mean, beyond the fact that both of these international success stories were launched in Hollywood. The answer lies in the ape-man's costume, skimpy as it is: his *pelt*, or "animal hide."

Film has its origin in a PIE root that flourished in words widely dispersed across the language family. Meaning "skin" or "hide," the root **pel-* underlies Latin words that preserved the initial *p*, such as *pellis*, for "skin," and related words that English gained from Latin via French, such as *peel* and, indeed, *pelt*. The Latin *pellicula*, meaning "a little skin," as in the peeling from a fruit, was passed down to Romance languages in various forms to mean "film," including, in some cases, the "Me Tarzan, you Jane" kind of film. And while

English did absorb the rarely used cognate *pellicle* to refer to the sort of "film" that you probably wouldn't be willing to stand in line to see, such as the scum forming on top of the yogurt that someone may have left for a little too long in the back of a fridge, it has also preserved its own native Germanic word, *film*.

An obvious question here is how does a root that starts with the sound *p* in early Indo-European become the sound *f* in English? The answer is that some influential person in the early communities of Germanic-speakers was pronouncing *p* sounds as *f* sounds, and that others then took up this pronunciation as well. This is one of the classic sound changes that allow Indo-Europeanists to reconstruct the prehistoric roots of the language family. Very consistently, the PIE **p* that shows up unchanged in Latin *pater* shifted in Germanic to the *f* we now have in English *father*. Similarly, in the case of *film*, the PIE **pel-* underlies Old English words such as *fell*, a noun still alive but not often heard in Modern English, in which it means "animal hide." But it was a variant form derived from this root that would produce the global entertainment industry's five-star word for its five-star medium: Old English *filmen*, meaning "membrane." Indeed, the first attestation of *film* shows up in a medical document from around the year 1000 AD, when, it appears, inhabitants of England might have been enjoying one or two too many cupfuls of mead:

> *Hēr sint tācn āheardodre lifre ge on þām læppum & healocum &*
> film*enum.*[1]
> Translation: Here are symptoms of a hardened liver at once on the lobes and the recesses and the membranes.

As *filmen* developed into the *film* that you'd be happy to shell out a few bucks to see in a cinema, its meanings widened. By the late

1500s, *film* could also denote a "layer," or "sheet" or "covering" of any kind of material, be it silk or suede. Or dirt. By then the word was also being used as a verb: *to film*. But this was strictly in the sense of "to cover with a film" of, say, silk or suede. Or dirt. Shakespeare was among the earliest to experiment with the verbal form of *film* in a passage from *Hamlet*. Here, Hamlet warns his mother not to take emotional refuge in his madness when what she really needs to do is tend to herself and examine her own "trespass," her sin:

> *Mother, for love of grace,*
> *Lay not that flattering unction to your soul,*
> *That not your trespass but my madness speaks.*
> *It will but skin and* film *the ulcerous place*
> *Whiles rank corruption, mining all within,*
> *Infects unseen. Confess yourself to heaven.*
> *Repent what's past. Avoid what is to come;*
> *And do not spread the compost on the weeds*
> *To make them ranker.*

(3.4.145–53)[2]

Not an auspicious start for the film industry. Thankfully, the word *film* continued to evolve. By the mid-nineteenth century, it referred as well to "a thin mist" or "haze," and also—now we're getting closer—to a "coating," including one "of light-sensitive emulsion." This latter coating was initially used on photographic plates made of glass or metal. But the American George Eastman discovered a way to apply it to celluloid in an easy-to-use roll form. Reckoning that his innovation had some business potential, Eastman prepared for possible success by registering the trademark Kodak in 1888. Film of this kind went on to become a staple of camera users around the world. Yet the global reach of *film* was cast even wider with the motion picture application of Eastman's innovation.

Coupled with a camera—or rather the Kinetograph, as Thomas Edison named the object he coinvented with his young assistant W. K. L. Dickinson—strips of Eastman's coated celluloid recorded still images that could, when viewed in rapid sequence, create the relatively fluid illusion of moving images. Mind you, the Global English *film* as shorthand for "narrative motion picture" was still to come. Until then, recorded episodes were comparatively experimental. For example, there was *Fred Ott's Sneeze*, which immortalized Fred Ott, an Edison employee, sneezing. But there were also signs of things to come: recordings of scantily clad ladies, violence, spectacles such as parades, and "unseen" sights, like dancing American Indians, or everyday life captured in "exotic" locales of East Asia, or in Mexico. These shows, while popular for a time in the United States and Europe, could only be "peeped," one viewer at a time, in another contraption bearing an Edison patent, the boxlike Kinetoscope.

Edison's innovations in film had been built on the breakthroughs of others, including the English photographer Eadweard Muybridge, whose still images, shown in rapid succession, magically portrayed motion; the French inventor Léon Bouly, who used film to record action; and his successors, the legendary brothers Auguste and Louis Lumière, who engineered sprockets that kept rolling film from sliding around, both when filmmakers shot scenes and when projectionists presented completed films to audiences.

In the United States and in Europe, technological and entrepreneurial advances made films increasingly lucrative entertainment for larger audiences. In 1902 there was Frenchman Georges Méliès's silent film *A Trip to the Moon*, which offered to viewers—no longer lining up for a solo peep, but gathered in theaters to experience film as part of an audience—a fantastic narrative experience replete with sci-fi plot and special effects. A year later, just as Hollywood grew into its own municipality, came *The Great Train Robbery* by American filmmaker Edwin Porter. While these early dramatic pictures were less than fifteen minutes long, they enraptured the public of their day. Seen retrospectively, they also demonstrate the unique potential of film as a medium of storytelling.

At the end of the decade, film studios had set up in Hollywood, where filmmakers could take advantage of the region's favorable climatic conditions, varied natural scenery, and abundant light. Hollywood was developed quickly, to the point that there wasn't enough water for its inhabitants. In 1910 the town was annexed to the city of Los Angeles. There, a new aqueduct would nourish the growing population of the Southern Californian ranch city as well as the country's young capital of *filmmaking*.

By 1912 Hollywood boasted its first generation of stars in such talents as Mary Pickford and Lillian Gish. That same year in the United States, the medium was accorded the recognition historically conferred only on written language. Thanks to copyright protection the film industry could profitably distribute its product to theaters around the country. Around the same time, in languages other than English, the word *film* began to refer not only to celluloid coated with a special emulsion but also to the rousing dramas presented in moving pictures. Initially, the term was used by insiders and devotees, but as Hollywood's reputation fattened thanks to those silent stars and directors who would command huge international followings, like Charlie Chaplin and Cecil B. DeMille, and as the new stripe of entertainment seized larger audiences, *film* became a favorite loanword around the world.

In Germany, "a film" would be *ein Film*, as with F. W. Murnau's intense 1922 vampire picture, *Nosferatu*. In France, it was *un film*, such as Jean Renoir's 1937 *The Grand Illusion*, realistically set during World War I and filmed on location rather than in a sound studio. In 1943 the rising Hindi film industry in Bombay released its blockbuster फ़िल्म, pronounced "*filam*," and sometimes "*pilam*," *Kismet*, which helped launch the career of India's first major film star, Ashok Kumar.

The American postwar period brought a new generation of films in color. Still, great films from around the world continued to be made in black-and-white. And around the world, most words for the form of entertainment continued to be variations of the native English *film*. From Japan, 1953 was a huge year for フィルム, or "fuirumu"—the Japanese pronunciation of "film." Masterpieces included *Tokyo Story*, by Yasujiro Ozu; *Godzilla*, by director Ishiro Honda; and *Seven Samurai*, by Akira Kurosawa. A few years later, the Arab world's فلم, or "film," capital in Cairo produced the remarkable *Cairo Station*, directed by Youssef Chahine. In 1963 Greek φιλμ, pronounced "film," gained Nikos Koundouros's earthy *Mikres Afrodites*, based on the myth of Daphnis and Chloe, with shepherds played not by actors but by . . . shepherds filmed in their natural settings.

In 1977 the Iranian director Abbas Kiarostami released the فلم, pronounced "fīlm," *Guzārish*, Persian for "report," the first of many features for which he would earn international renown. And 1982 brought *Private Life*, a Russian ФИЛМ, pronounced "fil'm" (with a "soft" *l*, as in the word "film" as opposed to the "hard" *l* in "luxury") by Yuli Raizman. Portraying everyday life in the Soviet Union as it was then rarely seen abroad, the film delicately enters the world of a man who loses his job. The noted Welsh *ffilm* of 1992, *Hedd Wyn,* offered a moving biographical take on its eponymous poet. And in 2003 there was *Aki na Ukwa*, a Nigerian "film" about two young brothers, Aki and Ukwa, who get into a lot of trouble. Like almost half of the huge numbers of movies produced in Nigeria, the picture, starring Chinedu Ikedieze and Osita Iheme, is in English.★

Film has proved itself an indispensable Global English word, even where it no longer has anything to do with films, or "coatings" of light-sensitive emulsions applied to plastic, or coatings of any kind. Digital cinematography, first marketed by Sony in the 1980s, has by now rapidly proliferated as a less expensive yet no less entertaining means to tell stories in moving images.

With new moving-picture technologies on the rise, the Global English word *film* now refers to stories, fictional or "true," told in any medium that projects pictures in motion. Including those about Tarzan in his pelt loincloth. Given that there have been close to a hundred Tarzan films since 1918, we can safely guess that we'll be seeing another about him before too long. And whether it's told in digital technology or a medium yet to be invented, its story will likely still be called a филм, فلم, フィルム, फ़िल्म, or *ffilm*. Or another version of the word whose roots go back to the Indo-European for "animal hide" and whose worldwide storytelling future is assured in Global English.

FROM *CINÉMATOGRAPHE* TO *CINEPLEX*

English inherited *film* from its Germanic roots, but borrowed the word *cinema* from French. In the late nineteenth century, the Frenchman Léon Bouly invented a machine that could both record and project motion pictures. He named the device a *cinématographe*, from the Greek terms *kínēma*, meaning "movement" (related to the English word "kinetic") +

★More films are made each year in Nigeria than in the United States. The affordability of digital filmmaking, and the popularity of widely distributed videos in English, Yoruba, and Hausa, have made Nigeria a thriving center of film production. Measured by numbers of films produced annually, Nigeria is second only to India: Mumbai is the world capital of moviemaking.

graphos, as in "writer" and related to the English *graphite*. A shortened version of the compound, *cinéma*, was then used to refer to films collectively, or to designate the space where films were projected. English borrowed the French word for these concepts of "the cinema," but also has alternative terms for the same ideas, including *film, the film industry*, and *movie theater* or *movie house*. Since the 1970s, speakers of American English have notably taken to using a shortened version of *cinema* in the compound word *cineplex*.

CREDIT CARD

Here's a strange fact: the first attestation of *credit card* appears decades before the thing itself. The phrase belongs to the utopian narrative *Looking Backward: 2000–1887*, by the American socialist Edward Bellamy. Writing in 1887, Bellamy set his story's action one hundred thirteen years in the future. By then, money has been replaced by pieces of pasteboard called *credit cards*.

In Bellamy's fiction, credit cards are not issued by banks looking to turn clients into rampant consumers and beleaguered debtors. (That glorious free-market story arc would only veritably begin some seventy years later, when Bank of America introduced the first nationwide credit card to the Eisenhower era, unleashing the miracle of washing machine and refrigerator "ownership" via wallet-sized debt-incurring pieces of plastic.) Instead, in Bellamy's book, the American government itself issues cards to men and women whose work earns them units of their share of the annual national product, exchangeable for goods and services. So instead of receiving a payment for himself, the family doctor, say, collects it "for the nation" by marking some of his patient's credit card units as used up. Bellamy imagined future American credit cards also working in European nations, where units, good as "American gold," could be exchanged for foreign currencies.[1]

Since the late twentieth century, no three syllables are more likely to animate global English-speaking vendors to finalize a sale than those of the question "Credit card?" Unless, that is, you're speaking to someone whose native language is syllabic, and therefore bound to break the consonant-heavy *credit card* into more than three syllables. In Japanese, for example, the phrase is delivered in eight syllables: "kurejittokaado," spelled クレジットカード in the Katakana alphabet.

Japan also happens to be a nation where the credit card is less popular than cash. There, consumers frequently carry out electronic transfers via their cell phones. If Japan sets trends in credit technology as successfully as it has in personal entertainment with devices like the Walkman and the camcorder, credit cards could eventually look about as up-to-date as letters of credit bearing a bank's wax seal. Until then, the world's buyers on credit fuss with jamming code-laden pieces of plastic into their billfolds.

Whether the stuff of socialist fiction or of capitalist reality, modern credit cards at first glance seem far removed indeed from any sacred concepts that were once wrapped around the roots of *credit*. If we look at the span of Indo-European branches from Tocharian to Celtic, we can see that languages at the far edges of the Indo-European spectrum share features that were missing in the more centrally located ones, such as Slavic or Greek. Linguists hypothesize that elements shared in distant parts of Indo-European territory are relics inherited from the ancestral prehistoric language. These relics preserve what appear to be especially archaic layers of Indo-European expression.

Credit is believed to be an exceptional example of this

phenomenon, a rare instance of an ancient locution in Indo-European: *kerd-* ("heart") + *dhē-* ("put"), meaning something like "to set the heart," and thus "to place trust (in)." Modern English has plenty of words built independently on these roots, such as the "heart" word *cardiac* and the "put" word *deed*, the latter of which in Old English captured the idea of a "thing done and set," including "a law."

Ancient phrases that reflect the combination of *kerd-* + *dhē-* show up in three distinct branches of Indo-European: Sanskrit, Latin, and Celtic. In all three, ideas having to do with "heart putting" carry religious significance.[2] In Latin, the linked forms are synthesized into one word: *crēdo*, "I believe" or "I put heart into." Old French had a number of words using variations of related Latin concepts of "believing" or "trusting," and among those that it passed on to English was *credit*, from the Latin *crēditum*, "a thing lent" or "a thing entrusted to another."

Card entered English in the early fourteenth century by a similar route: from the French *carte*, which was from the Latin *charta*, for "leaf of paper." But unlike *credit*, whose Latin form was inherited from Indo-European, the word *card* ultimately reflects borrowing into Latin from Ancient Greek. It comes from *khartes*, spelled χάρτης in Greek, meaning "a leaf of papyrus." Linguists don't see an Indo-European heritage in *khartes* but think it may be derived from an Ancient Egyptian word for "papyrus," not least because papyrus itself was made in Egypt.

If there is one realm of life that Global English does not particularly well serve, it's religion. True, American currency does profess trust in a higher power, but Global English is rather used for everything except spiritual beliefs, notably thriving in secular spheres like finance and commerce. The plastic credit card (seemingly tacit on the matter of faith, even as *credit* is at heart about little else) may, like paper and papyrus before it, be replaced by newer technologies. But *credit*, formed of sounds that were combined in sacred Indo-European expressions perhaps as long ago as ten thousand years (the earliest posited date for PIE), is unlikely to perish.

Credit systems at times lead us to conclude that we can't "put our hearts" or faith into them. But when it comes to the global economy, Global English-speakers will always be talking about some form of financial service that requires *credibility* if it's going to function properly. In the end, even something as seemingly nonreligious as credit only gains currency so long as it rests on shared cultures of belief. Recent turbulence surrounding the Global English word *credit* shows that the world is, for now, struggling to "put heart" into a planetwide system of financial practices.

LOL

Since the early twenty-first century, *lol* has been a must-have abbreviation.[1] Devised by internet users, it conveys mirth—"laughing out loud"—that is invisible and inaudible in purely onscreen interaction. This fresh addition to Global English has been adapted and refashioned with amazing speed, and to diverse uses. It seems too shiny new to have much to do with anything Proto-Indo-European. But intriguingly, it appears that the laughter of prehistoric people is echoed in the word *laugh*.

Laugh goes way back. While linguists can't tell us how prehistoric laughter sounded—or whether some Proto-Rodney-Dangerfield was telling mother-in-law jokes five thousand years ago—they have reconstructed a root for "to laugh": **klak-*. The concept of laughter is similarly (and thus tellingly) expressed in many branches of the Indo-European language family. Often words meaning "to laugh" feature sound repetition that appears literally to imitate the sound of laughter. Modern English does not preserve this imitative trait in the word *laugh*, but that's only because it's a shortened version of an earlier word that did. In Old English, "to laugh" was *hliehhan*, which evolved into *laugh*.

While Indo-Europeanists offer no reconstructed PIE root for "to laugh," they speculate that it must have sounded something like laughter itself, such as **khakha-*.[2] With *kh* sounding akin to the first *h* in Hanukkah, this isn't too far from the equally imitative English *ha ha*, which serves as a popular alternative to *lol*.

lol (it just looks wrong capitalized; like other vocabulary forged in cyberspeak it carries content indivisible from its form) is traveling the path that *OK* took in the late nineteenth century. That American abbreviation gradually came to embrace a broad range of affirmations around the world. (See section on O.K.) *lol*, launched in our era of sped-up communications, has naturally evolved faster.

We do find equivalents in other languages. Catalan has *mr*, *moltes rialles*, for "lots of laughs"; French, *mdr* for *mort de rire*, "dying of laughter."* But in these and many other electronically alive languages including Korean, Russian, and Hindi, *lol* is often preferred by younger interlocutors. The chat room visitor from Barcelona is likely to wind up in an exchange with a person in Mumbai, who won't get *mr*. So the global default setting? *lol*.

It can mean one's "laughing out loud," or just note that the "speaker" is kidding—laughing at his own joke. *lol* may also just

---

*Japanese has wwwww, or as many *w*s as you care to link, with more *w*s indicating greater hilarity. This isn't actually a word or acronym in Japanese, but some speculate that *w*s were adopted in the internet era to serve as invented symbolic characters akin to traditional kanji. When the internet caught on, traditional Japanese ideograms could not be employed, so the Latin alphabet was made to work in their stead. (As with "emoticons.") And wwwww adequately imitated, in the manner of a newly devised pictogram, the up-and-down body motions of the laughing person.

indicate a vague irony, as when a girl tags a snapshot in Bulgarian: "My mom and me! *lol.*" Or self-mockery, as in the Arabic caption to a photo of a luxury hotel: "My house *lol* in Dubai City." Or whatever it means when a Turkish-speaker reviews music: "I love this song—*lol*!" *lol* invokers are still generally on the young side, so they've fitted out *lol* to serve contemporary youth culture, along with its rampant ambiguities and awkwardnesses.★

As its users mature, *lol* gains gravity, and is retooled for use in still other contexts. (Before long, we should be seeing statements of this variety: "My shoulder replacement surgery *lol* went fine.") Moving from screen to talk, the abbreviation has also morphed into a one-syllable acronym: pronounced "lawl" but still spelled "lol." Here, *lol* resembles another Global English word that began as an acronym: *scuba*. Few people who use the word readily register the fact that its letters initially stood for words: *s*elf-*c*ontained *u*nderwater *b*reathing *a*pparatus. The acronym has since been combined in forms like *scuba diver*, and is used as a verb, *scubaing*.

But speaking of parts of speech, which would you assign to *lol*? None previously established. *lol* may be a pioneer, perhaps a new kind of Global English particle used in a plethora of grammatical senses to convey levity, irony, or reassurance: no offense intended! This is *lol*'s great virtue: in exchanges across cultures and oceans, its users learn to tread lightly, recalling that what sounds droll or goofy in Amsterdam could be fighting words in Addis Ababa. *lol!*

★American English in particular has long been seen by a good many non-Americans as an invigorated and invigorating source of new words and ideas, and generally as a language of youthfulness. As *lol* and other expressions of the internet era show, Global English is in many respects maintaining English's reputation as a "rejuvenator." An additional reason for English's ongoing associations with youth (apart from America's ageless distinction as an often naïve and indeed immature nation) is that English continues rapidly to spread, and is hence being learned—and used—by growing populations of children and young people.

SOME POPULAR ACRONYMS IN ELECTRONIC GLOBAL ENGLISH

k = OK

ruok = are you OK?

omg = oh my god

rofl = rolling on the floor laughing

gr8 = great (gr+eight)

asap = as soon as possible

afaik = as far as I know

btw = by the way

brb = be right back

bbl = be back later

ttyl = talk to you later

cul8r = see you later (c, u, l+eight+r)

imho = in my humble opinion

*$ = Starbucks (star+buck)

thx = thanks

10q = thank you (ten, q)

pls or *plz* = please

lol = lots of love, lots of laughs (alternatives to "laugh out loud")

OUT LOUD OVER MILLENNIA

Like *laugh*, *out* and *loud* are native English words with reconstructed roots in Proto-Indo-European. *Out* is from PIE **ud-*, meaning "up" and "out." *Loud* derives from **kleu-*, "to hear." But this was not just any verb for "to hear." It rather captured the important and prevalent Indo-European concept of "reputation" or "fame" or "what is heard about a person or deity and passed down for future generations to hear." With this sense, the root **kleu-* flourished as the *-cles* found in many enduring Ancient Greek names. One example is the heroic *Heracles*, whose name means "the glory of Hera" or "the undying fame of Hera." Another is *Sophocles*, the Greek dramatist whose name is a compound word meaning "reputed for wisdom."[3] Little wonder that the valuable **kleu-* root has been transmitted *loud* and clear over thousands of years. More surprising, perhaps, is that it has been diffused as never before in a Global English expression to do with something as fleeting as laughter.

BLOG

How likely would Global English be to absorb the word *shlog*? Would today's nearly 2 billion internet users embrace over 100 million *shloggers*, not to mention people reading and adding comments to so many *shlogs*?

The engineer of the World Wide Web, the Englishman Tim Berners-Lee, initially conceived of his creation as the "Information Mesh." If he hadn't changed its name, users of the new technology might have affixed the word *log* to that final *sh* in *mesh*, rather than to the final *b* in *web*, to *shlog* about the next elections or to download a "create your own *shlog*" platform—*Shlogger*? But things didn't turn out that way. Happily too, because the availability of the word *shlog* freed it up to become recent slang for, to put it politely, "slogging through sewage" and "school blog," uses that some English-speaking teenagers appear to find indispensable.

What's the story of this Global English word that has a significant fraction of the world typing and reading and arguing?

Web comes from the Indo-European root **webh-*, meaning both "to weave" and "to move quickly." This root has been reconstructed with a good deal of confidence because *web*-related words have flourished in so many branches of the language family. It has shown up in English but also in Albanian, Greek, Hittite, Sanskrit, and Tocharian B. Besides *weave* and *woof* and *weft*, English words related to *web* include *weevil*, from the Old English *wifel*, "that which moves quickly"; *waffle* and *wafer*, from a Germanic word for "honeycomb," with its woven appearance; *wave*, from Old English *wafian*, meaning "to move up and down," as the hand does when weaving rapidly; and *wobble*, borrowed from Low German *wabbeln*, meaning "to move from side to side."

And what were the Indo-Europeans weaving so energetically that their technology bequeathed words to do with speed and motion? Wool, mainly. Certainly nothing resembling the electronic data that race back and forth across the globe courtesy of the web that Tim Berners-Lee dreamed up.

In March of 1989, Berners-Lee was based at CERN, the European Organization for Nuclear Research, in Switzerland.* Well before the nonphysicist lot of us was introduced to the internet, Berners-Lee and his colleagues were accustomed to using computers to communicate with fellow researchers in labs scattered around the world. (One thinks of Alexander Graham Bell and how his invention was first used to link laboratories through phone lines.) Unlike other scientists, physicists, whose experiments require wide-scale collaborative efforts, embraced English as their professional lingua franca in the early twentieth century. The linguistic common ground has served their scientific community ever since. But while physicists' computer systems allowed data and ideas to be swapped in English, the machines themselves were set up like a string of islands, with user populations harnessed to pockets of information stored in isolated laboratory or office databases.

Berners-Lee pictured a system that would employ hyperlinks to interconnect all independent databases used by physicists. This would decentralize data and, in effect, *merge* databases, and their users, into a single, virtual space. In a proposal memo to his boss, Berners-Lee pointed out that the new system should be "future-proof," able to handle data packaged in ways that were as yet

---

*CERN: The "Organization" used to be called the European "Council" for Nuclear Research or, in French, the *Conseil Européen pour la Recherche Nucléaire*. Hence the original abbreviation CERN, which still has the old *C* even though it's no longer relevant. (See *SAT* for more on letters whose brand power is too valuable to give up, even when they no longer refer to anything.) CERN in fact stretches across the border between Switzerland and France, but Berners-Lee's historic idea was communicated on the Swiss side of the divide.

unforeseen. He added that it could "even" support data such as the laboratory telephone book, with hyperlinks connecting personnel by distinct criteria, such as their research group or office location.[1]

Wow. Did Berners-Lee, clearly a person of no little vision, foresee that, in just a few years, there would be a lot more to decentralize than telephone books and facility floor plans showing the visiting theoretical physicist the way from the coat room to the lab and, after a long morning among colliding protons, the optimal path to the closest WC?

Bye-bye, isolated islands; hello, World Wide Web. Just when Berners-Lee was nestled in the Alps, sketching out his dynamic concept, other isolated "islands," whole countries, were themselves stepping into a merged future. This other effort at fusion was unfolding in the realm of politics.

In the Kremlin, Mikhail Gorbachev had been cultivating *glasnost*, a policy of increased "openness" for the Soviet Union. In Poland, the first noncommunist workers' union in the Eastern Bloc, Solidarity, had fired up laborers of other nations, where governments were pressured to explore reform. By the spring of 1989, an Eastern Bloc nation was about to do something even more radical: open a physical portal to the West.

Hungary riveted the world's attention. Vacationing there over the summer of 1989, hundreds of East Germans took advantage of the opportunity—until then all but unthinkable—to cross over into Austria. This fissure in the Iron Curtain set off a chain of events, and by the end of the year the Berlin Wall had, at least conceptually, been razed.

By the time the World Wide Web, or WWW, was up and running with a user-friendly web browser, Mosaic, implemented in 1993, the Soviet Union was history. As were most of the governments that had been its clients. Not only did Eastern Europe and former Soviet socialist republics of Central Asia pursue new courses, so too did certain nations of Southeast Asia and Africa, such as Cambodia and Ethiopia.

These two independent developments—the rise of the World Wide Web and the end of the Cold War—now appear to be facets of a single phenomenon: the emergence of an openly interconnected, planetary community. The advent of that worldwide community, rooted not only in these momentous historical currents but also in the earlier adoption of a lingua franca by physicists and computer engineers, amounted to a great leap forward for Global English as well.

Web has since become a major Global English term, particularly in one of its elided forms: the critical *b* in *blog*. The contraction of *web* + *log* surfaced among English-based web users in the late 1990s, but gained global momentum after Google joined the web in 1998.[2] In 2002, William Safire, the late *New York Times* columnist, introduced *blog* and *blogger* to his readers, and floated his post–9/11 concept of all combined *blogs* forming *blogistan*.[3]

Blog is of course only one of many computer-related words that have gone viral in Global English. One thinks of *site*, *space*, *room*, *access*, *load*, *monitor*, *open*, *spam*, *mouse*, *text*, *clip*, and plenty more. And why wouldn't communications technology be driving—and accelerating—the evolution of Global English? After all, new communications technology is precisely the vehicle of new kinds of language use. And it's in these new technologies, rather than in any particular nation or region or municipality or river valley, that Global English can be said to be most "at home."

The internet has, faster than any other globally adopted technology, become very much the *web* envisioned by Berners-Lee. And it's retained his word's ancestral idea of weaving. In its latest guise, though, *weaving* is done on a loom that stretches clear across the world. And the *weavers* include some two billion daily internet users, as well as hundreds of millions of *bloggers*.

THE *LOG* IN THE *BLOG*

Web + *log* first appeared as the compound word *weblog* on December 23, 1997, when American Jorn Barger used it to describe his site, Robot Wisdom. *Log* is from a Middle English word of unknown origin. Barger used it in the sense of "a record," derived from the idea of a *ship's log*, "a book containing a detailed daily record of a ship's voyage." This seventeenth-century concept of the log was taken from the late-sixteenth-century idea of a "device for ascertaining the speed of a ship, a float attached to a line." Since the float was typically a log, as in a portion of a felled tree, the log cut from a tree gave its name to the log used for measuring a ship's speed in the water and, ultimately, to the book in which speeds and other details were chronicled. By chance, both *web* and *log* in this sense connote speed and motion.

DISCO

Few words have strayed so staggeringly far from their roots as *disco*, the American shortening of *discothèque*, a word English-speakers discovered in Paris in the mid-1950s.

French language authorities today define *discothèque* as follows:

> A. Room or building in which recordings [*disques*] are classified and preserved so that the public can, under certain conditions, come and listen to them.

Nice. This definition rhymes neatly with the French idea of the *bibliothèque*, or "library," as a similar kind of place, only filled with carefully organized books instead of recordings of music. But the following definition is the one that speakers of Global English would recognize:

B. Establishment where one goes at night to listen to recordings [*disques*], typically of modern music; to dance; and to drink.[1]

To understand the depth of the cultural divide at work here, consider that most Americans under age seventy-five would find even the idea of pronouncing the entire word *discotheque* too time-consuming. And over the postwar decades in which the discotheque has existed, and with the advent of file-sharing protocols, however piratical, exceedingly rare is that American who would take steps to inquire, say through a local library, whether and under which conditions certain recordings may be removed from archives for a listen.

The people who streamlined the word *disco* for what would prove to be its eventual adoption on a global scale would prefer to hit a disco to dance the night away. Or dance in their living rooms and dorm rooms. Or rock out from the waist up in their cars to disco anthems of the 1970s, like Donna Summer's epochal "Love to Love You Baby," or to the Bee Gees' "Stayin' Alive," as heard on the soundtrack of *Saturday Night Fever*. Or to "Dancing Machine," the hit by the Jacksons. Or to more recent tracks recorded by Gorillaz (from the United Kingdom), Justice (from the land of the *bibliothèque*), or Whitney Houston (America's own).

Disco's lexical ancestry gives few clues that the Indo-European root **deik-* was heading in the direction of serving conversations about nocturnal gatherings of alcohol-consuming youths who were to gyrate madly to recorded music. The root carries the idea of calling attention to something important, as in "to pronounce solemnly," or "to show," and, in its many derived forms, has to do with "directing" words or objects, literally pointing or sending them on a purposeful trajectory. Such objects have included "a thing hurled in a specific direction," or "the directed thing," or, to put it in Ancient Greek, the *diskos* of the athlete we know in English as the *Discus Thrower*.[2]

A related Greek word was *dikē*, meaning "the right direction indicated," or "justice." And in Latin there is the cousin word *iūdex*, for "the one who indicates the law," as in the related English word *judge*, and that *prejudiced* person who *judges* prematurely. An affiliated Latin word is *index*, whence the English "*index* finger" and the verb *indicate*. Latin also has *dicāre*, meaning "to proclaim," from which English-speakers have the words *abdicate*, *dedicate*, and *predicament*. Latin's closely related *dīcere*, meaning "to say" or "to tell," also underlies a litany of English words: *dictate*, *ditto*, *addict*, *condition*, *contradict*, *interdiction*, *jurisdiction*, and *predict*.

An alternative form of the Indo-European root, again to do with showing or indicating, is **deig-*, which appears in the native English words *token*, *betoken*, and that venerable one for pointing students down the best path, *teach*. But by far the most prominent Global English descendant of **deig-* is a word English has gained from the Latin for "finger," *digitus*. That would be *digit*, referring not only to a "finger" in English, but also to any numbers you can count on your digits, originally zero through nine. Thanks to the mathematical notation system that English-speakers gained from Arabic in the Middle Ages, *digit* is now heard in a host of expressions to do with *digital technology*.

What teaching, justice, predicting, index fingers, digits, and disks thrown by discus throwers all have in common is the idea that something or someone or some concept is being propelled in the right and best direction.★

And then came the American word *disco*. It's become global shorthand for *discotheque* in the nightclub sense of the word, as well

---

★Should this deep link between *disco* and the *index finger* prompt us to look anew at John Travolta's finger-pointing dance moves in *Saturday Night Fever*?

as for the musical genre that made *discos* the places to be (and dance and drink and much else besides, but don't direct the attention of any French academicians to these omissions) in the 1970s.

In the United States, disco as a culture left the mainstream in the early 1980s and discos were largely replaced by *nightclubs, clubs,* and *bars.* But you can still shake your nocturnal (and sometimes diurnal) booty at a disco in almost any city in the world, including New York and Miami but also Bangkok, Budapest, and Seoul. Or at the only disco on the desert island of Boa Vista, in the Cape Verde Islands, five hundred miles off the western shoulder of Africa. In all these places, you can also say "hello" in Global English to that latest incarnation of the Ancient Greek discus thrower, your *disc jockey,* or, to use the abbreviated form, your *deejay.* Or you can put in a request for your favorite disco CD. The DJ may not be familiar with KC and the Sunshine Band's "That's the Way (I Like It)." But until newer global technologies outdate the phrase, everyone will at least know what you mean by *compact disc.*

STAR

Star belongs to a class apart from Global English words like *shampoo, business, T-shirt, safari,* and *robot.* Elemental, natural, and visible to anyone able to observe the night sky, the stars belong to a group of select phenomena for which we can expect every language to have names. But for the vast majority of speakers in the world, the word for "star" is particular and culturally distinct. In Turkish it's *yıldız,* and in Swahili *nyota.* Thai-speakers say *duangdaw,* and Vietnamese *sao.* Japanese has *hoshi.* In the Marshallese language of Bikini Atoll, *iju* means "star."

Speakers of Cherokee say *no-qui-si*.* And in West Greenlandic, an Eskimo-Aleut tongue, the word is *ulluriaq*. Astronomers and astrophysicists alone use an international term; for roughly a hundred years, they (like physicists generally) have worked in English, and talk about *stars*.

For their parts, Indo-European languages point to a solid Proto-Indo-European root for *star*, telling us that speakers of their common ancestor language had enduring conversations about the pinpricks of light that shone down at night on the Eurasian soil they seeded and hoped to harvest. The root for "star," reconstructed from a sweeping range of evidence, underlies words in dead and living languages alike.

In the Celtic branch of the Indo-European tree there is Welsh *seren* and Breton *steredenn*. In the Italic branch, Italian *stella* and French *étoile* stem from Latin *stēlla*.† And from an eastern branch there is the living Persian word *sitarih*, descended from the prehistoric Iranian **stăr-*. The related Sanskrit form is *star-*. Armenian has *astì*. And in the Anatolian branch of the Indo-European language tree? Yes, a "star" word is attested in Hittite: *astiras*.

The simplified version of the Proto-Indo-European root for "star" is given as **ster-*. But the picture it paints is misleading. In this one enchanting instance, let's see how Indo-Europeanists have

---

*No-kwi-si is another way to render *star* in Cherokee, an Iroquois language in which syllables are used to build "words," or rather conceptual elements that can be expressed in multiple and creative ways. *Star* is written ℤℙℬ, with each symbol standing for one syllable of diverse pronunciations. For example, ℙ may be variously transliterated as *gwi*, *kwi*, *kw*, or *qui*, but the combined syllables meaning "star" are not frozen in place, and can be interwoven with syllables expressing other concepts to form new "words," which more closely resemble what in English would be sentences. For this reason, the very notion of a "word" is not well suited to *Tsalagi*, the Cherokee "word" for "Cherokee."[1]

†Interestingly, Spanish *estrella* and Portuguese *estrela* are not simply from Latin *stēlla*. Instead, they blend the Latin *stēlla* with the synonymous Latin *astrum*, the latter from the Ancient Greek for "star," *aster*.

used their full kit of nonalphabetic symbols.[2] The root for "star" is reconstructed as *$h_2$ster-, which looks scary, but it tells an amazing tale about how prehistoric speakers of PIE viewed stars. It turns out that the strange-looking reconstructed form, while usually referred to as a root, is in fact a root + a special suffix. If we break it down, we have the root *$h_2$es-, meaning "to burn," and *ter-, an agent suffix. Putting these parts back together, we learn that "star," in the ancestral language, meant "the burner." *

In Old English *steorra* was the word for one such luminous celestial object, in Old Norse *stjarna*, and in current Dutch *ster*. In Yiddish it's *shtern*. And in Danish *stjerne*. But among all these various related ways of saying "star," the only word to have gained planetwide recognition and use is English's own *star*. That is, German-speakers preserve their related word *Stern*, Arabic-speakers their totally unrelated word *najm*, and speakers of Mandarin Chinese their distinct *xīng*. But many millions among them have also adopted the English word *star* to refer to that creature who is anything but one among the scattered many: the human star, the person who stands out from the rest.

Given the prominence of theater in British culture, it's not surprising that the earliest uses of the word *star* in the world of entertainment refer to stage talents. The great Shakespearean actor David Garrick was indirectly acknowledged as "the big star" when actors

*One very ancient Indo-European word for "star" deserves a starring moment of its own. In the language known as Tocharian A, *śreñ*, "the stars," were perceived collectively. It was used only in the plural, so that stars themselves were perceived as a single, collective entity. This may sound strange, but English isn't unfamiliar with plural-only nouns. Some examples are *shorts*, *scissors*, *glasses*, and *binoculars*—all things we think of only in the plural. No native English-speaker is going to say, "Hey! I believe that's a red-throated pipit. Can you pass me a binocular?" Seeing stars in this plural-only way is akin to conceiving of "the heavens"—by which we refer not to a grouping of independent heavens but to one larger-than-life object of wonderment.

diminished by his presence were described, in 1779, as "the little stars." Stars of all magnitudes were subsequently sought by theaters to attract audiences. But with the arrival of cinema, *star* in this special sense enjoyed its first step toward meteoric success as a global term.

Famous movie actors were acknowledged *film stars*, a fitting adaptation of the theatrical idea of the *star*, not least because the cinema actor literally shone out on silver screens in darkened rooms. Even the first attestation of this newest kind of performing arts luminary hints at the reach of fame to come, with "the greatest film stars in the world" putting things globally in 1914. Soon thereafter, *star* was adopted by other cinema-going cultures of the day. It cropped up in French in 1919, although at first French-speakers weren't sure which gender to give the English word, so both the masculine *le star* and the feminine *la star* were freely employed. By now, the French have settled on *la star*, taking the gender from their own word for "star," *étoile*. Even a male star is referred to with the feminine article: *la star* of the film *Titanic*, for example, being the incomparable Leonardo DiCaprio.★

As so often where English has gained widespread currency courtesy of the arts and entertainment, we have Hollywood to thank for supplying Global English with *star*, one of its most brightly recognizable words around the world, just as we have the City of Los Angeles, and in particular its chamber of commerce, to thank for over two thousand bronze stars artfully embedded in otherwise

★As a loanword, the English *star* has been given diverse genders in languages employing gendered nouns. For example, it is the feminine *la star* in Italian and the masculine *der Star* in German. These are the two most-spoken languages in the border region of Italy and Austria where you can visit Ötzi, also known as the Iceman. At 5000-plus years old, his mummified corpse, clothing, hat, shoes, weapons, hunting gear, backpack, medical kit, and other belongings entrance visitors to the South Tyrol Museum of Archaeology in Bolzano, Italy. Named for the Ötz Valley adjoining the glacier where he was discovered in the Alps, Ötzi, Europe's most media-friendly Copper Age individual, is called a *star* in Italian and German.

soulless concrete to symbolize the immortality of real and fictional stars—from astronaut Neil Armstrong to Walt Disney, and from Marilyn Monroe to Mickey Mouse—who have culturally enriched audiences of mass entertainment, and financially enriched its symbolic capital. The Hollywood film studio Metro-Goldwyn-Mayer, or MGM, has long been understandably proud to boast, in its quasi-official motto, "More stars than there are in heaven."

Little wonder that the number of "burners" adorning the sidewalks along the Walk of Fame is now roughly equal to the number of natural stars visible to the naked eye in most parts of the world where light pollution only minimally interferes with stargazing. But as Global English makes planetary gains, we can expect media stars to outnumber their ancient namesakes in more populated locations. Around Las Vegas, where Hollywood stars abound on stages and screens from dusk till dawn, anyone scanning the firmament for signs of a celestial flicker or two will be lucky at this point in the city's synthetic-light-bathed sprawl to make out more than a handful. And even then, at least some astronomical knowledge is needed to distinguish the odd twinkle from so-called space trash, those man-made objects littering the sky in the form of aircraft, spacecraft, satellites, and discarded junk that reflect a ray of natural or artificial light from time to time.

Whatever their words for stars in the sky, speakers of Turkish, Portuguese, German, and other tongues turn to native-language media outlets named partly or entirely in Global English, often putting the word *star* in the limelight. Star TV broadcasts to Tanzania in Swahili. *Hello Star*, a magazine published in Thai (and English), contains sections titled "Star Focus," "Star Buddy," and "Star Fashion." Turkey has the newspaper *Star Gazetesi*. And the Dutch-created *Star Academy*, one of the most popular TV shows on the planet, now runs in dozens of national versions from sub-Saharan

Africa to the Balkans and Brazil. (By chance, *Star Academy* was first telecast in France in 2001, the year that a similar offering, *Pop Idol*, aired in the United Kingdom. The following season that TV show spawned *American Idol*.)

In most of its Global English manifestations, *star* preserves ideas of celebrity and media prominence. Or of realizing sensational dreams. Aptly, *Eurostar* was the name given to the high-speed train service that linked Continental Europe to Britain under a significant body of water. But *star* in Global English isn't always about the famous or the fantastic. The Taiwanese girl band S.H.E. ignited huge audiences with its 2003 mega-hit "Super Star." A sample of its lyrics:

wŏ	zhī	ài	nĭ	*You are my super star.*
I	only	love	you.	*You are my super star.*[3]

The core of the song is in Chinese, but its refrain is delivered in Global English, the language in which *you* get to be a *superstar*.

ANCIENT GREEK, LATIN, AND GERMANIC WORDS IN ENGLISH ALL DESCENDED FROM THE PROTO-INDO-EUROPEAN ROOT *STER-*

Building on its native Germanic word *star*, English has the verb *to star*; compounds like *stardom*, *all-star*, *stargazer*, *five-star*, *starstruck*, and *superstar*; and phrases such as *rock star* and *pop star*. English words employing the Ancient Greek for "star," *aster*, include *asteroid*, *astronaut*, *astronomy*, *astrology*, *asterisk*, and, combined with the Latin prefix *dis-*, meaning "apart," "removed," or "deprived," *disaster*. From the Latin for "star," *stēlla*, English has *astral*, *stellar*, and *constellation*. And of course who's likely to forget Marlon Brando as Stanley Kowalski in *A Streetcar Named Desire* bellowing "STELLAAA!"

3

MADE IN ÆNGLISC

D oesn't the word *English* look weird in Old English? *Ænglisc*. Anyway, that was one way to spell it.★ It's funny to consider that *Engl-ish* originally meant "Angle-like." Not an angle as in one of the three composing a triangle, but Angle as in the Angles, who migrated from their tribal territory, Angeln, in an area overlapping present-day Denmark and Germany, to Britain. They're usually remembered with the Saxons, as in "Anglo-Saxon." This hyphenate adjective survives as well in the name of their language, but today "Old English" is preferred, in part because it was not used *only* by Angles and Saxons. Still, the Angles were among the inhabitants of "England" (yes, Angleland) who spoke the oldest known version of "English." So, speaking "like an Angle" meant speaking *Ænglisc*.†

We're taking a look at the emergence of *Ænglisc* as a distinct

---

★*English* was written in dozens of different ways before spelling was standardized. In Old English, it usually appears as *Englisc*, with the *sc* pronounced "sh." Among the diverse spellings are *Æncglisc, Englesc, Onglisc,* and *Englis*. In Old English, -*isc* (and the -*isc* like variations on that spelling) more precisely carried the sense of "shares the nature of."

†Angles themselves would surely have been astounded by any suggestion that Anglelike behavior could, fifteen hundred years beyond their time, become a worldwide practice.

language, to see how it began its evolution into Global English. A natural temptation is to find signs of the language's future awaiting us in its past, as if English had been destined from the outset to turn into a planetary lingua franca. But for now we'll resist that temptation and try to see the language in its earliest phase for what it was, in its own time. English's current status is largely the outcome of multifarious historical accidents. By getting to know more about the language, too, we can better appreciate its fundamental building blocks. In this chapter, we'll explore some important features of Old English that still exist today—as well as those that have been lost—in order to gain a better picture of how and why English has come to be adopted even by speakers on whom it was never imposed. Let's now look at how and when English first differentiated itself from its various cousins both near and distant on the Indo-European family tree.

Clearly, languages can change a lot over so many millennia. Indeed, as we've seen, changes generate the clues that scholars use to reconstruct Proto-Indo-European (PIE) and other prehistoric languages. As we'd expect, then, Old English was different from the English you're reading now. Let's take a moment to set the "English" stage.

This may remind you of a "Who's on first?" routine. In pre-English England, speakers of diverse languages are hopping to new language bases around the mound, ditching languages in mid-inning, and being called out. It can be tricky to keep track of who's speaking what when and why.

First, we have the Neolithic natives of the archipelago we'll anachronistically call the British Isles. We don't know what that prehistoric population spoke; its language is out of the game with the arrival of Indo-European's Celtic branch. Celtic-speakers migrated into "Great Britain" several centuries before the region would receive a visit, in 54 BC, from its first historically attested celebrity: Julius Caesar.

The visit's purpose, formulated in Latin, was to conquer the island. But even though Caesar deployed boatloads of his legions, his first effort was unsuccessful. Rome never would manage to subdue the British Isles entirely, but it did eventually establish a province, Britannia, on part of the island that would later be called England. And to maintain order among often-unruly natives (descendants of earlier immigrants), the empire imported auxiliary troops and administrators from another of its provinces: Germania. Perhaps as early as the second century AD, and until the eve of the empire's withdrawal from Britain, in 410 AD, speakers of Germanic languages were transplanted to Britain to serve Rome's imperial mission.

So who's on first in linguistic Britannia when the Romans decamp to defend their beleaguered continental empire? When the Celts first arrived in "Britain," they spoke one language, named (retroactively, as are most of these languages) Brittonic, which evolved into Breton, Welsh, and Cornish. (Breton was spoken by Britons, who later migrated back to the Continent, where they inhabited the region that is now Brittany, in France.) We've got at least one unknown, probably eliminated language of the Neolithic era. Latin's out (the Romans have more pressing concerns than what's being said, and how, in the British Isles). And we've got a number of closely related Germanic dialects, spoken by Rome's former mercenaries. Those imported employees are now effectively jobless, but will eventually establish their own realms on the island, where Rome has left a power vacuum.

Meanwhile, long-mounting pressures that sent the Romans packing are also pushing new populations into Britain, and this time not to raid and leave, as some had in the past, but to stay. Shifting across Europe since the fourth century, populations of Huns, Visigoths, and other groups had been competing for territory and resources. Added to these man-made disasters, natural ones, such as floods and crop failures, also likely motivated Germanic migrations, including into former Britannia. What's more, by around 450 AD, Attila the Hun, with his so-called barbarian hordes, had entered the Germanic region on the continent, adding yet more good reasons for tribes from there to find new places to make their homes.

Chief among Britannia's freshest Germanic inhabitants would be Saxons, Angles, Frisians, and Jutes. By 600 AD, these tribesmen had forced the indigenous Celts into the west of former Britannia and established clusters of kingdoms in which their West Germanic dialects began to take new forms. Scholars have named these emergent dialects of English after the kingdoms where they were spoken: West Saxon, Mercian, Northumbrian, and Kentish. Note that these languages don't match up perfectly with tribal groups: the first was spoken in a kingdom founded by Saxons, the next two by Angles, and the last by Jutes.

And now we have yet another "meanwhile." For as ex-Britannia and its environs were, linguistically, now part Celtic and part West Germanic, an ejected language got back into the game: Latin. This time Latin wasn't a medium of military sway, or of imperial rule, but rather of religion and learning. In 597 AD, Augustine, Bishop of Canterbury (eventually canonized, yet not to be confused with the earlier Saint Augustine, author of *The Confessions*), undertook a successful mission to Christianize the island. Thereafter, growing communities of clerics dotted the region, introducing ecclesiastical Latin words and ideas into its evolving mix of languages.

One interesting point to consider is just how much people in the different kingdoms initially understood one another when circumstances required them to converse outside their own language groups. It is difficult to know exactly just how easily the diverse Germanic dialects were likely to have been mutually comprehensible. But it was probably without much difficulty, given their close linguistic kinships, that the clusters of West Germanic languages sporadically evolved into what would become the earliest manifestations of English.

So what's the start date for English? Arguably, it could fall in the fifth century, after the Romans left Britannia to its hapless Celtic- and Germanic-speakers (the latter, left in charge to cope with unraveling Roman rule, were all too aware that chaos was brewing in the empire). In this period, as more speakers of West Germanic dialects arrived from eroding Germania to settle in a crumbled Britannia, the dialects began to differ from those spoken on the Continent. These insular forms of West Germanic developed into early forms of spoken "English." If what one cares about is *spoken* English, then, the language surely "began" before it was written down, or rather inscribed on whalebone, as it was in the mid-seventh century.

Yet another approach to a start date would be to look at the historical moment when Old English is first seen not simply to be written but to flourish in writing. This would take us deep into the late ninth century, when the brilliant West Saxon king Ælfred, a poet and translator as well as a monarch, advanced the language in spheres of law, education, administration, and more. He was also the first sovereign to style himself king of England, when he united early English kingdoms to defeat their common enemy: the invading Danes. From the time of Ælfred's dramatic undertakings, English would head in a surprising new direction. Before we take a look at that big moment, though, let's pause to get a feel for Old English in its earliest phase, when it still closely resembled the languages from which it sprang.

· · ·

In today's English, a nose is a *nose* no matter what it's up to in a sentence. One can say "The nose smells the rose." Or "The rose attracts the nose." Or "I put the rose before your nose." In each case, the word *nose* remains the same, whether it's the subject, the direct object, or the indirect object in a sentence. In Old English, the word for "nose" was *nosu*. But this word took different endings depending on its grammatical role. If you wanted to say "The rose is under your nose," for example, the word for "nose" would be *nosa* instead of *nosu*.

Today English nouns take obligatory special endings in the plural. *Nose* becomes *noses*. But in Old English, special endings with other meanings were even added to the plural form. So, if many noses were sniffing your rose, you'd have said, "The rose is under your *nosum*." These are just a few examples of special endings used for the class of nouns to which *nosu* belonged. I won't burden you with added facts about how the adjectives describing your various noses would also have been "declined," or given special case endings, depending on your nose's or noses' grammatical functions. You can see well enough, from the nouns alone, that Old English used a different kind of grammar.

Another basic difference: in current English, *nose* and other nouns have no grammatical gender. We use specifying words like *the* or *that* for them all, across the board. You can say *the nose* and *the artichoke* and *the hippopotamus*. Or *that marmalade* and *that daydream* and *that theory of the universe*. We don't have to worry whether nouns are masculine, feminine, or neuter. But in Old English, as in almost all Indo-European languages, words for "the" and "that" vary with the gender of the noun they specify.

Let's stick with *nose* to see how this works. In Old English, *nosu* was a feminine noun, so if you wanted to refer to a particular nose, you'd say *sēo nosu*, "that nose." Yet with a masculine noun—say, *fugol*, meaning "bird"—you'd use *se*. And as if two genders weren't complicated enough, there was a third, the neuter. Hence, *lomb*, "lamb," would take *þæt*, which now looks odd because it employs some non-Latin letters but was pronounced somewhat like the current word it spawned: *that*. Keep in mind that these articles, too, changed depending on their grammatical roles.

These variable endings and shifts in words are collectively termed *inflection*. Old English was a highly inflected language. That is, to speak it, you had to know not only the genders of nouns, and how to modify them and their adjectives and articles, but also how to modify pronouns and verbs. English still has some inflection, even if native speakers are barely aware of it. Besides the added *-s* to form regular plurals, another *-s* comes into play with certain verbal forms, as when we say "He raids and plunders" as opposed to "Let's raid and plunder!" Plus, we add an *-s* generally to put a noun in the possessive case, as in "Mrs. Greider's desk globe." ★

We also have some vestigial inflection that's increasingly

★The possessive *-'s* is a special ending that Modern English nouns inherited from Old English, in which *-s* endings were used with certain nouns to designate possession. The possessive *-'s* isn't to be confused with the kind of *-'s* we see in "Where's Bill Perry?" That *-'s* is simply a stand-in for *is*, with the apostrophe replacing the missing vowel. While the possessive *-'s* ending is now widely used, it isn't obligatory in the same way as plural *-s*. For example, if I want to say "Alaya's Aymara village," I can also put the idea differently, as with "the Aymara village where Alaya lives." Or if I want to say "Jack's stinky rubber wet suit," Modern English allows me to get around use of the *-'s* by saying "the stinky rubber wet suit belonging to Jack." In Old English, nouns used in the possessive case simply had to take special endings. As it happens, the Modern English *-'s* was inherited from only one of several Old English noun endings used for this case, also called the *genitive*. That was the genitive singular ending on what are called masculine strong nouns. An example of this type of noun is our just-seen *fugol*, Old English for "bird." To say "of" or "belonging to" the *fugol*, the noun became *fugles*. It was the *-s* ending on this kind of noun that was later adopted for all nouns, and which appears as the *-'s* in Modern English. Things might have turned out differently for Modern English if the genitive ending for another class of Old English noun had prevailed over the one taking an *-s*. After all, singular genitive endings in Old English also included *-e* and *-an*.

optional, much to the chagrin of strict English teachers. We say
"Who is on first base?" But when "who" shifts from subject to object, we (now almost never) say "To whom did you pitch the strike?"
Most current English-speakers couldn't care less about *whom*, and
have little use for it. After all, no one is confused by sentences like
"Who did you pitch the strike to?" To put *who* and *whom* in perspective, though, consider that speakers of Old English had seven
distinct forms of the word *who*. The language was far more inflected
than even the most grammatically conservative English is today.[1]

The tenth century saw a noteworthy development in English's
transformation. The language began to show signs of influence by
the tongue of its speakers' aforementioned rivals: the Danes, a.k.a.
the Vikings.

Beginning in 793 AD and continuing for decades thereafter, Viking raids brought North Germanic clansmen to the coasts of Britain. These incursions became increasingly brazen, to the point that
they couldn't fairly be described as raids. Viking warriors began
instead to tack sojourns onto their pillaging expeditions. Eventually, rather than return to their homes in Scandinavia, they simply
settled, at first along the coastlines they had come to know so well
from seasonal raiding expeditions, and then in their own sizable territory, the Danelaw (as in "where the law of the Danes ruled").

King Ælfred spent much of his military life battling these aggressive cohabitants of the landmass that would later, in part because
of his effectiveness, become "England." The Danes pushed his
kingdom, Wessex, into a pocket of the island's southwest. Ælfred
therefore had occasions to negotiate peace treaties (for what they
would prove to be worth) with Guthrum, the leader of the Danes,
whose region bordered Ælfred's. The relative newcomers' language,
Scandinavian, also called Old Norse, was in fact related to the English spoken by Ælfred's subjects, but it was different enough for

confusion to arise. This "foreign," North Germanic language would alter the course of English.

With Ælfred's death, his crown passed to his children, including his daughter Æthelflæd and her husband. Under them, battles with the Danes continued, until Ælfred's grandson, Æthelstan, expanded English rule across the island. But from the late tenth century onward, for nearly eighty years, England's first royal family was unable to rule without interruption.

At various times, the Scandinavian-speaking Vikings gained the upper hand, and added England to their own kingdom. These periods of Scandinavian sovereignty and linguistic dominance left marks on English. Influence on English was especially strong in the north, where the Scandinavian presence was most entrenched. There, it appears that the English and Vikings set up house together, and raised bilingual children. By the time that bilingualism died out, English had prevailed over Old Norse to become the population's mother tongue, but not without being transformed by the Vikings' language. Consider the most spectacular instance of Old English grammar's retooling in the wake of its speakers' pivotal contact and intermixing with speakers of Old Norse.

The English words for *him* and *them* were initially one and the same: *him*. If we're using Old English to say "Give *him* your peace treaty," it could mean either "Give it to one male person (him)" or "Give it to several people of any combination of genders (them)." Take your pick. Old English–speakers were expected to infer intended meaning from context. But Old Norse left no such wiggle room. It had distinct words for these two ideas, each with its own grammatical function. Amazingly, English eventually dropped some of its own pronouns to make room for those it adopted from Old Norse.

While languages can easily borrow new nouns and verbs, it's

extremely rare for them to borrow pronouns. To picture how radical such a step is, think of it in terms of surgery. If adding nouns were akin to a face-lift, adopting grammatical elements as basic as pronouns would be closer to a heart transplant. Were it not for this grammatical porosity, English could now be using modern versions of its old plural pronouns *hīe*, *him*, and *hira*. Instead, these Old English words were replaced by Norse words that we still use today: *they*, *them*, and *their*. Borrowed from Scandinavian, these forms are helpfully distinct from the Old English versions that could so easily be confused with the singular male pronouns *hē*, *him*, and *his* (in Modern English *he*, *him*, and *his*) and the singular female pronouns *hīe*, *hire*, and *hire* (in Modern English *she*, *her*, and *hers*).

Exceptional as this grammatical shape-shifting was, it wasn't the only way English would change beginning in that era. With time, English would, dramatically, lose much of its inflection, those special endings and word alterations that so characterize many Indo-European languages. In fact, the very phrases used to distinguish linguistic periods of English—Old English, Middle English, and Modern English—were initially inspired by the observation of this gradual loss of inflection, Modern English being the least-inflected form of English to date. One clear possibility suggested in this progression is that, as English evolves into Global English, it could lose even more—possibly what little residual inflection it has left.

But just as critical in the story of the language's evolution as inflection, or rather the growing lack of it, has been English's extraordinary absorption of "foreign" words and concepts. In its Old English phase, English adopted words from all the various Indo-European languages that came into contact with it, including those from distinct branches—Celtic, Italic, and, by way of Latin, Hellenic.

Classical Latin supplied terms from its military and imperial culture, which English transformed into powerful words such as *mīlitisc*, meaning "military," and *port*, "harbor," as well as the practical measuring term *mēter*, now "meter." From ecclesiastical Latin, English gained not only the Latin alphabet but also the grand words *biblioðēce*, for "library," and *crīstendōm*, for "Christendom." That last word illustrates a case of compounding, or making one word from two or more, something that can be done with ease in Germanic languages, and that Modern English has not lost. The first part of the word, while introduced into English by Latin, is in fact derived from the Ancient Greek for "anointed," *khristós*, and the second part, *dōm*, is a native English word for "state" or "condition." This latter word has by now become a suffix, as in *freedom*, but the Old English version of *freedom* was a compound built of two words: *frēo* + *dōm*.

Compounding, a distinctive feature of Germanic languages, supplies English-speakers with an important and flexible means to borrow from other tongues, and to form new words built from diverse sources and elements. (While certain speakers of American English were delighted to hear such new compounds as *Batmobile* and *Batcave* or *Bat-time* and *Bat-channel* in 1966, few, apart from my then-partly-deaf grandmother, were so flummoxed by such linguistic creativity that they had to ask fellow TV watchers, "What is that man saying?" Then again, her grandparents probably asked her the same question when a voice on the radio used words like *airport* and *carwash*.) Speakers of English generally accept and innovate compound words with ease.

From Celtic, Old English mainly gained place names, and a few words such as *crag*, and *cairn*, for "heap of stones." From its fellow Germanic language Scandinavian, it absorbed a wide range of terms, including those for "sky," "birth," "steak," "skin," "skill,"

Building English[2]

English is a Germanic language, but even from the earliest phase its vocabulary came from a mix of tongues.

1 A Celtic language, spoken in "England" before the emergence of English, contributed a small number of words to English.

4 Vikings raid and settle areas of England beginning in the late 8th century. More than 1,500 Modern English words descend from their language, Scandinavian.

3 As the Roman Empire falls in the 5th century AD, Angles, Saxons, and Jutes dominate parts of England and speak dialects that evolve into English.

England

2 Latin arrives with Julius Caesar in 55 BC, and returns in the 7th century through the church and education. Nearly 25,000 Latin words from these eras remain in Modern English.

5 Between 1066 and 1500 AD, England was long ruled by speakers of French, which added close to 9,500 words still used in English.

THE ENGLISH IS COMING!

"time," "to take," "cake," "are," "happy," and "law" and "outlaw." The Old English lexicon was even augmented by a few words from beyond the Indo-European realm when its earliest speakers were Christianized. Words in Hebrew, which is not Indo-European but rather belongs to the Semitic family of languages, survived translations of sacred texts intact. Embedded in Koine Greek, and preserved in Latin translations of the Bible, a few Hebrew terms were widely employed in Old English, such as *amen* and *alleluia*, Hebrew for "so be it" and "praise Yah," more often rendered "verily" and "praise the Lord."

We should remember, though, that even the most learned figures of the era, including the Venerable Bede (also made a saint), had zero inkling that Hebrew was a language unrelated to English, Latin, Greek, and so many others. It was for them an article of faith that Hebrew was the primeval human tongue, spoken by Adam and Eve, and hence the source of all earthly languages.★

In spite of varied borrowings, though, the lion's share of the Old English vocabulary was what's been called "native," in that its words

★From Bede's day, it would take over a thousand years for the Christianized view of the world's languages to be displaced by theories, now fully accepted, that Latin and Greek were related to Sanskrit and not to Hebrew. One can imagine how shaken many in Christendom were by this hypothesis. The kinship between Sanskrit and Western languages of antiquity had been noted since the seventeenth century, when clergymen from Portugal and France, having traveled to India and learned Sanskrit, had occasion to contemplate its likeness to languages they knew. But while the clergymen were onto something, Sir William Jones is generally credited for setting linguistic study down the path it remains on today. On February 2, 1786, in Calcutta, Jones delivered these now-famous remarks to fellow members of the Asiatick Society of Bengal: "The *Sanscrit* language, whatever be its antiquity, is of a wonderful structure; more perfect than the *Greek*, more copious than the *Latin*, and more exquisitely refined than either, yet bearing to both of them a stronger affinity, both in the roots of verbs and the forms of grammar, than could possibly have been produced by accident; so strong indeed, that no philologer could examine them all three, without believing them to have sprung from some common source, which, perhaps, no longer exists." That common source first imagined by Sir William is none other than the one we now refer to as Proto-Indo-European. His observations were published in 1788, in the journal he had founded, *Asiatick Researches*.

were not borrowed, but rather passed down from its immediate linguistic ancestors. Consider some of these words, extracted from the epic *Beowulf.* These literary specimens, all compounds capturing the Germanic nature of the language, offer windows onto the Anglo-Saxon world as seen through the lens of its heroic poetry:

wīn-reced	wine-hall
medu-drēam	mead-joy
word-hord	word-hoard
benc-swēg	bench-rejoicing
niht-bealwa	night-evil
nīþ-grim	attack-fierce★
gūð-rinc	war-hero
upp-riht	up-right
morgen-lēoht	morning-light
rūm-heort	room-heart ("generous")

Of course, the nearly twenty-five thousand words known to be native to the Old English vocabulary didn't appear out of the blue. Indeed, at the heart of Old English are bundles of words rooted not only in the language common to all Germanic languages but also in its more distant ancestor, Proto-Indo-European. Even the masterpiece *Beowulf,* told in English that is about as "native" as it gets, employs some words imported from Latin and Old Norse. The basic story too was, in effect, imported into English. Its characters are Scandinavians, and its action is set neither in England nor in places that "native" English-speakers migrated from, but in Scandinavia.

So, was English made in England? Or was it rather assembled

★The letters "thorn," *þ*, and "eth," *ð*, were borrowed from the runic alphabet, and added by scribes to the Latin alphabet, to capture a sound that didn't exist in Latin: *th.*

there, of parts imported from diverse places? Or does neither option really capture English's provenance? An answer is supplied by the word *made* itself. Its trail leads to an elemental problem with all these questions about the origins of English. Let's take a closer look at the word *made*. Along the way, we'll also pick up a critical point about distinctions between "native" and "borrowed" English words.

The verb *to make* comes down to us from (or maybe better to say "through") the Old English verb *macian*. Its PIE root is **mag-*, meaning not only "to make" but also "to knead" or "to mix." Some Indo-Europeanists believe that dwellings of PIE-speakers were built of something that would have been kneaded or mixed—mud, for example. This idea is compelling because, in various branches of PIE, words derived from the same root carry meanings having to do with "building" and "constructing," as well as "making." An example from Old French is *mason*, which became *maison*, "house," in Modern French. A cousin word in Norman French, *maciun*, was renovated into *mason* in English. (We'll take a closer look at both of those influential languages in the next chapter.)

All from the same PIE root, related "construction" words in English are *match* and *mate*, as in a person or thing "well-fitted" to another. (The word *make* can still convey this old concept of the perfectly formed object, even when that object is a day, as with Dirty Harry's famous exhortation in 1983's *Sudden Impact*: "Make my day.") Formed on a Germanic variant of the PIE root **mang-* are *mingle*, *among*, and *mongrel*. These are from Old English words classified as "native" because they were inherited directly from a Germanic root—in this case one meaning "knead together," with emphasis on the blending effect of kneading.

Old English itself was *made* in this mixed sense, from its outset composed of a mixture of preexisting idioms. Those spoken by the

Angles and Saxons were, as we've seen, among others in the motley pedigree of English, a *mongrel* tongue even in its earliest known phase. Other expressions of the "knead" root entered English later, and from other languages. These are considered "borrowed" as opposed to "native," even in cases where the lending language is another Germanic one. Dutch provides an instance of this, via French, with *maquillage*, for "makeup." (To the Middle Dutch *maken*, French-speakers had added their telltale suffix *-age*, and the rest of the word captured how people pronounced that mix of borrowed verb and native ending.) While Dutch is very closely related to English—both are daughters of West Germanic—*maquillage* in English is nonetheless deemed a "borrowed" term.

From the Hellenic branch, English took other words derived from the same root: one is Ancient Greek *magma*, "molten rock"; another is *mass*, a "kneaded" lump of barley cake, from the Greek *massein*, "to knead." In this case, the Greek word for "lump" traveled a classic route: Greek passed it over to Latin, which kneaded it into *massa*; Latin then passed it down to French, which remolded it into *masse* (and gave it the sense of "material" or "substance"); and it was in this form that, around 1400 AD, English received it from French as yet another "borrowed" item.

Some three hundred years on, that Greek-coined word for a blob of dough was used in a different sense among English-speaking physicists contemplating *mass*. And by the time Einstein was making news with the *m* in $E = mc^2$, *mass* was well on its way to further immortalization in such phrases as *mass production*, *mass media*, *mass culture*, and, perhaps inevitably, *mass hysteria*. *Mass* was used for masses of other concepts too, save Church *mass*, which isn't from *massa* but from *missa*, Latin for "dismissal," or "thing that's sent," such as a *missive*.

So what do *make* and *made*, and *mass* and *maquillage*, tell us?

They show how English has used both inherited and borrowed elements to generate a lexicon that is notably different from that of other languages sharing so many of its prehistoric roots. These words also illustrate a signature trait of English: absorption of a profusion of "foreign" words that are nevertheless related, through common Indo-European roots, to "native" words that English possessed from its earliest phase. That is, English has expanded its vocabulary, beyond that of any other known language, by drawing on its Indo-European roots both directly and indirectly. This mixed heritage helps to explain why English, when spoken, sounds as varied as it looks.

Now some six thousand years into the story of Indo-European languages, English would, on October 14, 1066, take an astonishing leap in its unique course. King Ælfred's eventual successor, Harold II, king of England, was on that date slain at the Battle of Hastings. His vanquisher was William the Conqueror, a Norman.★ William seized the English crown and installed a French-speaking court in London. For some three hundred years, virtually all official conversation was conducted in medieval French. The royal administration, the judiciary, the elite and its educators, the military, key clergy, and leading writers were all French-speakers.

Had the Normans integrated the English-speaking peasantry into their way of life and language, they might well have turned England into a French-speaking island even to this day. Alternatively, the Normans might have given up their native language in favor of English.

★Around the time that Vikings were raiding and settling England, they were up to the same on the European continent. On the French-speaking coast, they settled, intermarried, and eventually adopted the local language. Like Old English, the region's French evolved, after the arrival of Vikings, differently from French spoken in other regions, including Paris. Normans thus became what linguists call a *speech community*, a group of people sharing a common language. They took the name *Norman* from a shortened version of a Germanic word for "Northmen," or "Norsemen," as in the Scandinavian Vikings who had spoken Old Norse when they first arrived in the region of France that is now called Normandy.

But no French-speaker fell in love with English as far as we know. (There is, however, surviving evidence of contempt for the language.) Apart from a few aristocrats and bilinguals, English-speakers were kept at linguistic arm's length from their rulers. No longer a language of influence or administration, or of study or enduring literature, English in effect went underground. But while English literacy waned, spoken English continued to evolve unfettered. In fact, it did so more freely than it would have as a written language, not least because writing was, in the preinternet era, capable of "freezing" language to an important extent, slowing even its spoken transformations.

By the time it resurfaced as a language of political and cultural prominence, in the fourteenth century, English looked and sounded remarkably different from Old English. It had remained a Germanic language yet had quietly absorbed a gigantic number of French words and ideas, as well as a French musicality to bind them together. Its grammatical character was also altered. All the same, in spite of its curiously hybridized form and content, the core of English remained recognizably, unshakably, true to its roots.

But let's now leap much farther ahead, to the present, and delve into the more contemporary guise of English. We'll see that words in this next batch have, through an array of routes, survived the linguistic upheavals that transformed Ænglisc into English. And they've been kneaded, mixed, and mongrelized anew to serve vast and growing populations who speak "Anglelike": *business, parking, T-shirt, FREE!, bank, STOP.*

BUSINESS

Business or pleasure? Either way, English plays an increasingly vital role.

Let's say it's pleasure. You want to order tickets to the Tashkent Tennis Open in Uzbekistan but don't speak Uzbek, or the regional lingua franca, Russian? English is your language. Across the world, are you ready to hire that guide who can explain the mysteries of Machu Picchu? The most effective tongue would be English, unless you happen to speak the local language, Quechua, or the regional one, Spanish. The pleasure map has expanded beyond measure for those who speak English. Even honeymooners who used to dread the language factor of a romantic stay in Paris can now add "speaking with French people" to their list of trip highlights. Unless, of course, the honeymooners don't speak English, the language du jour even in the world's once notoriously "English Not Spoken Here" city.

But *business* holds a special place in the Global English lexicon. The word alone is a magic talisman for many who seek access to opportunities on a planetary scale, rather than a local or regional one. It's a verbal symbol for promise and prosperity, increased standards of living, success, and even motion, exchange, dynamism— modernity itself. For some, business is the reason to be alive in our times. Enter the word on your favorite search engine, and see if the number of hits doesn't exceed those you get with words as basic as *life* and *love*.

What is it about the word *business* that makes it . . . *the business*? Even when the word is having a bad season—or a bad year—in native English-speaking quarters, it can continue to buzz with upbeat energies and results-oriented possibilities for those who embrace it as the jewel in the crown of Global English.

Business is often what draws new speakers to Global English in the first place. After all, what's the point of learning *business English* if not doing business, looking businesslike, keeping business hours, forming business plans, writing business letters, dressing business casual, negotiating business deals, using business centers, traveling business class, reading business pages, being antibusiness, earning a business degree, running a business, tracking business cycles, taking business initiatives, becoming a business leader, charging it to the business, and perhaps eventually wrestling with business ethics?[1]

By now, business of some form or other has become a descriptor of whole aspects of human experience. Does any part of your life *not* have to do with business? Aside from those moments when you are meant to be pursuing pleasure? If you don't happen to be a slacker, a full-time parent, or a cloistered nun, or have some other means to carve out a non-business-related moment or two in your day, the answer could well be no. But lucky us: one of the fine things about the word *business*, besides the fact that it finds much profit attaching itself to virtually any noun, verb, or adjective, is that, altogether in its many varied manifestations, *business* invests life with a guaranteed minimum level of action, vibrancy, immediacy, purpose, status, and existential plenitude.

Except when it doesn't. Because, of course, along with business comes its dark side, today captured by terms like *stress, jet lag, burnout,* and *depression,* and phrases like *flight delayed* or *meeting canceled.* These less-attractive facets of doing business in the twenty-first century can be found in the earliest appearances of *business,* a word that is native to English. In Old English, it was *bisignis,* or "busy" + "ness," the suffix meaning "state of being." But "being in a busy state" also suggested being worried or fretful. The verb was *bisgian,* meaning "to make busy," as in "to occupy" or "to employ." At the same time, it meant "to afflict" or "to trouble." Business that occupied the body also preoccupied the spirit. This distressing character of "busy-ness" in the Old English sense has never been fully exorcised from the word *business*. For good or ill, there is something perpetually agitated about the word and, for that matter, about the world as seen from the *business sector* of life.

It was not until the Early Modern period that *business* generally acquired meanings more starkly to do with industrious, productive activity. Then, the *man of business* first entered the English language, a figure taken up with the secular affairs of public office, or with mercantile pursuits, or with his occupation as a lawyer. And as all of them would now be as busy across space as the busy formerly were chiefly in spirit, each was prone to travel. But even the Early Modern man of business had inherited a somewhat duplicitous and deliberately frazzled streak from an earlier, also very "busy" man, Chaucer's own fictional but emblematic and influential lawyer, the Man of Law. He is described in the *The Canterbury Tales*, where (more for pleasure than for business) he has joined others on a pilgrimage to Canterbury. But he also distinguishes himself among them:

Nowher so bisy *a man as he ther nas,*
And yet he semed bisier *than he was.*[2]

Translation: *Nowhere was a man so* busy *as he;*
And yet he seemed busier *than he was.*

(General Prologue, 321–22)

Shakespeare also was attuned to the unsettled inner lives of the busy. He used the word *business* frequently, often with a disturbing ring. We hear in his works of "unlawful business," "swift business," and "the strangeness of this business." Chillingly, the ambitious Macbeth talks of witches' dire predictions as "that business." Other

memorable Shakespearean *business*es are linked to adjectives by alliteration, a poetic effect of sound repetition that reaches back into
the earliest layers of Old English battle poetry, suggesting that the
Bard is tapping into archaic matters. We are deeply unsettled to
hear of "bloody business," of "the bleeding business," and, from
Hamlet, who stirs himself to avenge his murdered father, of "bitter
business":

> *Now could I drink hot blood*
> *And do such* bitter business *as the day*
> *Would quake to look on.*

(*Hamlet* 3.2.397–99)[3]

Will *business* ever be entirely free of its ties to unholy matters?
The word did gain a new lease on life with the Industrial Revolution, when it was brushed off and put to work for a new era. The
phrase *business man* was first recorded in English in 1826, and by
1840 there had been so many factories popping up in the northeast-
ern United States, and hence so much new business to conduct, that
in Boston the business of making *business cards* also appeared. Soon
thereafter, so too had the idea that life was divided not into pleasure
and pain, but rather into business and pleasure.* Fascination with
the new concept of the *business suit* arrived in 1870. And the phrase
business school caught on from 1916, first mentioned in a bulletin

---

*As if trying to keep up with the demanding schedule of the word *business*, English-
speakers during the Industrial Revolution formed many compounds employing *pleasure*.
There was the *pleasure horse, pleasure car, pleasure trip, pleasure cottage, pleasure cruise*, and so
on. There was even the *pleasure party*, which sounds redundant until you recall that it may
otherwise have been mistaken for a *business party*. One may be interested to note that, while
business is a "native" word that English gained from its Germanic ancestry, *pleasure* was
"borrowed" from French sometime around the beginning of the twelfth century, in the era
after William I was crowned king of England.

published by the National Education Association of America. *Business lunch* did not join the language of English-speaking business culture until 1926. But by then, there were only a few hundred business days available for lunching before the crash of Wall Street popularized another phrase: *business crisis*.

Viewed alongside child labor, slavery, migrant labor, workplace dangers, financial meltdown, the rise and fall of workers' unions, corporate corruption and monopolization, and other busy-making issues of the business epoch, however, much business language has lost its sparkle. *Business* has frequently struggled to shake off its associations with greed, ruthlessness, cheating, and cleverness to a fault, especially in the form of *big business*.

Even so, there's no reason to fall completely out of love with the word. *Business* can still rhyme with entrepreneurial innovation, human creativity, and wholesome employment. The language pendulum of *business* naturally has its way of swinging in step with *business cycles*. Little wonder that English-speaking *business culture* was accused of being "square," "unhip," and "establishment" during the troubled Vietnam era, yet preened with power-breakfast-fueled confidence during the go-go eighties, especially in Reagan's America and Thatcher's Britain. From its earliest appearance in English, *business* has itself been a busy word, darting about in all directions, as magnetized to the miraculous diligence of bees as to the handiwork of the devil.

Now that *business* has played such a central role in taking English global, what's to become of the word? In the era of Global English, it appears that *business* will have a fresh chance to shed its burden of worry, vexation, and deeply secular anguish. Over recent generations, the base camp of global business has been the United States. Will business remain a critical word even if that base shifts to another country or region, one where another language is dominant? Or will speakers of Global English no longer rely on the wealth and influence of the "American empire" to keep doing business, and talking about business, around the world? Nonnative speakers of English have already played their parts in enlarging *business*'s stock of meanings. Speakers of Thai, Turkish, and Tongan rarely hear Shakespearean word ghosts haunting *business*, but they do use the word to refer to auspicious careers and educational avenues and, for that matter, as a prestigious global term for profitable activity of any kind. Were the word *business* a business, which it is in some respects, we'd have every reason to see it as a swelling *business opportunity*.

PARKING

Thanks to Detroit's burgeoning manufacturing plants and the Roaring Twenties' insatiable appetite for automobiles, lots of American cars suddenly needed a place to park. Hence *parking lot*, first attested in 1924.★ Since World War II, American automotive language has been tacitly (and explicitly! see *STOP*) licensed to drive Global English, the default worldwide idiom for *parking*.

With the world's car population accelerating toward the one billion mark, there are rising pressures to find places to stow four-wheeled vehicles in Earth's most densely populated zones. Automobilists know what to look for when they're ready to turn off the ignition away from home. In French, Spanish, and Polish it's *parking*. In many languages, the official word can be slightly

★The first attestation of *parking lot* reads, "Some of the people still lingered under the arc light, with its summer collection of bugs still in it, waiting for the two to come from the *parking lot*." It is from *R.F.D. No. 3*, a work of fiction by Homer Croy.[1]

different, but it typically starts with a *p*—when capitalized, it's also the Global English one-letter symbol for *parking*. In Czech, that *P* stands for *parkoviště*. In Japanese, it's *pākingu*.* In Romanian, *parcare*. German uses *Parkplatz*. Turkish, *park yeri*. And depending on how you feel about cars and car culture, you'll perhaps be unhappy to encounter the *P* with a diagonal line across it, symbolic Global English for *No Parking*.

But even in languages where *parking* is not a so-called dictionary word, it frequently finds its way into names of parking lots or onto road signs directing drivers to them. There's Easy Parking in downtown Rio de Janeiro. And C-Park Parking in central Sapporo. Or Spinney's Parking Lot in Beirut. Throughout China too, a prominent white *P* on a blue background spells "parking," even where speakers of the national language, Mandarin, use a compound, literally "stop car," *tíngchē*, to say it. (Note the absence of a spoken *p*. And for that matter, the absence of anything resembling a *p* in Chinese characters widely used to write the compound, 停车.) *P* is also the one-letter symbol for "parking" in Quebec, where opposition to English gives rise to linguistic rivalry, and where French-speaking Canadians proudly employ the non-English word *stationnement* to say "parking." However effective the Official Languages Act of Canada remains on terra firma (parking lot terra firma included) in an age replete with transnational internet and texting, *P*s appear in parking and no-parking signs alike throughout the nation's French-speaking province.

A reconstructed form of the English word *park* is **parruk*, used in its prehistoric ancestor language West Germanic, which was spoken until around fifteen hundred years ago. But in this very early

---

*In formal discussions, the Japanese word for "parking" is *chūshajō*, but the *P* symbol refers to the more casual term.

form, the word appears to have denoted fencing, rather than any given area that real or notional barriers could enclose. In Old English, a related word is *pearroc*, which refers to an enclosure holding farm animals, just as its descendant word *paddock* does today.

The word *park* was added to English during the medieval period, but it came attached to specific meanings introduced by speakers of French, whose rule of England deeply influenced English. A *parc* at that time referred to something that had blossomed in the French-speaking court culture of the twelfth century: "an enclosed preserve for hunting."[2] Occupiers of this English *park* were game animals like deer and boar, not domesticated sheep and cows.

In the late seventeenth century, however, *park* in English referred to a different kind of enclosure, one catering to humans who sought respite from the noisome distractions of city life. And if fencing was to be involved, it would be used to keep urban elements *out*, rather than to keep animals *in*. These parks grew into *public parks*, *municipal parks*, *state parks*, and, most monumentally, into *national parks*. American English would globalize a homegrown concept when Yellowstone National Park, in 1872, became the first of its kind in the world. That park contained fauna no French-speaking courtiers or English-speaking sheep farmers of the High Middle Ages knew existed: grizzly bears, rattlesnakes, bison, bald eagles, and moose, to name only a few of the New World creatures inhabiting America's first national park.

Eventually, the enclosed area known as a *park* came to include things other than animals or people. The first known use of *park* as a verb came in 1531, from the idea of setting up camp in a park to prepare for battle. English here once again adapted a concept from French, in which the verb *parquer* initially had to do with putting animals in a park, but was later used to refer to stashing artillery and gunpowder and, eventually, military vehicles. This earlier concept of *parking* as a military activity may help to explain why parking now often comes with the idea that someone is standing sentry over your Corolla, providing it with protective surveillance. Or at least appearing to do so.

The related phrase *parking space* also shows how completely English has by now forgotten its *parking* roots. Here, *parking* refers to the action of placing the car, and it requires another word to tell us where the car is being *parked* (precisely not in a park). The absence of any concept of enclosure, guarded or not, makes room for the word *space*.

But *parking* is one of those rare Global English words that could go full circle to reclaim some territory of its earlier meanings. Environmentalists note that the huge paved surfaces of the world's parking lots trap heat that adds unwanted degrees to the Earth's surface temperature. They also point fingers at polluting substances—gas, oil, battery fluid, and more—that gather on parking lot floors, often to be swept away by rain that flushes them into land and watersheds.

City dwellers have also begun to look anew at the idea of publicly owned parking spaces, including those spaces rented out to individuals who use *parking meters* to pay for them. In 2005, Rebar, an arts collective in San Francisco, potently employed a set of parentheses to inaugurate *PARK(ing) Day*, an annual event inviting the public to set up enjoyable miniature parks within metered parking spaces. The practice has gained popularity in car-congested cities within and beyond the United States, and has urged people to take a fresh look at the forgotten *park* encased in the word *parking*.

Over the lively course of its English career, the *park* has held farm animals, hunted animals, people, military equipment, large expanses of nature, and, in its *parking* guises, automobiles. And the stray Winnebago. What next? The future of this Global English territory will no doubt be shaped by the future of automotive culture itself. And automotive culture is geared up to be reengineered. So we can expect *parking* to mean new things in coming years. Will *parking* in 2017 instantly denote electrical or solar battery recharging facilities? Watch your local parking spaces and lots to see how this word will shift course. Or join the park(ing) movement and contribute your own new meaning to the word.

DETECTING THE DEEPER ROOTS OF *FARKING*—OOPS, I MEAN *PARKING*!

Comparative linguists use diverse methods to figure out whether a word is rooted in earlier layers of its own language or is borrowed from speakers of another one. *Parking* presents a fascinating example of the kinds of facts that word detectives can uncover. The earliest attested *park* words suggest that the root flourished first in Germanic languages. But this doesn't necessarily mean that there was no borrowing going on somewhere or other. The root that shows up in *parking* appears to have been borrowed by speakers of a prehistoric Germanic language that eventually split up into different languages, including English. So where do language detectives see "foreign" fingerprints on *park* words? Their key clue is the letter *p*. Recall that the PIE **p* became an *f* in Germanic. But since Latin preserved the *p* sound, it could have lent an early form of *park* to prehistoric speakers of Germanic.[3]

T-SHIRT

The American T-shirt, now a global garment attached to a globally recognized amalgam of a Latin letter and an English word, is nearly one hundred years old. By 1920 the noun *T-shirt* denoted a collar-free, short-sleeved, cotton undergarment that replicated the letter *T* when laid out neat and flat. But wider interest in the T-shirt was stirred only when Hollywood, in the 1950s, offered up the T-shirted torsos of idolized stars in films like *The Wild One*, *A Streetcar Named Desire*, and *Rebel Without a Cause*. These movies gave the humble item an edgy flair for the postwar generations of men in, and well beyond, the United States.

Macho characters portrayed by Marlon Brando and James Dean were fleshed out with brazen working-class energies in their American T-shirts, until then seldom worn uncovered save by laborers. Alone, the word *shirt* carries plenty of manly associations, at least if one looks widely enough into its roots. In Old English, *shirt* is related to *skirt*, not typically associated with hunky heroes of the silver screen, unless one is willing to make an exception for kilt-clothed Scottish warriors in Mel Gibson's *Braveheart*. Both *shirt* and *skirt* stem from the Indo-European root **sker-*, meaning "to cut," and have to do, in this case, with "a cut piece" of fabric. *Shorts* is also in the same family of words, conveying the idea of pants that have been cut, shorn, or *shortened*.

The Germanic roots of *shirt* produced a bonanza of English words affiliated with the idea of cutting: *scar*, *scissors*, *shear*, and even *share*, a portion that has been cut from a whole. Sports fans will be happy to note that *score* is a related word, borrowed from the Vikings. It captures the idea of marking goals by making notches or incisions. *Scrimmage* and *skirmish* also share the same root.

Those who prefer cerebral competition may be surprised to discover that *scrabble* is also a **sker-* word, from a medieval Dutch verb for "scraping," one of many Indo-European verbs to do with actions of cutting or of removing and reshaping surfaces. The famous board game indeed involves a surface that is constantly reshaped with new words. A closely related Dutch verb supplied English with a word in the cleaning department of life, *scrub*, which also concerns surfaces, this time the removal of unwanted ones. And from its Germanic side, English has inherited other words describing cut pieces or rough and sharp edges, like *shard* and *shrub*.

The English verb *screw*, as both a mechanical and impolite verb, may also emanate from this group of words and ideas whose origins date from over four thousand years ago. Some have argued that *screw* is from the Latin word *scrōfa*, meaning "sow," so named for the beast's rooting and digging behavior.[1] There is also the *scabbard*, a word that has preserved the concept of "cutting" captured in its prehistoric root. Just as the roots of *shirt* extend back into earliest layers of Indo-European languages, there are similarly related words from the root **kar-*, a variant of **sker-*, in the Italic branch of the Indo-European language tree. So, thanks to French and Latin, English-speakers now sink their teeth into *cuirass*, *carnage*, *carnality*, and *carnivore*.

The *T* part of *T-shirt* is no less suited to global rebels, those with or without a cause. The letter *T* comes from the Latin alphabet, which was introduced to English-speakers when their territory was a province of the Roman Empire. For its part, the Latin alphabet was adapted from the Etruscan, which came from the Greek, which had modified the Phoenician alphabet, which around three thousand years ago was an innovation of far-reaching and radical impact. The Phoenicians spoke a Semitic language, a non-Indo-European tongue related to Hebrew and Arabic. As active merchants pursuing trade throughout the Mediterranean, the Phoenicians adapted a long-evolving writing system to their own geographically far-ranging purposes. Until they did so, writing had taken other forms in places where the Phoenicians circulated. One was Egyptian hieroglyphics, which relied heavily on knowledge of numerous visual symbols standing for people, gods, things, events, and concepts.

Another was cuneiform, a system passed down by the ancient Sumerians, early inhabitants of Mesopotamia's so-called Cradle of

Civilization, who had developed it initially to keep track of crop surpluses. Cuneiform, which involved making coded markings with a sharp tool, or "stylus," was eventually used by Sumerians and others in their region to record language. But each of these previous ways of writing could be used and understood only by initiated priests or by trained scribes. Literacy was therefore a rare and closely guarded skill, typically reserved to realize the priorities of royalty.

Perhaps motivated by their commercial endeavors on and around the Mediterranean, where so many different languages were spoken, the Phoenicians developed a writing system that could, approximately, record speech in any spoken language. Their alphabet captured consonants, leaving readers to infer the vowels that should be vocalized between these consonants. Still, with its focus on broadly recognizable sounds rather than on culturally specific ideas, such as peculiar symbolization for the Egyptian sun-god Ra, this new alphabetic system of writing was nothing short of a revolution.

Phoenician-derived alphabets adopted the strategy of representing not the things or ideas that words referred to, but rather the key sounds, or at least close approximations of sounds, made by people as they uttered these words. The Ancient Greeks pioneered a new approach to alphabetic scripts when they added letters to represent the sounds of vowels along with those of consonants, in the dialects of their language. The Greeks passed their model on to others, who used it to develop the Etruscan, Latin, and Cyrillic alphabets. Latin letters were then used to write English as early as the seventh century, when missionaries used them to translate sacred texts into the language. But it took longer for the Latin alphabet to come into use for the Romance languages of western continental Europe. For one, most of those tongues didn't begin to emerge as distinct languages until after the Roman Empire had fallen. And even when they had emerged, words deemed worthy of being set down in writing, such as those used in contracts, would generally have been in Latin until roughly 1000 AD.

One enormously influential aspect of the Phoenician system of writing was that it allowed the average person to learn its phonetic symbols and sounds fairly easily, and so to attain literacy at a time when reading and writing—long shrouded in mystery—were effectively monopolized by members of a privileged and impermeable caste. The phonetic alphabet rapidly put paid to the awesome authority of high priests and members of a social stratum who had, for thousands of years, controlled access to all forms of recorded, enduring knowledge.[2]

With the advent of the Phoenician alphabet, then, and following other alphabets that appeared in its wake, time-honored social orders were reconfigured, and wider populations gained access to literacy. Indeed, Ancient Greek institutions and ideals—from schools to democracy—would have been unlikely, probably unthinkable, without the alphabet and the doors it opened to literacy. From there, the unbroken chain of the Western tradition of liberal education is directly traceable to its apex: spring break, and the wet T-shirt contest.

Of course, the *T* in *T-shirt* makes no strict reference to the alphabetic revolution, but it nevertheless remains a direct descendant of the Phoenician breakthrough in writing. And mass-produced T-shirts, bearing messages for all to wear and many to read, will always be partly indebted to those ancient tradesmen plying the coasts of the Mediterranean.

Like *blue jeans*, *T-shirt* is now a global phrase for a sensationally successful item of clothing that had its international start in America. By the late 1960s, with the civil rights movement well under way in the United States, and with the Vietnam War raging overseas, the white shirt popularized by cinema's sexy antiheroes gave way to yet a new generation of T-shirts: those carrying slogans of protest and political change. A T-shirt without a message of some kind was, from then on, a wasted canvas opportunity. T-shirts in Global English carry all kinds of messages, from the tame, and even quasi-meaningless, to the incendiary, but the vast majority of them for the moment propel branding campaigns of one form or another, whether I ♥ NY, *Coca-Cola*, or a more homespun declaration, such as this one created by an international outfit representing language teachers: "I speak Global English."

THE PHOENICIAN ALPHABET

Note that the *T* appears as a wheel-shaped letter, containing an *X*-shaped marking. It was this *X*-like symbol that evolved into the *T* of the Latin alphabet.

𐤀	'	⊗	T	𐤐	P
	B		Y		C
	G		K		Q
	D		L		R
	H		M		Š, š
	W		N		Th
	Z		S		
	Ch		'		

FREE!

Shoppers practiced in the art of combing department stores, souks, flea markets, and the internet will be on guard when they catch sight of *FREE!* It's often little more than a

ploy to trap your eyeballs and get them to persuade your brain that something can be yours for nothing, *if* you buy another thing for more than it's worth.

But some things really do turn out to be free, such as the tremendously powerful tool that is a foreign language. There are lots of ways to learn another language without spending a penny. You can listen to radio shows programmed for children, swap language lessons with a native speaker of a tongue you'd like to learn, persuade a foreign-language-speaking relative to switch you on to their way of putting things, lend that spare room to a recently arrived exchange student, or check out a teach-yourself-Tagalog book and audiotapes from your public library.

On top of all this, free internet access has become a lure to establishments from cafés to hotels to airline lounges. And once you have that internet access, there are free tutorials, blogs, and chat rooms that can get you started on a language you'd be curious to learn more about.* Would it be Mandarin Chinese? How about Dutch, or Irish? Or perhaps a more scarcely heard language, like Chukchi, spoken in northern Kamchatka, the Siberian peninsula renowned for its volcanic wilderness. What would things look like through the lens of that language? Or Warlpiri, spoken by a small indigenous population in Australia's Northern Territory.

In addition to seeing *FREE!* as your pass to a new cell phone saddled with a burdensome contract, or as your ticket to some additional frequent flyer miles, consider it a doorway to a free pair of magic glasses. By the time you pick up that phone, or those miles that could land you on the glittering Adriatic coast, you may also be able to get by in Italian,† and that would be an altogether different kind of trip from the one you'd take with Global English alone.

---

*One good site to explore for free lessons in dozens of languages—including Basque, Breton, Coptic, Javanese, Kurdish, Lithuanian, Nahuatl, Swahili, Wolof, and many of the most widely spoken tongues—is www.lexilogos.com. From the home page, click on the Union Jack to consult the site in English.

†I'd rather have said "Serbo-Croatian" here save that, if you try to put Serbo-Croatian to use along the Adriatic, you'll quickly discover that many Serbs and Croats would rather you refer to their language(s) as Serbian and Croatian. And there are also those Montenegrins who will remind you that they speak Montenegrin, the national language of another country on the Adriatic coast: Montenegro. And let's not forget inland Bosnia-Herzegovina, where many identify themselves as speakers of Bosnian. There are also certain nationals

Since the fall of the Berlin Wall and the rise of a relatively all-encompassing "single" global market, global sightings of the word *FREE* are continuously on the rise. In France, Free is the name of a leading internet service provider. It's not free in the sense of "gratis," but it does facilitate individual freedom of communication across national boundaries. In India, once more concerned with freedom from underdevelopment than with aggressive marketing language, the English *FREE!* now shows up alongside Hindi, Urdu, Tamil, Bengali, Gujarati, and other expressions of the concept in one of India's many official languages. *FREE shampoo!* Nowadays, *free* speaks to customers not only in a regional or national market, or even in a random troop of tourists from an English-speaking country, as may have been the case not long ago, but rather in a wider English-speaking world.

From the spots around the planet where it's posted, *FREE!* also suggests that someone may be interested in speaking Global English and implies that you may be interested in that person's language too. Not only is conversation *free*, it could enrich your life in unforeseen ways. You can't get a better deal than that.

Free has come to mean "at no expense to you, dear consumer." The word is native to English via its ancestor language Germanic, and it was passed down from the PIE root **pri-*, "to love." By now, you won't be surprised to see that the *p* in this PIE root became the *f* in the Old English word for "free," which is *frēo*. Many related

---

of Bosnia-Herzegovina who insist that they speak Serbian, or Croatian, and believe that the language spoken by their Muslim compatriots, referred to as "Bosniaks," should not be called "Bosnian" but rather "Bosniak." Are you now baffled? *Dobrodošli!* Or rather, "Welcome!" (in Serbo-Croatian) to the Balkans. By the way, none of this is to suggest that the designation "Serbo-Croatian" is or should be politically or culturally neutral, or that its use effectively sidesteps the fact that the languages of the former Yugoslavia have indeed evolved on distinct paths since the Middle Ages.[1] But to get back to your free trip to Italy, there are arguably at least as many tongues on that side of the Adriatic. Will you be heading to Venice? If so, you may prefer to learn Venetian.

words in Germanic languages share this idea of "love" and "belonging to loved ones" being linked to *freedom*, in the sense of "freedom from bondage." And while we don't know exactly how the very early ancestor language of English shaped expressions of loving and being loved, we do know that the Germanic languages commonly express these wonderful experiences in words intimately intertwined with the concept of being free from enslavement and oppression. (Being a "slave to love" may seem a predicament of the Romantic poets of yore, but the condition still resonates in the lyrics of lower-case romantics such as Bryan Ferry.)

Was there a cataclysmic event behind this remarkable association of words long before English existed, at a time before the Germanic languages split off to go their own ways? One is tempted to picture some prehistoric hostage-taking of Germanic-speakers and to imagine their rescue or escape or release—and their eventual return to those they loved. Such a scenario would explain how love and freedom became linked ideas. But there is of course no historical record of any such scenario. There are only puzzle pieces contained in language itself.★ Perhaps unsurprisingly, a related word in English is *friend*, a "loved one." And *Friday*, that merciful day of the week that now happens to release many English-speakers from their workplaces . . . at least until a new workweek begins on *Monday*, named for the moon.

Free enjoyed a special peak in native English usage between 1981 and 1986, big years for discussions of *tax-free* alternatives and *free trade* and, not accidentally, the *Free World* standing

★The *OED* proposes: "This sense perhaps arose from the application of the word as the distinctive epithet of those members of the household who were 'one's own blood,' i.e. who were connected by ties of kinship with the head, as opposed to the unfree slaves. In the context of wider society only the former would have full legal rights, and hence, taken together, they would comprise the class of the free, as opposed to those in servitude."[2]

shoulder-to-shoulder with President Reagan against the unfree Evil Empire and its political friends.

Overseas, the picture has been different, with Global English *FREE!* still on the upslope of a stunning, sixty-plus-year growth phase. The world has become better acquainted with the word over recent decades, in expressions like *free jazz, free time, Free Nelson Mandela!, free press, duty free, free love, free range, free fall,* and *Radio Free Europe.* Most recently, though, the internet has introduced masses of *free downloads, free software, free online games, free ringtones, free shipping,* and planetwide concern about the implications and long-term impact of free access to so much free stuff, from recordings of Bach cello suites to movie reviews of *THX 1138,* and from recipes for Karla's black sesame butter cookies to codes used to design applications for electronic devices. All *free, free, free*!!! And if all these free items aren't enough, there are *free radicals,* which—as radicalisms generally do—provoke their own brand of anxiety even though, and maybe precisely because, so few of us get what they actually are.

But this multivalent sense of the word *free* looks likely to shift. At its core, the Germanic roots of *free* remain first and foremost about *freedom from* something bad: enslavement, imprisonment, dark days, disturbance, war—things that prevent you from being with and belonging to those bound to you by love, and so from loving. Is the root **pri-,* "to love, and *therefore* to be *free*"? Or "to love *because* one is *free*"? Either way, free not to accumulate, consume, obtain, use, and discard. (Where *does* that packaging for the "free" cell phone end up once it's tossed in the recycle bin?) Global English for the moment is more taken up with free *things* than with *free*ing anyone from anything, least of all from bondage to those things.

Still, no one knows what *free* will come to mean in forty years, when speakers of languages other than English may free this very old word from its current hell of being used predominantly to describe goods and services to be had (or so hope the naïve and unwary) at no cost.

BANK

If I say *bank*, quick—what do you see? Is it a lobby appointed with inoffensive artwork and sort-of-comfortable chairs? An unreconciled statement? Let's skip that one, too toxic a sight. How about a glassed-in ATM targeted by a security camera or two? Or a member of the Wall Street elite stepping into his chauffer-driven luxury sedan en route to a splashy event with his bejeweled wife? Whatever you're seeing, it likely has little to do with marijuana or the Boston Red Sox. And yet the *bank* word trail leads in unexpected directions.

Bank—as in the financial institution—comes into English, possibly via French, from the Italian *banca*. In turn, Italian had taken it from the Late Latin *bancus*, meaning "workbench," a counter-like surface that could be set up by those who manned them—"bankers"—in town squares dotting the Italian Peninsula. There, the *banca* operated as a mobile office, offering money-changing and coin-weighing services. This was especially valuable at a time when curious currencies circulated freely throughout the Mediterranean, including coins of values that were not self-evident.

At the height of the Roman Empire, Latin had no word akin to *bancus*. Instead, in commercial hot spots of the Roman Forum and elsewhere, coins were handled in an *argenteria*, a stall whose name came from the word *argentum*, meaning at once "silver" and "money."★ Not sure whether my pouch of silver-looking coins is worth your three hundred jugs of olive oil? Let's take the coins to an *argenteria*, where, for a fee, an expert can assure us that they're real silver and, after weighing them in his balance, confirm that we're looking at three hundred jugs' worth.

So how did Latin gain the word that would eventually become the English *bank*? From English's own cousins on the Germanic side.

As we've seen, Latin-speakers were in contact with speakers of Germanic languages whom they had battled and ruled and employed to build the Roman Empire. But there was to be more contact between speakers of these two language groups when the Roman Empire collapsed. At that time, in the fifth century, people remaining in Italian regions continued to use Latin. But they were also ruled for hundreds of years by speakers of Germanic languages. Latin then naturally absorbed certain Germanic words.

One such word was *bancus*, for the ancient "workbench" whose name has a common ancestor—in the Germanic line—with the Modern English word *bench*. And just as Germanic languages were injecting fresh words and ideas into Medieval Latin, so too did the culture of financial services shift under new influences from the East. The *argenteria* was then replaced by the *bancus*, a raised surface that resembled the worktable used by money changers in Greek-speaking Byzantium.

★Paper, including receipts and transferable credits for commodities—say, a note granting to you ownership of a portion of my recently harvested stores of wheat—were familiar financial tools in ancient Egypt and Greece. But coin-loving Romans preferred cold, hard cash—the minted kind having "intrinsic value." The handling of metal money was therefore something of a cultural specialty, particularly because the long Italian Peninsula, surrounded by commercial activities of merchants and traders, was a valuable land-and-water crossroads.

Indeed, since ancient times in Greece, the traditional locus of money changing and related financial services was the "table" or *trapeza*, from the Ancient Greek *tra*, or "four," + *peza*, "footed," referring to the feet supporting its surface.★ In the New Testament book of Matthew, 21:12, when Jesus enters the Temple and overturns the "tables of the money changers," the Koine Greek uses precisely this noun, *trapeza*, referring to the work surfaces employed by *trapezites*, the Greek versions of the Italian *banchieri*, "bankers," who worked on *bancas*, "benches." †

Around the year 1000, with Romance languages replacing Latin as the spoken tongues of territories formerly within the Roman Empire, the Late Latin word *bancus*, on loan from a Germanic language, yielded the Italian word *banca*. And while *banca* at first referred strictly to the old money-changing workbench, it soon came to refer to something else: the place where money or valuables were "mounded," "piled," "raised up," or simply "banked." Gradually, a new concept of banking arose in medieval Northern Italy, where bankers were to do far more than weigh coins, exchange them, and occasionally mint them.

As early as the twelfth century, the city of Venice found that public debt could be paid off by having taxpayers contribute to a "mound" or "bank"—the words *monte* and *banca* were then used interchangeably in this sense—of funds in exchange for certificates of credit that, at least in theory, included interest payments to

---

★*Trapeza* remains in use in Modern Greek. Greece is one of the few European countries that did not adopt a variation of the Italian *banca* or the Global English *bank*. *Trapeza* became *trapezoid* in English, a geometrical term referring to a quadrilateral with one pair of parallel sides, which is also the shape formed by the aerial contraption of the *trapeze* artist.

†In fact, Jesus is overturning the "banks" of the money changers, but we have come somewhat confusingly to think of them as "tables" because of how the passage has been translated into English from the Latin version by Saint Jerome. In his translation of the Greek Bible, Jerome had used the Classical Latin word *mensas*, meaning "tables."

citizens.* The piled-up money in such a public bank could then be used to pay for publicly funded projects, such as wars. Over time, prominent families in flourishing cities like Florence and Milan replicated this practice, accommodating private as well as public interests. Their services included not only money changing, deposit taking, and transfers, but also credit for clients hoping to reap financial rewards through high-risk activities, from pursuing commercial ventures to waging wars.

A notable bank of this pivotal era was in Genoa: the Banca di San Giorgio, or "Bank of Saint George." Founded in 1407, it set new standards for other banks of Northern Italy.† While the bank was family owned, it was overseen by a board of directors and chartered by the Genoese government to serve the public. It had dealings with prominent Europeans of the day, including that most famous of the Genoa born: Christopher Columbus. But the Bank of Saint George would also gain notable foreign clients, and eventually add the crown of Spain and Portugal to its list of account holders.

Within a few decades, English-speakers began to refer to the Italian idea of the *banca* or *monte*, anglicizing only the first, as *bank*. Some Italian banks by then had branch offices in London. But bankers based in Italy and elsewhere—notably Holland and France—would in time find themselves competing fiercely with

---

Monte and *banca* were fused in the Italian word *montimbanca*, from the expression *monta in banca*, literally "mount on bench." In the late sixteenth century, English borrowed this word, now spelled *mountebank*, to refer to those roaming charlatans who would step onto a box or bench to attract the attention of potential buyers of such dubious offerings as "snake oil" medicine.[1]

†One of these banks, operating since 1472, still carries the medieval word *monte*: the Monte dei Paschi di Siena. It was founded in the then-fresh spirit of Northern Italian banking. In 1624, the ruler of the Republic of Tuscany, a Medici grand duke, guaranteed the deposits of the bank's clients by tying up the republic's pasturelands. This agricultural means of backing the bank's holdings gave it its enduring name: *paschi*, meaning "pastures" in the Tuscan idiom of the era.

those in England. The word *bank* reached new heights following the successful commercial enterprises of the East India Company. Established in 1600 under charter from Queen Elizabeth I, "the Company" eventually transformed London into a burgeoning financial center for privileged movers and shakers of international trade, working regions as far from London as Asia, Africa, the Middle East, and the Americas.

With London's growing economic influence through colonization, military conquest, treaties, and other profitable activities— London's current status as the world's capital of finance can be traced back to the seventeenth century—the word *bank* was absorbed by many other languages, including Bengali, Persian, Arabic, Russian, and Hebrew. Even in countries like China, Japan, and Greece, where other words are used to capture related ideas for "banking," the English word *bank* is freely recognized.★

While the Global English word *bank* finds its *financial* roots in Italy, whose *banca* descended from the Germanic north, English had its own related Germanic word, *benc.* Meaning "bench" or "long seat," this native term was entirely devoid of any association with Roman coins or Italian mounds of real or theoretical silver and gold.† Quite unlike the "workbench" that Mediterranean bankers adapted from Germanic languages to describe work surfaces for their money-changing operations, the Old English *benc* had potent Germanic associations. We can sense the word's cultural intensity

---

★For example, in Japan, the traditional word for "bank" is from Chinese, *ginkō.* But Japanese-speakers also use the word *banku,* introduced into Japanese by foreign banks. Examples of specific banks include *banku obu amerika* for "Bank of America," and the rather unfortunate sounding (at least to some ears) *shitī banku* for "Citibank."

†The closely related Germanic word *bank,* as in "riverbank" or "bank of clouds," also captures the idea of a raised, flat surface. But while *bench* was native to English, *bank* appears to have been borrowed into English from Scandinavian, via contact with Vikings in the early Middle Ages.

in the Old English masterpiece *Beowulf,* the epic that was set down in writing in the early eleventh century, but whose story elements were passed down orally over previous hundreds of years. This time frame is central to our bank story: at the very historical moment that a Germanic root for a "workbench" was evolving into a *banca* in the Mediterranean, speakers of Old English were shaping the same root into the word *benc,* which was equally indispensable to their culture.

In *Beowulf,* exhausted warriors collapse on benches. When the time comes for them to feast, a bench is lovingly cleared so that they may sit together in a banquet hall.* And when the heroes have succeeded in their mission, and the story's king finally takes his seat among them to celebrate, an exquisite moment of bonding produces the compound word *bencswēg,* a pretty clamor (*swēg*) rising up from—you guessed it—the benches. We glean from *Beowulf* that speakers of Old English had strong feelings about benches. They were not merely raised platforms designed to relieve more than one person of the tedium of standing. Rather, they filled minds with ideas of team effort, leadership, heroism, celebration and feasting, and creative forces driving out destructive ones. The Old English "bench" even assured a kind of sacred order in the world: people found their places among prized kinsmen and allied clans on the *benc.*

Airs of the Beowulfian *benc* still hang about words in living languages whose common ancestry is Germanic, including English. Like-minded members of Parliament share a bench. So do athletic teammates like the Boston Red Sox. The athletes' coaches also critically determine which players to call from (or send to) those

---

*The current English word *banquet,* which shares the same root as *benc,* preserves this association between benches and feasting.

benches. Great authority is vested in a prosecutor's or defense attorney's being told to "approach the bench." There's also the bench as commanding metaphor for the very dispensing of justice. And let's not forget that big compound word *benchmark*, without which many institutions today (including banks) would be unable to measure their relative successes (and failures).

So *bank* is an English word of mixed heritage, a fusion of native mead-hall Germanic and imported *pasta alla Italiana*, an heirloom received from both sides of the family. Its Global English usage stems from an English that was retooled by Italian that evolved from a Latin that borrowed it from Germanic-speakers whose native words shared common roots with English. Phew! As exhausting as this journey must have been for the word *bank*, it has served English-speakers well, and richly. If the older Germanic *benc* had delayed its journey by fifteen hundred years or so, it could have circulated among languages in less time than it took a banker in Florence to weigh a mound of silver coins. Or than it took an Old English storyteller to recount one of Beowulf's epic deeds. Indeed, *bank* gives us a slow-motion picture of the kind of travel words now carry on at lightning speeds, out of and into Global English.

BANK'S HINDI COUSIN

Distantly related to *bank* on the Indo-European language tree is the Hindi *bhang* (sometimes spelled *bang*), meaning "dried leaves and stalks of hemp," as in marijuana. The Hindi word traces its own roots to the ancient Sanskrit *bhangha*, meaning "pounded" or "broken up," potentially with reference to the processing of hemp, the extracted fiber that has been used since prehistoric times to make things like ropes.

ANCIENT IOU

Laws regulating financial interactions survive from as early as the eighteenth century BC, when King Hammurabi of Babylon had a number of them written in Mesopotamian stone, or rather rock, namely superhard diorite. We know from his code that debt was a fact of life for ancient Babylonians, but that even in this early era there was the idea of a "grace period" and, well before Mutual of Omaha got into the insurance business, the "act of God": "If a man owe a debt and Adad [the deity holding sway over storms] inundate his field and carry away the produce, or, through lack of water, grain have not grown in the field, in that year he shall not make any return of grain to the creditor; he shall alter his contract tablet and he shall not pay the interest for that year."[2]

BLOOD BANK

The first attested use of the phrase *blood bank* dates from 1938, when it was used to describe stores of human blood available for emergency transfusions at Cook County Hospital in Chicago. From this phrase, which other languages have adopted, using the Global English word *bank* alongside their own for "blood," countless other phrases have been formed, including *eye bank, sperm bank, egg bank, kidney bank, organ bank, food bank, milk bank,* and *data bank.*

STOP

If events had unfolded in a slightly different order, one of the following words might have become a common sight on roadways across the globe: 止まれ, 停, *HALT*, 정지, *PARE*, *ARRÊT, ALTO*, रोको. Starting with Japanese and passing through Chinese, German, South Korean, Brazilian Portuguese, French, and Spanish to Hindi, the polylingual list represents national languages of the most productive automobile-manufacturing countries in the world, aside from the United

States, which would by the way currently rank third. But the word that you're most likely to see adorning crossroads not only in English-speaking lands but also in Lithuania and Senegal, and on the islands of Fiji and Iceland and the Seychelles, and a lot of other places, is in English.

The French and Germans were the first, in the eighteenth and early nineteenth centuries, to build automobiles, those mobile vehicles that are *auto-* or "self"-powered. But English was the language spoken at an intersection where a highly influential road sign cropped up, in 1915, in Detroit, Michigan.[1] A few years earlier, near that city, Henry Ford had set up the first major car-manufacturing plant, and his Model T, affordable and sturdy, was rapidly transforming the lives not just of a fraction of a land's wealthy elite, but of an entire national population. By the time of the 1929 crash (financial, not vehicular), Ford would sell over fifteen million of his colossally popular cars, a number roughly half of all cars then registered in the United States. For the first time, an enormous percentage of a nation's population was mobilized by internal-combustion engines.

America's love affair with cars wasn't only about numbers—although by sheer numbers alone, U.S. factory output left Europe's in the dust. Even such early car-making heavyweights as Panhard-Levassor in France, or Daimler and Benz in Germany, designed models that were driven away by at most a few hundred or few thousand buyers. But America's thralldom to the automobile was something qualitatively different as well, so basic as to transform the American way of life, reshaping America, its economy, its society, and even its landscape.

Main Streets and country roads were the first to be transformed. And urban settings. Later, roadside and suburban ones, with homes and ice cream parlors, banks and pharmacies, fast-food joints and commercial zones of massive surface areas containing malls, outlet stores, entertainment complexes, and of course car dealerships, filling stations, and the "motor hotels" that Americans contracted into "motels." They were designed and built—and sadly often not exactly what you'd call designed but built anyway—as much for cars to access and idle in and park triumphantly before them as for people to use and enjoy.

In fact, America is, in many spots, a country more about its cars than its people. Or its natural resources. Interstate routes, bridges, ramps, highways, toll roads, and freeways cut straight through old farms, divide neighborhoods, are elevated right on top of town squares, and menace quiet parks, many of which had served communities long before 1893, the year that the brothers Frank and Charles Duryea in Springfield, Massachusetts, built the first American car to run on gasoline.

Detroit's innovative road sign was little more than a piece of sheet metal cut in the shape of an octagon and tacked onto a post. It bore bold, black capital letters over a white background spelling out the word STOP. And while the sign's colors would change several times before settling down to the familiar white on red, that initial basic design, selected by committees of highway safety researchers for its shape's ready recognizability and then standardized throughout the country, would, within forty years, (in theory) stop motorists virtually worldwide.

Curiously, when one of the research teams was scouting around the United States for ideas to inspire the optimal stop sign, its members noted the effective design used at railroad crossings: two crossed sticks derived from earlier and more broadly used "caution" signs graced with a skull and crossbones. (In some places, actual animal skulls and bones were used to signal warning, especially in the rugged West.) Perhaps the Detroit-style stop sign gained additional appeal from its multiple edges loosely resonating with those vivid, archaic crossbones.

Shifting the color to red also brought the stop sign into line with railroad conventions, where red had long symbolized danger or cause for alarm. Just as the form and color of the stop sign seem matter-of-fact yet are linked to rich visual cultures, so too is its verbal *STOP* deceptively simple. It works as a verb in the command form, instructing you to STOP! And equally, as a noun, it represents the act of coming to a STOP where it is posted. It also serves as an interjection: "Hey! Here's a STOP sign."

A chief reason such a sign was deemed necessary in 1915 Detroit is that the cars being built there were not only numerous but, thanks to engineering advances, ran all too well—to the peril of other cars and objects and beings, not least the unsuspecting pedestrians and animals who had previously congested roadways without such lethal competition from the machine world.

The now-unmistakable octagonal red sign instructing motorists in white letters to STOP was adopted throughout the United States in 1954, just in time for a new generation of fast, powerful American cars. The old Ford Model T by then looked about as modern as a Wells Fargo stagecoach. Instead, Ford was equipping some cars with robust V-8 engines that more than tripled the 40-odd mph top speed attained by the Model T. The same era saw a host of muscular or simply beefy new models hurtling across the United States, from Chevrolet's Bel Air to General Motors's athletic Cadillac Coupe de Ville and Chrysler's sensational New Yorker Deluxe, which featured everything from cigar lighters and ashtrays and carpeting to a 235-horsepower engine and, happily, power brakes.

Cars built in America and overseas were even racier by 1968, when the United Nations Economic Commission for Europe, seeking to reduce roadway accidents across nations of diverse languages and driving habits, took steps to standardize use of the stop sign in Europe. The resulting Vienna Convention on Road Signs and Signals introduced America's red geometry, along with its white-on-red *STOP*, to a large population of non-English-speakers by the time it came into full effect in 1978.

Not that Europeans hadn't beheld or heard variations on "stop" before the new traffic signs riddled their intersections. In Latin, the noun *stuppa* means "tow," the course part of flax that was used in antiquity as a stopper-upper of flowing water. In Late Latin, the noun became a verb, **stuppāre*, meaning "to plug up with tow." Borrowing produced the Old English *forstoppian*, "to stop up," and a verb, "to plug," which has been reconstructed as **stoppian*. This last became the Modern English *stop*, both as a verb and a noun. While some Romance languages also found use for **stuppāre*-derived words, the Late Latin concept—and the associated technique of using tow to form plugs in breakwaters—was helpful where the Rhine flowed, and where seasonal flooding called for seasonal stopping up of rising river waters. But only in English would words related to *stop* be used for the idea of coming to a standstill.★

Well before the Vienna Convention, some Europeans used or at least recognized the anglicism *stop*. It was the misfortune of Frenchmen, for example, to hear the British order them to 'Stop!' as early as 1792. French revolutionaries were shortly to decapitate their sovereign. England's George III, his own head at least still physically

---

★Then again, only in Yiddish does **stuppāre* appear to yield a verb meaning "to whack" and "to push" and, in slang, "to have sex with": *schtuppen*.

on his shoulders, was determined to prevent the new French political thinking from gaining a foothold on his country's shores.
With the French Revolutionary Wars heating up, and with conflict
brewing on the high seas, *stop* entered the French vocabulary as a
maritime term.[2]

Some five decades later, American telegrams began to make *stop*
a familiar word in electrically transmitted messages. By the 1920s,
millions of telegrams were sent worldwide, with *stop* continuing to
indicate, in French and many other languages, breaks between sentences. And *stop* had by then been exported from the United States
for key moments in certain sports, such as boxing. Still, the stop
sign made *stop* an everyday sight rather than a word reserved for rare
occasions and rarified vocabularies.

Throughout the motorized world, *STOP* went on to become
almost as familiar as the red octagon that so often presented it to
drivers nearing potential collision. The sign's idiosyncratic shape
and color trumpeted independent authority, no less effective for
being nonverbal. In the United States, the sign's shape was initially
favored as a national roadway symbol because the word *stop* alone
could so easily go undetected—say, because invisible at night or
because the driver was illiterate. Indeed, the sign's verbal message,
shape, and color fused into a distinctive case of language being
at once literal and symbolic, and readily transplantable to foreign
soil.

Little by little, *stop* has seeped out of the traffic sphere to generate
new nouns and verbs in European languages. The French now officially recognize *stopper* as a verb roughly equivalent to their native
arrêter. Yet while stop signs in France say "STOP," those in Quebec,
where French-speakers assert their powerful linguistic rights amid
Canada's English-speaking majority, typically say "ARRÊT." In the
Canadian tradition of protecting the vitality of minority languages,

some signs also say "STOP" in Cree, Inuit, and other languages native to Canada.

The Quebecers are not alone. Other *STOP* words on the planet's roadways similarly employ local languages, including Arabic قف, Thai หยุด, Chinese 停, and even the WHOA that may charm tourists where America's Amish still get around by horse-drawn carriage. Nevertheless, the U.S. road sign has made *STOP* a fantastically successful four-letter word around the world. It is also an extraordinary case of an English word's being globalized by international contractual agreement. Over fifty countries signed on to the Vienna Convention, and even in many territories where the convention is not in effect, the U.S.-born stop sign has been adopted as the way to go. Or rather the way to stop.

A SECOND GLOBAL *STOP!* FROM MOTOR TOWN, USA

Four years after the red stop sign became a national fixture on U.S. roadways, Detroit found itself not only the world's greatest automobile-manufacturing city but also home to a new record label, Motown. Specializing in the city's pop genre known as the Motown Sound, with *Motown* condensing the phrase *Motor Town*, a nickname for Detroit, the label released "Stop! In the Name of Love." Recorded in 1965 by the Supremes, the track topped the charts. As one of the world's favorite pop tunes, it augmented the global prestige of *stop*. Today, pop music lovers everywhere understand the title lyrics and know the song's catchy melody by heart. On dance floors and within earshot of radios, Global English-singers also deliver the palm-out stop signal that Diana Ross and her fellow Supremes legendarily used each time they belted out "STOP!" Motown fans may be surprised to know that a similar palm gesture serves as the roadway stop sign in one of the few countries that has not adopted the U.S. design: Israel.

COUNTRIES CURRENTLY OBSERVING THE VIENNA CONVENTION OF ROAD SIGNS AND SIGNALS, WHICH INCLUDES USE OF THE STOP SIGN

Albania, Austria, Bahrain, Belarus, Belgium, Bosnia and Herzegovina, Bulgaria, Central African Republic, Chile, Côte d'Ivoire, Croatia, Cuba, Czech Republic, Democratic Republic of the Congo, Denmark, Estonia, Finland, France, Georgia, Germany, Greece, Hungary, India, Iran, Iraq, Italy, Kazakhstan, Kuwait, Latvia, Lithuania, Luxembourg, Macedonia, Mongolia, Montenegro, Morocco, Norway, Pakistan, Philippines, Poland, Romania, Russian Federation, San Marino, Senegal, Serbia, Seychelles, Slovakia, Sweden, Switzerland, Tajikistan, Tunisia, Turkmenistan, Ukraine, Uzbekistan.

4

MADE IN ENGLYSSHE

Shakespeare loved the adjective *fire-new*. And so he should have; he coined it. Or at least, if it was circulating in London, he's the first person known to have set it in writing. One of the phrase's earliest appearances is in *Love's Labor's Lost*, when one character describes another, the comically conceited Don Adriano de Armado, as "a man of fire-new words." [1] Indeed, Armado does have his own way with language, as when he speaks of "the posteriors of this day, which the rude multitude call the afternoon." [2]

Fire-new evoked gleaming, fresh-forged metalwork. And it recast another phrase then already in use: *brand-new. Brand*, initially "torch" in English, and a word that had come to mean "sword" or "a recognizable mark made with hot iron"—as in *branding iron*—was, like *new* and *fire*, inherited from Proto-Indo-European via Germanic roots. In fact, as crisp and modern as Shakespeare's words sounded in the 1590s, and still do today, every one of them—*a, man, of, fire, new, words*—is native to English, derived from its ancient word-hoard.

But by the time Shakespeare was adding over a thousand new words to English, much less of its vocabulary could be called native. We've seen how English began to acquire foreign words even in its Old English phase, especially through its contact with Scandinavian. After that period, English would go on two more word-absorbing sprees. One took place before the Bard's time, and the other occurred during the English Renaissance, the cultural moment that Shakespeare has come to personify. We'll see that, in each of these transition phases—one that reshaped Old English into Middle English, and another that changed the latter into Early Modern English—vocabulary wasn't the only thing being substantially transformed. The basic sounds and atmosphere and even a few of the major organs of the language—notably its grammar—changed as well.

One of the most engaging things to consider about any language is how poets, lyricists, playwrights, and the occasional blogger are able to wake us up to words we use every day but seldom hear in depth. No less fascinating is how speakers reshape words and languages. How do people come to agree that *groovy* no longer expresses what it once meant? Or that *brand* should refer not only to those identifying marks burned into the rumps of livestock, and the heated objects that make them, but also to pretty much everything under the sun that large numbers of us among the rude multitude can be conditioned instantly to recognize, from Mick Jagger's lips to donut shop signs?

Most of us are too busy wrangling language, or too encompassed by it, to glance around from time to time and look at what we're making it do. Language is so integral to our lives that it seems to just happen on its own, as if it weren't akin to a technology that we constantly retool to serve life in the herebefore. Yet even those of us who wouldn't brand ourselves poets tirelessly participate in the ongoing collective process of remaking whichever languages we use.

With so many words now flooding into English, and with people using its old words in new ways, the language bears illuminating kinships with the English of Shakespeare's time. In that short era too, some twenty thousand new words were added to the language, and English-speakers—within the British Isles, as English was yet to emerge as a major export commodity—had to decide, "voting" with their palates and their pens, which would remain in circulation and which were to be relegated to obsolescence. During the English Renaissance, words came and went, often with the rapidity that electronic gadgets do now.

Of course, speakers and writers can't be worrying about which words will be useful centuries into the future. (Who speculated about life in the twenty-second century, let alone the next millennium, before throwing *groovy* into the recycling bin?) Nevertheless, the words we have to work with today are with us, for the most part, because past speakers found them useful and kept them in circulation.* Speakers of twelfth-century English, of Renaissance English, or of rapidly evolving Global English play decisive roles in fabricating the language that's taken up—and resculpted—in English's ongoing future. The addition and deletion of words happen

---

*Consider how words like *lufu, lif, heofon, eorðe, weorc,* and *hlūd* have survived (albeit in their modified forms "love," "life," "heaven," "earth," "work," and "loud"), along with roughly 40 percent of the known Old English vocabulary, in Modern English, whose speakers have come to take them for granted. Would English-speaking life today be somewhat different had words like *wuldor, scop, dryhten, hyge,* and *līc* (or "glory," "poet-singer," "lord," "thought," and "body") survived as well? These terms, along with some 30 percent of the known Old English lexicon, simply didn't make the journey down to our time. The remaining 30 percent of the words used in Old English neither stuck nor strayed. Instead, they were markedly reshaped by speakers who needed them to mean new things or wanted them to look and sound substantially different.[3]

continuously, but we'll see how it accelerates in these major-shift phases.

Not that there's a rule about how many words a language can at any moment employ. The known Old English vocabulary totals around twenty-five thousand; English today boasts over one million. Global English, by midcentury, may embrace two million terms. Or (more likely, I'd think) settle in with closer to twenty-five thousand of the most useful.* To sharpen our perspective on English in its current transition, and to see what raw materials Shakespeare had to work with, let's go back a bit before his time, to the period when Middle English arose.

We noted that Old English sparkled with cultural output under King Ælfred, but that it was forced to contend with the arrival, in 1066, of a French-speaking king. English then cohabited not only with William the Conqueror, but also with tens of thousands of French-speakers who followed him into England. The environment would no longer foster those wordsmiths who might otherwise have been more visibly adding words to the English word pool, or magically new-minting old ones. Had history taken a different course, I might have been writing this book in French, inviting you now to

---

*Jean-Paul Nerrière, the French proponent of a simplified English he calls "Globish," finds that fifteen hundred words suffice for basic and effective discussions among nonnative speakers. Nerrière and coauthor David Hon argue that, as only 4 percent of international communication in English takes place between native speakers, language users involved in the massive 96 percent of those exchanges need a form of English that is quick and easy to learn, and reliable to use. Their book on this subject, *Globish the World Over*, is not only about Globish. It's written in Globish.[4] The idea of using a limited vocabulary had been central to the work of British linguist C. K. Ogden, who developed a form of Basic English employing fewer than one thousand core terms. Basic English (with Basic being an acronym: *B*ritish *A*merican *S*cientific *I*nternational *C*ommercial) gained wide attention after World War II, when the utility of English as a transnational lingua franca became starkly evident. But with his coauthor I. A. Richards, Ogden had by 1923 already begun to rethink language in general, and to demystify English in particular.[5]

look at our Indo-European language family diagram to see where a daughter language of West Germanic, English, became extinct. (Though in all likelihood, such a turn of events would have obviated this book's basic observations; Global French would be, to put it conservatively, a different entity.) Instead, English survived by mutating. That is, its speakers reassembled it, and to the point that, after three hundred years of dominance by French, English only somewhat resembled its former self.

Keep in mind that the bones of English have remained Germanic, and through all its "international" makeovers. But if Old English *donned helmets* and *horns* and *brandished swords* (all italicized words are native), we'll see that, as Middle English, it *dressed* in *elegant robes* and *armor* and *stored* those in *wardrobes* and *armories* (these italicized words are from French). And while the French courts in England would cultivate no Shakespeare, or any other author who would add these and other fire-new terms to the language, there were whole populations of nameless creators of English who did: its speakers. Clearly, a lot of talking had been going on in English, and with ears open to the French languages in its midst.

I say French *languages* in the plural because more than one variety of French was to remodel English. First, there was William the Conqueror, a Norman who spoke Norman French. As it was used in England, the language would be called Anglo-Norman, a French that took its own path, distinct from the Norman spoken on the Continent. Norman also differed from the French of Paris (later to evolve—and to be prodded, reassembled, and rationalized by French academicians—into Modern French). But Old French—used in Paris, and heard in the London court and in other "frenchified" quarters of England—would influence English as well.

Fresh batches of French, from an even wider field of parts suppliers, arrived after 1154, when the English crown passed from the

Normans to the House of Plantagenet. Under Henry II, king of England (but also Duke of Normandy and Aquitaine, among a host of other titles), French acquired prestige among English-speakers in much the way that Global English has among native speakers of so many languages today. We pictured Ali Baba's cave to imagine why so many people are now drawn to phrases in English as powerful as *Open Sesame!* Medieval English-speakers similarly had good reason to employ the most effective door-opening devices of their era. A few of those were in Latin, but the most broadly useful were in French. Looking for work in the royal stables? Heading to court? Hiring a scribe to write a letter? Meeting with your mayor? You're probably not fluent in any idiom of medieval French, but a few words could go a long way. *Sésame, ouvre-toi!*

Henry's reign sparked what's been called the twelfth-century Renaissance. He overhauled the kingdom's government, which spoke French. And Eleanor of Aquitaine, his queen and the epoch's great patroness of the arts, encouraged the kingdom's best talents to compose literary works. You probably see what's coming, and it's not English—yet. This extraordinary cultural moment was also made in French.

But while Normans held the throne for nearly a hundred years, and while brilliant poets and storytellers enchanted French-speakers under the Plantagenets, English-speakers were remaking their language in an utterly "unsponsored" way, below the radar of official French. Exposed to different varieties of French, they gradually adopted words from them, even when distinct kinds of French provided English merely with different ways of saying roughly the same thing. Such roughly interchangeable terms nevertheless became valued alternative expressions, often because speakers adopted them, and then diffused them, with distinct meanings. For example, English-speakers had a word for "pig," as in the domestic farm animal, before the Norman Conquest. For speakers of Norman French, the word for "pig" was *porc*. English-speakers then adopted the French word and diffused it with a distinctive culinary meaning, "pig meat to eat," or *pork*.

In some cases, alternate terms were preserved simply because they enriched the vocabulary with nuance, or added poetic sounds. If we listen to English as music, it can sound like it's being played on an unusual variety and range of word instruments. It is. And this, along with the ensemble of languages it borrowed from, is one of the reasons why. (This will inform our attempt, in a final chapter, to hear and see English of the future.)

Consider an example from Norman and Old French. As they shared a common linguistic ancestor, Latin, those tongues resembled one another closely in structure as well as vocabulary and sound. For instance, the Late Latin *captiare* generated the Norman verb *cachier*, which English recycled into *catch*. But speakers of Old French turned the same Latin verb into *chasser*, rebranded as *chase* in English. Here are some examples of English words gained from both kinds of French after the Norman Conquest. As you'll see, where speakers of Old French pronounced a hard *g*, Normans used a *w* sound.* And while some French-speakers accused the Normans of speaking an inferior, less cultured tongue, English-speakers didn't discriminate. Instead, they just took from both:

Norman French	Old French
wardrobe	garderobe
wage	gage
warden	guardian
warrant	guarantee

*French dialects are not alone in demonstrating shifts of sounds between *g* and *w*. In the Spanish of Panama, the anglicism *watchman* has become *guachiman*.

Middle English received a major word transfusion from "French," which, as we've seen, was in fact more than one language. Non-Norman varieties of French also injected double terms, such as *real* and *royal*. We'll never know just how many borrowings from French fell by the wayside. There were surely more circulating in spoken English than those that survived, especially in London (where the *sésame* factor was bigger than it was in places farther from the throne's sphere of influence), once English was put back on the country's front burner. Here's a mini thought experiment: English-speakers borrowed the word *war* from the Norman French, but what if they'd passed down to us its non-Norman twin, *guerre*, as well? Would we now philosophize that all's fair in love and guerre? Or read a book review lauding the latest translation of Tolstoy's *Guerre and Peace*? Or head to a friend's house for a marathon viewing of all the *Star Guerres* movies? As it happens, English-speakers did employ the word *guerre* toward the end of the Middle English period, and they kept it in circulation for roughly ten generations. But for better or worse, *guerre* was ultimately thrown into English's lexical junk pile, where it's been joined by an antiguerre generation's *groovy*.★

Today, around one-third of the English vocabulary is "French," borrowed from one or another of its medieval and modern versions. Consider a sampling of these words that would help to transform Old English into Middle English. Some are being remodeled yet again, this time by speakers of Global English. While these terms taken from different varieties of French initially looked and

---

★Speaking of *groovy*'s era, the French-speaking population of Vietnam would refer to a certain war as the *guerre américaine*, or the American War. Thus, had English-speakers beyond the early seventeenth century continued to use both terms, that same war—known in the United States as the Vietnam War—might instead have been called the Vietnam Guerre.

sounded somewhat different in English, their current forms are *story, soldier, war* (as we saw, from the Norman; the *w* is the hint), *oil, money, labor, rescue, random, reward* (ditto), *engineer, nurse, attorney, garden, oyster,* and *beef.* Plus a couple of personal favorites: *magic* and *mushroom*, from the French *mousseron.* (That last term was a reminting of the Late Latin **mussario*, which sounds like a word Shakespeare could have used for an Italian character in one of his plays.) As for the phrase *magic mushroom*, it would have to wait until 1957, when it first turned up in a *Life* magazine article that a young Professor Timothy Leary would read with interest before trying magic mushrooms himself and exhorting everyone else in the USA similarly to indulge.

A funny thing happened to French in the fourteenth century. It re-became a foreign language in England. How could such a thing occur? The reemergence of English was a long and slow process. Let's spotlight a few of the major events and influences that helped English regain its lost role as a language of stature and of official business in England. In 1204, King John, the Plantagenet son of King Henry II, and the brother of Richard the Lionheart, lost his Norman holdings. With this development, speakers of Anglo-Norman (the Norman French then spoken in England) were cut off from their continental homeland. As a result, Anglo-Norman would very gradually lose prestige, while English, still spoken by the peasantry, would become more attractive to French-speaking inhabitants of England.

Then, in 1348, the plague swept through England, killing over 30 percent of the population. Rural survivors of the Black Death, almost exclusively English-speakers, moved in significant numbers to London and other cities and towns. This population shift widened the use of English in places where French had long been established. In addition, once-more-subdued peasants revolted,

raising their voices in an English that their sovereign could no longer ignore. English was also crucially advanced by John Wycliffe's
translations of the Bible into English in the 1380s. By this time,
"French" rulers of England had become native speakers of English.

Among the new English literary talents in London to be supported by Henry's descendant Richard II was one who stands apart:
Geoffrey Chaucer. Often called the "father of English literature,"
Chaucer translated French and Latin works into English, but
also used English to write original poems and lyrical narratives.
Through these compositions, English reclaimed the standing it
hadn't enjoyed since the bygone era of Ælfred's line. In his most
renowned work, *The Canterbury Tales*, Chaucer conveyed the voices
of sharply defined speakers in a society much more layered than
those of Kings Ælfred, William, and Henry. *The Canterbury Tales*
was an unfinished work when Chaucer died in 1400, and it appears
that he had been writing the work for over a decade. This was the
Comeback Kid moment for literary English although, by the late
fourteenth century, it was coming back into a very different world.

Unlike the glittering literary gold of *Beowulf*, Chaucer's astonishing creation was built on centuries of English-speakers' listening to
French, and their creative mongrelizing of its "nonnative" words.
One can understand why Chaucer became a favorite author in his
day (the numerous surviving manuscripts of *The Canterbury Tales*
attest to the work's popularity), and imagine the thrill it must have
been for people to hear and see their native tongue put to such
captivating use. In a selected passage from the *Tales*, we can also
sense Chaucer's enjoyment, his relishing of remade English, as he
plays with its French verbal accessories. At the same time, we glean
how greatly English (and England) has changed since the days of
Beowulf. Here Chaucer's narrator tells us a bit about a fictional prioress. She has reportedly learned to speak a brand of French, and

Historical Events in the Evolution of English

English developed with pushes from history. Key events are as varied as the arrival of a foreign monarch, the spread of a disease, a technological advancement, the flourishing of a playwright, or the founding of a distant colony. Without these influences, English would not be the global language it is today. Here are some events that changed the language in its phases as Middle English (from 1066 to 1500) and Early Modern English (1500 to 1800):

DATE	EVENT AND WHY IT WAS IMPORTANT
1066	William the Conqueror rules England and introduces Norman French words; some 900 of these survive in Modern English[6].
1154	The English crown passes to the House of Plantagenet, adding more French words to English.
1204	King John loses Norman holdings, so ties to French-speakers on the Continent are cut. English becomes more attractive as French loses prestige.
1348	Black Death. The plague wipes out more than 30 percent of the population. Surviving peasants move into cities from rural areas, bringing English with them.
1380s	John Wycliffe translates the Bible into English and adds more than 1,000 words from Latin to the English language.
1400	Death of Geoffrey Chaucer, author of *The Canterbury Tales*, which establishes English as a literary language and paves the way for Shakespeare.
1476	William Caxton sets up England's first mechanized printing press. Foreign words enter English as works are translated for publication.
1582	Richard Mulcaster's *Elementarie*, a word list and guide, shapes the teaching and learning of English.
1595–96	William Shakespeare's *Love's Labor's Lost*. While most English-speakers use around 4,000 words, the Bard's plays employ 30,000.
1599	Globe Theater built in London. With each performance, over a thousand commoners are able to hear English used in new ways.
1600	The East India Company is chartered under Elizabeth I. Words and products reach England from Asia.
1607	The Jamestown Settlement in Virginia is colonized under James I. English begins to spread and gains words from the New World.
1611	The King James Bible deeply influences speakers and writers of English.
1755	Samuel Johnson's *A Dictionary of the English Language* attempts to standardize English during the so-called Age of the Dictionaries.
1776	Representatives of "the united States of America" pen the Declaration of Independence, heralding a new era in the history of English.

to exhibit English manners made in French. (At first glance, the Chaucerian English can look alien, but if you read these lines aloud, you'll see that it's easy to get the gist of them.)

> *And Frenssh she spak ful faire and fetisly,*
> *After the scole of Stratford atte Bowe,*
> *For Frenssh of Parys was to hire unknowe.*
> *At mete wel ytaught was she with alle;*
> *She leet no morsel from her lippes falle,*
> *Ne wette hir fyngres in her sauce depe;*
> *Wel koude she carie a morsel and wel kepe*
> *That no drope ne fille upon hire brest.*
> *In curteisie was set ful muchel hir lest.*
> *Her over-lippe wyped she so clene*
> *That in hir coppe ther was no ferthyng sene*
> *Of grece, whan she dronken hadde hir draughte.*[7]

(General Prologue, 124–35)

French influence on the English vocabulary is on full display in Chaucer's versions of *school*, *morsel*, *sauce*, *courtesy*, and *grease*. And in references to *French*, and *Paris*, and even in the character's "French" concern that no bits of her meal escape onto her breast or into her cup. Notice too that English no longer has gendered nouns and adjectives, although in the many nouns ending with *e*, such as *drope* and *coppe*, medieval versions of "drop," and "cup," there are still graphic vestiges of more-inflected Old English. Yet not all nouns in the passage dangle case endings. For example, *morsel* has none, though it's the object of a verb, which would previously have obliged it to take one.

Listen to some words that English gained from medieval French:

largesse, gentle, honor, courtesy, noble, messenger, chivalry, amiable, conscience, visage, manner, melody, inspiration, adversity, beauty, art, and *romance.* Along with new ideas, English acquired a new sound world. Indeed, French had overhauled not just the English vocabulary, but its phrases and rhythms as well.★

Within eighty years of Chaucer's death in 1400, English-speakers faced a fresh onslaught of unfamiliar terms. But, compared with those before them, whose Old English language was altered by conquest and by the French-speakers living among them, those who lived through this next transformation had more in common with English's native speakers of today: their language was being altered in part by technology, as well as by contact with speakers of many tongues, spoken in near and distant lands.

The item to play the critical role in the next phase of English's globalization arrived from the Continent, but not by force. It was the movable-type printing press. Devised in German-speaking territory (Germany wouldn't properly exist for a good while to come), where the Englishman William Caxton first encountered it at work, mechanized printing technology revolutionized not just dissemination of literature and ideas, but also linguistic contact.

Caxton established the first press in England in 1476. Among the works he initially published was *The Canterbury Tales.* (Like so many others, he was a Chaucer fan.) In short order, another

★Old English poetry had been formed in shorter arcs, built on three to five beats. And it used alliteration—the repetition of initial sounds—for effect, as with a phrase we could update to *"He fought the fiend in the fire."* But in Chaucer's English, the language has discovered the end rhyme, as in his *allelfalle* and *clenelsene,* and prefers more elongated phrases, each built of an enduring ten syllables. Shakespeare would preserve this Chaucerian innovation and widen its possibilities in "free verse," which didn't require rhymes. While poetry of course isn't the same as everyday language, it does condense for us the exceptional ways in which Germanic English had, over the course of three centuries, been "frenchified."

character portrayed in the *Tales* would be cast in a new light. The Clerk, a mature student of philosophy at Oxford, is described as having twenty books, and as being poor for having spent his money on them. In Chaucer's day, books were indeed expensive and rarely owned by anyone who wasn't an aristocrat, scholar, or cleric.★ While block-printed books existed, the philosophical texts belonging to someone like the Clerk would have been copied by hand, and onto costly parchment rather than paper.

With the advent of modern printing, and rising literacy, speakers of foreign languages didn't need to invade the island in order to supply speakers of English with thousands of new words. In fact, speakers of those foreign languages didn't even have to be alive. At the heart of England's enormous cultural shift from the Middle Ages to the Renaissance was a burgeoning demand for works in translation. And not only of texts in living languages of the Continent but also notably of those in the prominent languages of classical antiquity, Ancient Greek and Latin. Translations of texts in these languages were prized by students, storytellers and poets, philosophers and historians, and those in the "reborn" realms of mathematics, medicine, science, architecture, technology, rhetoric, and, of course, that center stage of the English Renaissance, the theater.

The consequences for the language, remade into Early Modern English during this period, would be as profound as its "frenchification" during the Middle Ages. How was the language changed this time around, as England entered a new era? To some, it seemed to be the "polyglotification" of English, by scads of new words coming in from all directions.

★After Chaucer's death in 1400, such was the popularity of *The Canterbury Tales* that members of the growing middle class also owned copies of the work in manuscript.

Among the titles Caxton printed were his own translations (from the French) of works originally written in Classical Latin, such as Ovid's *Metamorphoses* and Virgil's *Aeneid*. In his preface to the latter, Caxton acknowledges that his translations had required him to introduce an abundance of "curyous termes." Other translators and setters of movable type likewise had little choice but to cram printed pages with sights never before seen: *illecebrous, fatigate, abequitate, questitious, anacephalize,* and *obtestate.* We've no idea what these Ancient Greek- and Latin-inspired terms mean, because Renaissance English-speakers, fabricating their lexicon anew, didn't see fit to embrace them and hence to pass them down to us.★ These words were instead deposited in the *groovy* dump site, where they now commingle with *guerre.* But plenty of polysyllabic words, which to some then looked just as bizarre and absurd, did make the cut, including plenty we now can't imagine doing without: *necessitate, contemplate, parenthesis, monopoly, thermometer, algebra, illustrate, skeleton,* and *anonymous.* Even shorter words were to be wrestled with and eventually accepted: *fact, species, climax, plus,* plus *larynx.* Among other current and probably future English must-haves were *crisis, chaos,* and *catastrophe,* and *comedy, tragedy,* and *drama,* all from the drama-loving speakers of Ancient Greek—but used differently by us. (Aristotle would have scratched his head to hear a CNN anchor refer to an aviation accident as "a tragedy.")

The great unleashing of so many weird terms, most of them reading like code that couldn't be cracked without an Oxford degree in classics, produced excitement but also moaning, dismay, and passionate objection as English then experienced a drastic case of

★Some of the weirder-looking terms adopted in this period remain in the English lexicon today, but are spelled quite differently. For instance, *adnychylate* looks awfully foreign but is readily recognizable in its Modern English form, *annihilate.*

preglobal growing pains. One of the troubled was Thomas Wilson, author of an influential treatise, *The Arte of Rhetorique*, first printed in 1553 (eleven years before the birth of Shakespeare, who would read it). Wilson advocated "plainnesse," a concept that was especially appealing during the reign of Elizabeth I, when clear translations of the Bible, such as William Tyndale's, would allow literate Protestants to engage directly with sacred texts. (The King James Version, published in 1611, recycled much of Tyndale's translation for readers under the Stuart succession to Elizabeth.) Wilson claimed to deplore the use of "inkhorn terms," those wrought words that sounded pretentious, unnatural—un-English. In Wilson's view, inkhorn terms didn't arise in the honest way, as products of speakers' collective making, but were rather concocted free of any organic communal participation, by individuals dipping pens into horns that served as inkwells.

Inkhorn terms understandably struck many of their readers as incomprehensible, verbal zombies scarily mixed among—and feeding off—unsuspecting, humble English. But even Wilson, in spite of himself, was caught in the word wave of the moment, introducing in his work such now-familiar made-in-Ancient-Greek ideas as *metaphor*, *allegory*, *image*, and of course *rhetorique* itself, his Renaissance English for *rhetoric*. He also put out his share of terms soon found to be of less use, like *exornation*, *abusion*, and *transumption*. The rhetorician's objection to the invasion of English by phalanxes of alien and alienating words was therefore—how shall we put it—*hypocriticalulatory*? As proof of how aggravating the new terms could be, Wilson produced a letter he said was written by a man seeking help in obtaining employment. (Some scholars suspect Wilson of having fabricated the letter to make his point.) Here's an excerpt from the letter, showing the transgression of good English that Wilson aimed to illustrate:

*I being a Scholasticall panion, obtestate your sublimitie, to extoll mine
infirmitie. There is a Sacerdotall dignitie in my natiue Countrey con-
tiguate to me, where I now contemplate.*[8]

Are you wondering what on earth Wilson's job seeker is talking
about? If so, then Wilson has probably persuaded you that inkhorn
terms are not terribly helpful additions to the English language. But
even as he was forcefully making his point, Wilson was trapped in
an "I say I hate even as I fervently embrace" relationship with the
word craze. He and other debaters had stepped into what's now
called the Inkhorn Controversy—is English enriched by foreign
words, or rather ravaged by them?—for a hundred years. Siding
with Wilson as the controversy gained momentum, a Cambridge
University classicist, Sir John Cheke, was equally repulsed by the recent developments: "I am of this opinion that our own tung should
be written cleane and pure, unmixt and unmangeled with borowing
of other tunges."[9] But Cheke's objection happens to contain the
words *opinion*, *pure*, and *unmixed*, only a few of the borrowed words
that he used to argue that borrowed words were not legitimate English. Nor good English. Though the Inkhorn Controversy was
quieter by 1650, its echoes were persistent.

What to do? Should speakers of English simply refuse to employ
"non-English" terms? Or rabidly seek them out? Like English-
speakers in any era, Sir John and his fellow anti-inkhornians would
have been hard-pressed to avoid borrowed terms. For, as we know,
English was born of "mixt" and "mangeled" tongues, and has only
grown increasingly "mixt" since then—perhaps especially during
the Renaissance, when far-flung non-Indo-European "tungs" added
long lists of new reasons for some to cheer and others to despair.
From Chinese came *tea*, first recorded as *Chaa* in 1598, and from
Hindi there was *guru*, spelled every which way you can imagine

starting in 1613. Even languages to the north, where English picked up *parka* in 1625, supplied words that became Angle-like, or "anglicized." And we mustn't forget a certain spot across the Atlantic Ocean. In 1607, the Jamestown Settlement (like the King James Bible, named for England's then sovereign) initiated the enduring colonization of Virginia. Along with shipments of *tobacco* grown in America, English-speakers would soon be in receipt of Native American words such as the Algonquian *powwow* and *moccasin*.★ But given that *Renaissance* is yet another borrowed term, French for "rebirth," perhaps Cheke would have preferred that we refer to his day, more "natively," as the *Birthagaindom*?

And of course *Birthagaindom* brings us back to Shakespeare, whose language so often hums with the concord of terms native and borrowed. Had the Bard entered the fray of the Inkhorn Controversy, one might expect him to have been in favor of such raging verbal inventiveness. In a way, Shakespeare did leave us his take on the matter: the classical verbiage mania offered great material to include in plays. It produced some of the most striking voices in Shakespeare's midst, both in Stratford-upon-Avon (where the young Will was schooled) and in London. Shakespeare was certainly attentive to inkhorn-term fanatics around him. They figured as voices in the larger dialogue then going on in English, about English. Indeed, one can read all of Shakespeare's plays as dramatic, impersonated explorations of these vast questions: What is English? How do we make it and hear it? What do you mean when you speak it? What do I? How do we understand one another in it? And how do we not?

One stock character in Shakespeare's plays is the pedant, a cross between a tedious schoolmaster and an avowed, outright possessed

---

★The word *tobacco*, from the Carib language spoken in Haiti, had entered English via Spanish in the 1570s.

enthusiast of inkhornery. *Love's Labor's Lost* features one of these fellows in the character of Holofernes, who can't help spewing out Latin terms, even when no one has a clue what he's talking about. Here's the sound of his voice: "Yet a kind of insinuation, as it were, *in via*, in way of, explication; *facere*, as it were, replication; or, rather, *ostentare*, to show, as it were, his inclination" (4.2.13–16). We can be fairly certain that Shakespeare would have been disgusted at the idea of a world filled exclusively with English of this stripe—or a world filled exclusively with any one kind of talk. He was rather listening out for varieties of voices and, as a dramatist, putting them into conversations with one another for audiences to recognize or discover. Thanks to his plays, English-speakers have long had the privilege of being able to hear themselves making language—and of using varied kinds of voices to speak English in different ways.

Before we move on from Shakespeare's day, note one important development apart from its vocabulary boom. From 1590, Shakespeare's works were written over three decades that lie solidly within Early Modern English. Old English had lost inflection as it evolved into Middle English. More inflection was lost when Middle English evolved into Early Modern English, a phase of English's evolution that dates from 1500 to 1800. Consider that, by the end of this period, the word generally used to say "you" was *you*. Another example is the verb "to do." In Modern English, dated from 1800 to the present, forms of the verb show little inflection in the present tense: *I do, you do, we do, they do*. The exception is the third-person singular: *he does*, or *she does*, or *it does*. But look at this famous Early Modern English line from *Romeo and Juliet*: "O Romeo, Romeo, wherefore art *thou* Romeo?" And another, from *Hamlet*: "The lady *doth* protest too much, methinks." Inflected forms of *you* then included *thou* and *thee* in the singular, and *ye* and *you* in the plural. And forms of *to do* in the present tense alone included not only *do* but also the now bygone *dost* and *doth*. In Early Modern English, these grammatical matters were in flux. Speakers then often had the choice of using inflected forms or dropping them. As English entered what's been called the Age of the Dictionaries, marked by Samuel Johnson's *A Dictionary of the English Language* in 1755, spelling and grammar moved toward standardization. At the same time, much of the inflection that characterized Shakespeare's English was lost.

What do we make of the latest English word explosions within the context of past linguistic fireworks? Today telecommunications technologies, chief among them the internet, are the new printing press. They're in the process of remolding English yet again. Former eras have shown us English borrowing roughly equivalent to a bag of coins from Celtic; taking out a college loan with Scandinavian; mortgaging the penthouse and automobile to French and Latin; and bumming tobacco, coffee, and tea off hundreds of others. But English's lexical indebtedness has largely been to other Indo-European languages. If English's past indicates its future, its next phase will be marked by two trends. One is more big borrowing sprees, only this time from languages that have not as yet been in extended close contact with English. The other is the *fire-new* phenomenon: terms minted from the existing *word-hoard*. Or *vocabulary*. Or *lexicon*. Even with those three terms, each from a different branch of the Indo-European tree (Germanic, Italic, and Hellenic), there's plenty of word metal for speakers to work with. And a Global English answer to the *Beowulf* poet, or Chaucer, or Shakespeare, can be expected eventually to hammer out lots more.

Meanwhile, we're perhaps now experiencing a digital revival of the Inkhorn Controversy era, trying out copious quantities of new words, finding them excessive, some of them irritating, and sitting tight to see which will be generally adopted by speakers and writers of Global English. Users of the technology-driven word *blog* have already put into circulation hundreds of variations on it alone. Here's a sampling: *blogosphere, blogalicious, schlog, blogwash, blogaholic, blogarrhea, the blogeoisie* (as in *the bourgeoisie*), *the Bloggerazzi, to blogify,* and, last but not without reason, *blogging a dead horse.**

It looks like it may be time to invent yet another, one that would describe the countless words now up for grabs, those that trigger discussions about what's acceptable or should be standardized and where, if at all, to draw limits when so many novel words are cascading into English. My vote: *bloghorn.* And I'd be for the coining of a word to represent that graveyard where English words go to rest when speakers no longer employ them. *Groovydom* could fit the bill. Although I suppose that would be on the *hypocriticalulatory* side, since it would bring *groovy* back from its grave, even if in a new guise.

When we next consider the big picture of English, we'll take a different perspective. Instead of seeing how it has altered through time, from its prehistoric roots and into the *blogiverse*, we'll look at how it compares with other languages that have spread out to serve populations far greater than just their native speakers.

Let's now investigate some words from the Global English vocabulary and *blogabulary.* Unlike that last word, these have already been adopted around the world, and are unlikely to spark

---

*For more—a lot more—*blog* words and phrases, see the lists on urbandictionary.com.

inkhorn-style controversy. As a group, they show how English-speakers of the medieval and early modern eras reworked words, native and borrowed, that continue to evolve as we speak: *check, penthouse, cookie, taxi!, job, fun.*

CHECK

Check out the Global English uses of *check*, a word that mobile and interconnected populations have adopted for a surprising range of activities.

Travelers *check in* for flights and *check out* of hotels. To make payments, they may use *checks*, and where the standard variety is not accepted, *traveler's checks* often are. When there's spare time between one kind of *check* and another, some Global English–using venues invite patrons to *check* hats and coats before taking a break over a meal or stepping into a museum. And if checking in and out of too many places has taken a physical toll, entertainment might be forfeited for another plan incorporating the word *check*. Are you in Istanbul? Like practitioners in many of the world's medical centers, Turkish-speaking doctors now administer *checkups*. If what's ailing you is your hard drive, mechanical variations on the medical theme are also available on a planetwide basis. In case a Global English *systems check* failed to solve your computer problem in Timbuktu, the laptop can undergo a *checkup* even there, in the heart of Mali.

And to which language is English ultimately indebted for this immensely useful and flexible word? The answer is its distant Indo-European cousin Persian, a daughter language of Indo-Iranian.*

---

*Just as English is at base a Germanic language with roughly 30 percent of its lexicon borrowed from Latin, Persian is at base an Indo-Iranian language with a large percentage of words borrowed from Arabic. But while Latin is in the Indo-European family of languages,

Check is from the Persian word *shāh*, meaning "king." In Ancient Persia, it designated not only the sovereign "shah" himself, but also the chess piece that would become the "king" in English. After Muslim Arabs conquered Persia in the early seventh century, Arabic-speakers took up chess as well, and eventually introduced the hugely popular board game into western Europe.

By the start of the twelfth century, French-speakers would refer to the game in the plural as *eschecs*. It no longer looks much like *shāh*, but here's at least a partial explanation. Affixed to the *esche*, there's a *c*, pronounced as a *k*. It might have been added owing to association with a preexisting word in Old French, *eschec*, meaning "booty" (in the sense of "loot" or "stolen goods"). When the sound of one word colors or "contaminates" the sound of another, linguists refer to the phenomenon as *phonetic convergence*.★ Speakers of Old French had perhaps come to think of chess as a game associated with "booty," or at least with taking opponents' chess pieces as booty. In any case, players didn't have to know that a word resembling *shāh* referred to the king on their chessboards; had this been common knowledge, the game may well have been renamed *roi*, or "king," in French. Instead, *eschecs* was named for the signature sound uttered when one player notified the other that his king was threatened. This time the word was used in the singular: *eschec!*

Arabic is not, so Persian represents an unusual example of an Indo-European language with a significant non-Indo-European vocabulary. In Iran, the Arabic alphabet was adapted to write Persian; and in Afghanistan, Arabic was similarly adapted to write Dari, a language closely related to Persian. In certain former Soviet republics where Tajik, also related to Persian, is spoken, the Cyrillic script has been used to write the language since the Soviet era. Like the Latin alphabet, the Arabic and Cyrillic alphabets are phonetic writing systems descended from the Phoenician alphabet.

★English-speakers did the same thing to the French word *longue* when, in the early nineteenth century, they heard it as the unrelated word *lounge* to form the phrase *chaise lounge*. In French, the recliner is a *chaise longue*, "long chair."

In French, words and ideas to do with chess didn't stray too far from the chessboard. *Eschec*—meaning "check!"—would later take on the sense of "failure" or "defeat." But *eschecs* didn't go on to mean anything apart from "chess."

But the word's itinerary in English was another story. Following the conquest of England by a French-speaking sovereign in 1066, English came into contact with many French words and ideas. And activities, including chess. English-speakers then absorbed the French word for the game, employing English variations of the French plural *eschecs*, including *chesses* and *chestes* and *chesse*, before settling on *chess*, which carries the vestigial -*s* ending inherited from the French.

Check!, the English pronunciation of the French exclamation *eschec!* (with the initial *e*- chopped off, to please the English ear) was nonetheless preserved to warn of a king's exposure to capture. This alert naturally gave an opponent a chance to explore alternatives and to prevent *checkmate*, loss of his king and, hence, the game. *Check!* became tantamount to exclaiming "Examine options!" or "Restrain from acting without due consideration!" It also gained the sense "come to a sudden halt."★

In time there would be another kind of *check*, initially (and still in the UK) spelled *cheque*: a token in place of cash that initially provided a means to verify or "check" the collectability or legality of payment. Later there would be checkbooks, bank checks, checklists, checkouts, cross-checks, double checks, checked luggage, checked

---

★Medieval speakers of English used *check* to mean other things as well, such as "make a checked pattern," like the one on the chessboard, as in this example from a mid-fifteenth-century work including recipes and manners: "*Whan ye þat venesoun so haue chekkid hit, with þe fore parte of youre knyfe þat ye hit owt kytt.*" Translation: "When you've checked the venison, with the forepart of your knife you cut (a piece) out of it."[1]

tests, spell check, fact-checkers, checks and balances, Checkpoint Charlie, bikini-clad chicks to *check out* on the beach, Top 40 rap hits to *check for* on YouTube, baked Persian apples (stuffed with spiced lamb) to *check on* after twenty minutes in the oven, and more.

In French today, *chess* is still expressed in the plural for "shah," and is now spelled *échecs*. In Persian, however, chess is now called, as it has been since the seventh century, *shaṭranj*. This Persian word reflects borrowing from an ancient Sanskrit compound, *caturaṅga*, meaning "four arms," and referring to distinct branches of the military represented by pieces in the game that developed into chess. Arabic, and some languages historically in close contact with Arabic, including Spanish and Portuguese, preserve versions of this Persian word for *chess*, even as French, English, and other European languages instead refer to the game using its climactic Persian alarm for "king!"[2]

Check, however, English's much-altered version of *shāh*, is now a word recognized in Persian, as well as in French, Arabic, Spanish, Portuguese, and all other languages that have found Global English entering their vocabularies *unchecked*.

CHECKMATE!

Checkmate is from the Arabic *ash-shāh māt*, meaning literally "a king died" but used here in the sense of "Your king is dead!" Absorbed into Romance languages from Arabic, the phrase was altered. In French it became *échec et mat*, or "check and dead." But, like English-speakers using the word *checkmate*, French-speakers typically hear no Persian or Arabic meanings in their phrase. In Russian, the word for the game of chess employs a plural form of the phrase: шахматы, or *shakhmaty*. "Checkmates!"

PENTHOUSE

Nope, not that *Penthouse*. But if you're looking for titillation, stick around. You'll see that *penthouse*—the word—sizzles.

Penthouse is a solid compound built of two parts: *pent + house*. Right? Well, that's what it looks like. And that's how the word sounds in most pronunciations. So firmly built is the *house* in *penthouse* that we're now persuaded it's really there. And maybe it is, by sheer virtue of collective word reforging in sixteenth-century England. But when it entered English from French, *penthouse* was not a compound word. It was simply *pentiz*, Anglo-Norman French for, well, "penthouse."[1] But what the French meant by it, and what the medieval English meant as well, was rather a humble structure de*pend*ing on another, as in "lean-to" or "attached building."

The idea of one thing "hanging from" another had come from Latin's *appendere*, "to depend" or "to belong to"—familiar in medical English via a shared root with *appendix*. Medieval Latin had built its own word for a "depending" structure, the *appendicium*, which medieval French had reworked into *pentiz*.

The French word appears to have served Middle English perfectly well. The concept of a simple, ground-level structure was even useful to sermonizers describing Bethlehem's renowned edifice, today usually termed a "manger." One sermon speaks about Joseph and Mary in their *pendize* (one of many diverse spellings of *pentiz*) and notes that it was *wawles*, "wall-less." Clearly, we're as far as we can be from a classy or enviable address.

But speakers of English in Shakespeare's day retooled the medieval word. They attached the English word *house*, as a kind of verbal lean-to, to the word's core syllable: *pent-*. Thus the Early Modern English rendering of *pentiz* became *penthouse*.

Why did this happen? English-speakers, looking back on the earlier word, created their own folk etymology. That is, *pent-* in the original *pentiz* was "reheard" as a familiar element, as the *pent-* in words like *pentangle*. With *pentiz* heard anew in this way, its *-iz* ending made little sense, but sounded close enough to the more familiar *-house* to be replaced by it. *House* was therefore a kind of inorganic addition to *pent-*, a renovated Germanic structure attached to the older, Franco-Latin outbuilding. When we see the word now, it's difficult not to picture the "house" that seems to be its most vivid component: *penthouse*.

So where's the sexy part of the *penthouse* story? As so often with things sexy, it's before and after the medieval period. We'll discover some prehistoric sexiness in *house*. For its part, *pent-* is derived from the earlier Latin verbs *pendēre* and *pendere*. They, respectively, mean "to cause to hang" and "to hang," or "to weigh." Apart from the aforementioned *appendix*, some English words that stem from them are *append, depend, pendant, penchant*, and even *stipend*. Also in this family of Latin verbs is *pēnsāre*, as in "to weigh with the mind," "to think," as captured in the English word *pensive*. If we go very far back, these Latin words come from **(s)pen-*, a Proto-Indo-European root meaning "to draw," "to stretch," or "to spin." Independently of Latin, English inherited its own native **(s)pen-* words, with specimens including *spin, spider*, and *spindle*.

And now for *house*. When English-speakers saw fit to add *house* to *pent*, the new compound word would carry a fresh set of potential associations.

I say *potential* because the etymology of *house* remains uncertain. Carl Darling Buck, a linguist who specialized in the relationships among words in the Indo-European language family, asserts that *house* very probably derives from the PIE root **(s)keu-*,[2] which happens to have put out bundles of captivating words. It means "to cover" or "to conceal." And it often comes packaged with secretive, erotic, or mysterious associations in the many languages to which it was passed down. In Old Norse, the root appears in the word for "cloud," *skȳ*, that thing that conceals the sun, and from which English takes its own bright and glorious word *sky*, a welcome alternative to the heavier *heofon*, an Old English word that Modern English has preserved as *heaven*.

In Latin, the same prehistoric stem produced the intriguing word *obscūrus*, meaning "covered" but also "dark," and the source of English's *obscure*. Again from the same root, Latin has *cūlus*, that part of someone's body that remains unseen when we look at the person face-to-face: "the buttocks." Related English includes *recoil*, as well as a sassy word imported from French, *culotte*. A variation on the stem produced the Latin *cunnus*, meaning "sheath," or that covering that conceals something else, also a Latin word for "vulva." Here Latin provides English with the mission-critical *Penthouse* magazine word *cunnilingus*.

The *k* sound present in the variant form **kus-* shifted to an *h* sound in the ancestor language of English, as seen in the Old English words *hosa* and *hose*, covering for the legs, and early versions of modern *hose*, as in *pantyhose* and *hosiery*. Another related word in Old English is the verb *hȳdan*, from which we now have the sometimes disturbing verb "to hide." An affiliated Germanic word passed into French, which reshaped it into the noun *hutte*, from which English has a word evoking folktales and their forbidding forest settings replete with magical transformations: *hut*. Football fans will perhaps be pleased to know that the word *huddle*, from a Germanic verb to do with "crowding together" (could it come from a primeval idea of a group hiding from animals or people, or protecting someone or something from being found or seen by others?), is also in this ancient family of powerful words for concepts to do with concealing, sheathing, covering, hiding, darkness, and shelter.

But back to *penthouse*, that medieval, attached, subsidiary building, *appended*. It remained a lowly architectural object, indeed literally low since it was a ground-level phenomenon for roughly four hundred years. Then, in the United States, in the 1890s, the *penthouse* was, for a time, to be a *Pent-House*.★ We still don't have a swank residence. Instead, a real estate guide of the period explains that the term refers to the "extension of a building," where "a habitation for a janitor and his family" sits on the roof.[3] The nineteenth-century penthouse was still a "depending" structure, only now it is attached to a building vertically, instead of horizontally.

Finally, in the 1920s, following the arrival of the towering residential skyscraper replete with quality plumbing and reliable passenger elevator service clear up to roof level, the lackluster penthouse enjoyed a blessed upgrade. The pinnacle-attached janitorial shack was then remodeled into something no janitor could dream of affording: the modern penthouse, luxury accommodations situated on the highest level of a metropolitan monument, a place of topmost privilege. (Not to mention closer to the *sky*, that old cousin word of *house*.) From this new, awe-inspiring spot, urban power brokers could gaze down on the city where their ambitions would be realized. Other much-mythologized denizens of the penthouse would be playboys and femmes fatales, whose setting ensured that

★This is a dynamic example of a word in the process of being renovated by its users. Note the capitals and the hyphen: *Pent-House*. As so often, words undergoing transformation need a while to be vetted by speakers before being admitted as full members into the English club. Consider how words like *internet* and *email* were first used as *Internet* and *e-mail*, probationary versions of their current selves. Similarly, *bikini* was written *"Bikini"*—with both a capital letter and quotation marks—when it was first used in English to refer to the swimsuit. In this spirit, our imagined *bloghorn* terms should perhaps for now be referred to as *"Blog-Horn"* until such time as the compound is widely used. Like almost all other new words that gain wide acceptance, it would undoubtedly later be simplified to *bloghorn*.

they would attain new heights in romance or intrigue, perched between twinkling city lights and twinkling celestial stars.

The penthouse thereafter became an object of global attention, and *penthouse* became a Global English word whose stock rose sky-high. In languages spoken by some of the world's wealthiest individuals—Chinese, Arabic, Russian, Japanese, Korean, French, German, Dutch, Italian, Spanish, and of course English—*penthouse* is shorthand for "coveted high-rise address."

But forests of skyscrapers, along with urban contexts that compare with the first penthouses of the 1920s, haven't cropped up everywhere. Indeed, increasingly, *penthouse* means little more than a nice apartment, possibly with a sliding glass door and a balcony, and probably a view from at least a few floors off the ground.★

As a result of this gradual demotion to lower levels on the world's luxury meters, the word *penthouse* may no longer suffice for that knock-me-out top-floor apartment. Global English may soon have to come up with a new term for those rare addresses that *penthouse* no longer truly denotes. My own suggestion, inspired by the sensational **(s)keu-* root, would be the compound *skyhut*. And yours?

PARK AVENUE AND EAST EIGHTY-SIXTH STREET, NEW YORK, NEW YORK

The address of the world's first modern penthouse remains a mystery, largely because the first penthouses built on top of skyscrapers had yet to show their full potential. But one penthouse stands out as the first of the highly visible top-floor luxury accommodations favored by the fabulously rich in the Roaring Twenties. It can still be seen today at 1040 Park Avenue in New York: the penthouse built for magazine magnate Condé Nast, who had made his fortune with such publications as *Vanity Fair* and *Vogue*. Wrapping

★Given the direction the word has been heading, *penthouse* seems doomed eventually to designate in Global English any living space not physically located in a basement.

around the apartment was a generous terrace where, on January 18, 1925, Nast hosted a glamorous dance party to celebrate his new home. It may have been on the chilly side for an outdoor event, but guests would have been warmed by the sight of quite a few celebrities. And at least one of them was sure to cause a stir dancing on the penthouse terrace: Fred Astaire.[4]

COOKIE

Like many people who have attained global recognition, the word *cookie* is of Old World ancestry but born and raised in New York. In 1625 an established Dutch fur-trading settlement became known as *Nieuw*, i.e., New, *Amsterdam*. There, some respite from the trials of colonial life came in the form of traditional goodies known as *koekjes*. To the Dutch word for "cake," *koek*, the suffix *-je* had been added to mean that the *koekje,* pronounced "KOOK-yieh," was a "little cake," something that might have been called a *cakie* or a *caken*, or even a *cakeling* or *cakelette*, had it first been named in English.

The New Amsterdam *koekjes* remained their Dutch selves for some decades, until the British definitively gained control of the colony in 1674 and renamed it New York (in honor of the Duke of York, whose idea it was to wage war against the Dutch in the first place). Even under British rule, "little cakes" kept their Dutch name for roughly a generation, or twenty-odd years, the time it takes for a newborn to learn a native language, grow up on milk and *koekjes*, enter the adult world, and pass a language on to young ones. By the end of that cycle (during which so much can happen in a linguistic context), Dutch-speakers were increasingly using English in their English-ruled territory. The word *koekje* was then naturally anglicized.

Given how popular the little cakes became within and beyond New York, one can safely guess that *koekjes* were talked about in English a good bit before they were referred to in written English, for which there is compelling proof that the word had, as linguists put it, entered the language.

Cookie's first appearance is reportedly from 1730. Rather, that of the appearance of *cookies*, since the first recorded mention of the "little cake" refers to no fewer than eight hundred of them provisioned (along with rum and beer) for a funeral.* At this debut, they are spelled *cockies*.[1] And the rest is history.

Today, U.S. cookie manufacturing is a $10 billion–plus industry, including extensive trade with nations of fellow cookie addicts. Not a bad little business, or perhaps one should say "not a bad *businessje*" in honor of the seventeenth-century Dutch spoken by the bakers of those minicakes.

In America, cookies would go on to inspire perfect moms (and dads of course, but especially moms); White House chefs; R & D wizards behind the industrial cookies that make consumers water at the mouth; and such venerable institutions as the Girl Scouts of America (our household was always divided between the thin mint and the peanut butter). Creative Asian Americans were also motivated by the cookie to rethink message-bearing cakes and crackers from the Far East. Those ancient concoctions, some used in sacred ceremonies and ritual practices, first resurfaced in California as the *fortune cookie*. By now, they've appeared globally in Asian restaurants, often delivered in the form of a cookie consolation along with

---

*Word trackers have not yet found an explanation for the fact that the first solid, *OED*-certified attestation of *cookie* is from Scotland, circa 1730. Could the word have been introduced by a Scot who'd been to New York earlier in the century? Or could a Dutch cookie maker have introduced the word directly into Scotland? Another possibility is that *cookie* arose independently in Scottish English; this seems to be the best explanation, since the Scottish *cookie* barely resembles the American one. It rather refers to an unsweetened bun.[2]

a bill. No one bats an eye when a four-year-old in Brussels, having supped on wontons with her parents, pleads with them to read what's inside her cookie. Or, as she puts it, "*mon cookie!*"

Sweet bite-size finger food is of course not a Dutch-American invention. The Middle East is renowned for delectable treats such as clove-studded and honey-drenched baklava, or crunchier, sesame seed–packed *barazek*. Speakers of Lithuanian are more familiar with flaky and buttery *sausainiai su obuoliais*, or "little pastries with apple." Persian-speakers are more likely to talk about, and reach for, a *nān-i bādāmī*, a small "bread-of almond" that bursts with flavor as it melts in the mouth. And Cherokee-speaking bakers refine recipes for *se-lu i-sa u-ga-na-s-da*, little cakes named for their key ingredient, sweetened cornmeal.

Elsewhere there are minicakes linguistically related to the American *cookie*. An example is the Italian *biscotti*, the "twice" (*bis*) + "cooked" (*cotti*) goodie, hardened by its double journey into the oven and therefore better prepared to serve snackers on long journeys away from the oven. *Biscotti* were built to travel, as were *biscuits*, English for the often cheerless sort-of-cookielike items that seem to have been baked for durability rather than delectation. French-speakers have their own version of the sweet little double-baked cake in *biscuits*. Like *cookie*, all of these words are built on an Italic root reconstructed as *$k^w ek^w$-*.

The prehistoric root flourished in many Indo-European languages, mainly carrying ideas to do with "cooking" and "ripening," as seen in numerous words that English has borrowed: *cook, cuisine, kitchen, kiln, terra cotta*, and even *precocious*, as in "pre-ripened," or "mature ahead of time."

All such *kek*-sounding and *cook*-related words derive from the related Proto-Indo-European root *pek^w-*, preserved in Greek words that also have to do with "cooking" and "ripening," as well as "digesting," and heard in some English words taken from Greek, like *pumpkin* and *dyspepsia*. But let's not be distracted by tummy problems when we're meant to be obsessing about cookies.

What's so special about cookies? The king of cookies is of course the *chocolate chip,* which appeared quite late in the cookie game, initially in the guise of the Toll House cookie of the 1930s. But it captures the special nature of the cookie as opposed to its European cousins, biscuits. Whether soft or crispy; layered or flat; containing crunchy nuts or spices conjuring trapped airs of distant worlds released from their shipments, like cinnamon and nutmeg suddenly unboxed on saltwater piers, or apricot morsels and chunks of butterscotch; decorated with ginger glaze or coffee icing; sandwiched around hazelnut cream or painted with colored sugars for holidays, or not—cookies have managed to conquer a sweet tooth or two thousands of miles from Amsterdams old and *Nieuw.*

Still, actual cookies are only part of the word's global success story. Thanks to the widely followed TV show *Sesame Street,* Cookie Monster has been added to the planetary jar of *cookie* words in over one hundred countries. In Afrikaans, spoken in South Africa and closely related to Dutch, he is *Koekie Monster.* In Swahili, he goes by *kuki monster,* but in Malay he's *Cookie Rakasa.* Persian- and Arabic-speakers have their own versions of the wacky monster who wants a *kūkī,* as do East Asians and Filipinos. In their Katakana alphabet, Japanese-speakers write his name: クッキーモンスター, or "kukkī monsutā," Japanese pronunciation of the English "cookie monster." In Yiddish, the object of monstrous desire is a *kikhl,* sometimes written *kichel.* And in Modern Dutch, the googly-eyed one is *Koekiemonster.* Of course, had Sesame Street creator Jim Henson been born some centuries earlier, and had he become the puppet master of Nieuw Amsterdam, his blue-furred creation would perhaps have first appeared with the name *Koekjemonster.*

Meanwhile, global citizens who don't watch TV, or who don't hang out with Cookie Monster fans, could be using *cookies* in its post-1990s computer sense. So-called cookies are packets of friendly-sounding but controversial electronically dispatched data routinely sent by search engines or internet service providers to track activity on individual computers. Like the eight hundred cookies delivered to a funeral in New York, *digital cookies* are a plural phenomenon, delivered to computers in batches. What does come in the singular is *cookie technology*. It may have deleted charm from the Dutch-American word for "little cake," but cookie lovers won't be fazed. For them, a cookie recipe will simply never include things like encryption or binary pairs. Cookies are about sugar, fat, and flour. And maybe some raisins. And a *dashje* of rum.

TAXI!

On a corner in just about any city on Earth? Need to be somewhere *now*? Chances are high you'll want to call out a favorite word in Global English: *taxi!*

Taxi is one of those words that come fully into their own only when spoken (or yelled). Nonnative English users don't need to worry much about pronunciation of words like *spam*; people are too busy identifying and blocking it. Or sending it. But *taxi* is a word people actually need to utter aloud. Generally with at least one exclamation point. *Taxi!!!*

Would *taxi* have gone global so loudly if the word had rather been *thaxi*, *staxi*, *braxi*, *praxi*, *chaxi*, *glaxi*, or (hard to imagine) *splaxi*? *Taxi*'s tricky *x* differs a good deal across foreign pronunciations (see the box on page 189), but its critical initial *t* is more reliable, easy to e-nun-ci-ate with the requisite assertiveness across even the world's noisiest avenues. A test hail with the word helps us hear why it's a Global English gem: *ta-xi!!!* Even where it wasn't phonetically available, as in Hawaiian, the *t* sound has, happily, been a pretty easy one to borrow.

Short and crisp, the global-friendly *taxi* of course didn't just pull up out of nowhere. Like much of the core vocabulary of Global English, its assembly used parts from multiple sources.

If you've gotten where you need to be, and if you have a second to spare, whom do you want to thank for a word that serves you in every cosmopolitan center of the world?

Should it be Wilhelm Bruhn, the German inventor of the *tax-ameter*, a device that measured (the *-meter* part of the compound) distance or time, and calculated thereon a charge (*taxa-*)? Or the Germans in Stuttgart who, in the late 1890s, equipped motorized vehicles with Bruhn's instrument? They initiated a trend that would see the new technology shift from horse-drawn carriages to automobiles.

Or should it be the French, who rebranded the device a *taximètre* while others were sorting out whether the German compound should remain unchanged in English?

Or those speakers of Latin, whose medieval *taxa*, for "tax" or "charge," had supplied the first term in the German compound? (*Taxa* stems from the Latin verb *taxāre*, meaning "to assess" and related of course to *tax* but also to *touch*, *task*, *taste*, *tangible*, and the much-used Global English word *contact*.)

Or how about the ancient Greeks, whose *metron*, "measure," cruised through Latin to Bruhn as *meter*?

You may want to acknowledge Parisians (even if you have had an unpleasant experience with a Paris taxi driver). They began calling the for-hire motorized passenger vehicles *taxis* once the national

French Academy determined that *taximètre* would replace the German *taxameter* to become official French.* Rushed Parisians are, after all, fond of shortening multisyllabic words.†

So, you are likely asking, why are we even discussing *taxi* as an English word?

Taxi, like *bikini*, is not "native" English, but it powered into Global English all the more swiftly for having been broadly internationalized by French and English alike. It got its English jump start in London. As early as March 1907, an item in the *Daily Chronicle* noted that *taxi* was among likely candidates to designate the new *taximeter-cab*. But while the British now use *cab* more often than *taxi*, the terms London was then test-driving included *motor-cab*, *taxi-cab*, and even *taximo*, a hybrid of *taxi* and *motor*.

Still, in 1907, few taxis actually circulated in London. Meanwhile, American entrepreneur Harry Nathaniel Allen was founding the New York Taxicab Company, whose six hundred gasoline-powered, cherry-red and green taximeter-equipped Darracq Landaulets soon plied the city's streets and ferry piers and train stations. (They had been shipped in from France; New York would have to wait a few years for its seminal U.S.-built *yellow cabs*.) Manhattan was for a time the most taxi-crammed spot on Earth, and so enjoys a fair claim to the title World Capital of the Cry *Taxi!* (Probably as fair

---

*When the *taxameter* era had dawned in France, Professor Théodore Reinach, a specialist in Ancient Greek, argued that the word should be modeled on the Greek *táxis* (τάξισ), meaning "order" or "arrangement," as in the English words *syntax* and *taxidermy*. With the French language being Academy-ruled, and with Professor Reinach himself closely tied to the Academy, action was taken in 1905 to employ the Hellenic prefix *taxi-*, even though the Latin idea of "tax" better captured the raison d'être of the new technology. Curiously, perhaps, these Greek and Latin words share no common root.

†Not that *taxi* couldn't be even more truncated. In the 1950s, the French capital's university students and bohemians, always pleased to drop the verbal deadweight of nonessential syllables, injected the even-snappier *tac* into colloquial French. It didn't take with a wider population, but certain French-speakers can still be heard saying (and shouting) *tac* today.

a claim to the cry *taxi!* as Castroville, California, has to being the Artichoke Capital of the World.)

New York is also the uncontested, most-globally-recognized setting for taxi-driven screen entertainment, thanks particularly to Martin Scorsese's 1976 film *Taxi Driver*. But hey, wasn't that a yellow *cab*?

New Yorkers, and Americans in general, are indeed given to using *cab*, cropped from the back end of the word *taxicab,* interchangeably with *taxi*. Yet whatever reference they slot into "Call me a—" and "Just my luck, pouring rain and I can't find a—," they don't throw up a hand to shout, *"Cab!"* Just doesn't work. The United States may hold out on the metric system, but when it's time to get somewhere, Americans go with the world standard: *"Taxi!"* (I doubt that anyone would remember Travis Bickle if Scorsese had titled his film *Cab Driver*. And why does that sound so unmenacing?)

While the older compound word *taximeter* yielded the shorter *taxi* in English, that shorter word took a shortcut of its own in China. In Cantonese, *taxi* would be pronounced *diksi*. In Mandarin, the Cantonese word became *díshì*, but Mandarin-speakers have also shortened it to *dí* and then attached it to other words, including a verb, *dǎ*, to form the compound *dǎdí*, meaning "take (a) taxi."

In Shanghai, London, and New York—and in Paris, Stuttgart, Bangkok, Tel Aviv, and all the world's bustling cities—the fare totaled up by a taxi's meter can be brutally high given the realities of global-era rush hours; local parade, protest, or pedestrian routes; or that scourge of the urban roadway, gridlock.

In many locations around the globe, taxis have never met their namesake, the taximeter, so you may have no clue how much you're to be charged for your journey. Taxing indeed. Global English has yet to offer solid common terms to negotiate such details with the

world's taxi drivers. But as the planetary idiom spreads, we may well
be taxiing in that direction.

HOW TO HAIL A *TAXI* IN GLOBAL ENGLISH

Bengali	*taksi*	Lithuanian	*taksi*
Bosnian	*taksi*	Persian	*tāksī*
Estonian	*takso*	Slovak	*taxi*
German	*Taxi*	Swahili	*teksi*
Greek	*taxi*	Thai	*taksee*
Hungarian	*taxit*	Vietnamese	*tắc-xi*
Japanese	*takushī*	Welsh	*tacsi*

JOB

A Kenyan from the Rift Valley, training to be a nutritionist, is looking for an
internship not too far from home, maybe
in Entebbe, Uganda, where he aspires to
work for a semester. He speaks Kalenjin at home, and on campus he
mainly uses Swahili. In another valley, on another continent, a teenage girl interested in biology is seeking summer work. In her Glen-
dale, California, household, and even at her high school, Spanish
is the common language. She's excited to be applying for positions
offered by research camps in the rain forests of Guatemala, where
her parents were born. And in the high-tech city of Sendai, on the
island of Honshu, a young engineer is exploring salaried posts available in Europe. He speaks the regional dialect, Tōhoku, with his
family, and Japanese at work.

All of these individuals turn to the internet to explore options,
and the keyword that each will enter into a search engine is *job* (or,

in Japanese, *jobu*). One or two of our applicants may initially be perplexed by English *-job* phrases and compounds circulating in the electronic universe, like *nose-* and *paint-*, not to mention *blow-*, but they will eventually discover a wide range of employment opportunities of the kinds they're looking for: *student jobs, summer jobs, full-time jobs*, and much more. They've entered the employment sector of Global English, far ampler in opportunities than those available in the languages they most comfortably speak.

Over the last decade, the word *job* has gone planetary. Even for a local job search, it will pay, literally, to recognize and use the word *job*. In Russia, an employment service company, GogoJobs, uses GogoJobs.ru as its fetching Global English web address.* In Peru, some job seekers respond to advertisements for white-collar *jobs* offered by the Lima branch of the medical outfit Merck & Co., while others apply for far more dangerous *jobs* in nearby copper mines. For job searchers keen to find posts farther from home, *job* is an even more essential word. On a discussion thread bearing the English title "who needs job," posters on a Lithuanian site write such Global English notices as "We looking for job in the country skotland. Can you help us?"†

Why didn't another term for remunerative and likely career-oriented activity gain such worldwide use? English alone also offers *work, employment, positions, posts, occupations*, and *professions*. And other languages have plenty of broadly workable variations on

---

*The CV and résumé tips page for job seekers on the GogoJobs website notes in current Global English (with a light Russian accent): "In Europe as well as in USA resume (CV) can consist of 5 or more pages. If you apply for Russia you resume can be short and exact. It is better to rely on professional who deals with resumes every day and knows employers requirements in details. The market situation is changing very fast and you should follow its requirements, keep up with the times."[1]

†Curiously, in Old World French, the noun *job* is masculine, *un job,* while in Canadian French it's feminine, *une job.*

concepts for paid labor. Besides joblessness, what draws global opportunity seekers to *job*?

One thing that's particularly useful about the humble word *job*: it captures all manner of employment. It can refer to the *top job* at a major corporation paying salaries as well as handsome bonuses; a *summer job* as Denzel Washington's personal assistant on location in, say, Budapest to film a romantic thriller (the kind of job that pays next to nothing because so many would kill for such fun employment that they can add to their eye-popping résumés and use to get an even better job later on); a full-time *union job* with a construction company that offers health benefits and workers' compensation; a *part-time job* in a convenience store; and even a *two-hour job* raking and bagging leaves in Mrs. Greider's backyard.

In fact, *job* is so flexible a term that it can also refer to a job within a job, as when your boss at the Dallas–Fort Worth International Airport branch of Alamo Rent A Car, where we'll imagine you have a *night job*, asks if you could take on the *job* of supervising the trainee who hasn't yet learned how to use the computer system. You're not going to be paid for that latter effort, but you may not want to pass up a chance to prove that you're *job-promotion* material.

How did English gain such a fantastically flexible word for so many different kinds of labor, paid and unpaid alike? At least a piece of the answer can be found in the earliest uses of *job*.[2] When it was first employed in English in the mid-sixteenth century, *job* was not a stand-alone word. It came prepackaged into the phrase *a job of worke*, or rather a *iobbes of worke*, meaning "a piece of work." Nowadays, "a piece" or "a bit" of work is different from ongoing employment, but what's even more interesting about the Early Modern phrase is that it distinguished *job* from *work*. Apparently, *job* alone didn't initially mean "work." In the later seventeenth century, *job* on its own was used to mean paid work of any duration and according to any arrangement with an employer, but it still carried the older idea of "a piece" of work as well. Even today, native speakers of English hear in the word *job* a range of occupational senses from the lowly and hourly to the permanent and fabulously remunerated.

If we try to get a fuller picture of this crucial addition to the Global English vocabulary, we run into a dispiriting dead end. The sources of *job*, beyond *a job of work*, remain a question mark. Some linguists think it's a variation on an earlier medieval English word, *gobbe*, as in "gob" or "lump." Just as *a bit* comes from the idea of "a bitten-off piece," or "a bite," *a gobbe* meant "a mouthful," a portion of something larger.

And if this were the case? What about *gobbe*? In fourteenth-century England, it was adapted from an older French word employed for "mouthful," *gobe*. A verbal form of the French word is still used in its medieval sense in French today: *gober* now means to "gulp," or "swallow down without chewing."

And this brings us to an engrossing fact about medieval French. We noted how, before Latin spread across a large part of western Europe, other languages were spoken, including those of the Celtic branch of the Indo-European family. When a language, Latin in this case, imposes on a preexisting one, as Latin did Celtic, the original local language is called a *substrate* language: it sits on a *stratum* under (*sub*) the new language. In most cases when this happens, certain words and phrases of the substrate are integrated into the newly adopted language. It happens that *gobe* is from the substrate language that was spoken by people who became speakers of Latin and, in time, French. And that language? Gaulish, which, as you can see on our handy Indo-European languages diagram, is a now-extinct tongue of the Celtic branch of Indo-European languages.

But, as interesting as the *gob-job* theory may be, it hasn't convinced everyone.

Meanwhile, large numbers of people are using Global English to look for jobs—and to perform them. One of the most sought-after skills in today's job market is, after all, the ability to speak English.

JOB AT WORK IN GLOBAL ENGLISH

Phrases that can confuse job seekers for whom English is not a native language: *job lot, nose job, blow job, inside job, Steve Jobs, nut job, paint job, snow job*, and *the Book of Job*.

FUN

Why is *fun* a favorite Global English word? Isn't there just as much fun to be had in foreign terms that capture related ideas of "amusement," "diversion," "entertainment," "merriment," "recreation," "jocularity," "pleasing experience," or something as simple as "enjoyment"?

The answer is a resounding Global English "No!" Spanish-speakers plan "very fun," or *muy fun,* motorcycle trips; French-speakers consider dyeing their bangs purple *pour le fun*, "just for fun"; and in Vilnius, friends set out to have "fun," or rather *faina* in Lithuanian, at a new nightclub.

Officially, *fun* is a noun, but it does equal duty as an adjective. Both are probably from an earlier Modern English verb, *to fun*, meaning "to cheat" or "to play a trick on" or "to hoax." It's also possible that the Middle English verb *fon*, meaning "to make a fool of," or "to be foolish" and so "to be infatuated," is the medieval source of all this *fun*. And if *fun* came from *fon*, then it looks like there's also close etymological kinship with *fond* and *fondle*. Still, and fittingly, the origins of *fun* remain impishly elusive.

Native English-speakers are still able to hear a whisper of the earlier, British English sense of mischievous *fun* in such phrases as *funny money*, and such oft-heard schoolyard complaints as "Freddy made fun of my lunchbox!" But Global English *fun* was Made in the USA, a postwar export conjuring the good times to be had with markedly American activities like jitterbugging, watching 3-D movies, building campfires or tree forts, making obscene phone calls, and hacking into the FBI's mainframe computer. The American idea of having fun was part of the American lifestyle package: youthful exuberance, a dash of hipness, and a brand of personal fulfillment that put the accent on bold individualism.

From the land whose Declaration of Independence elevated the "Pursuit of Happiness" to a God-given and inalienable right, *fun* would eventually be exported as a concept of global reach. One can't help but notice that *happiness* has not entered Global English with anything near the frequency and force that *fun* has. But whether *fun* is what the Founding Fathers had in mind when they signed the Declaration, as a human right it has come to resonate hardly less powerfully than "Life" and "Liberty."

Fun was of course alive and well in prewar American English. Fitzgerald and Hemingway put it to frequent use in describing diversions like jumping on a diving board, or the pleasures to be expected during a trip through Spain. They also added to *fun* evocations of recreation so deeply unstructured as to stand for the existential mode of their so-called Lost Generation. In *The Great Gatsby*, a restless Daisy Buchanan sums up the prewar picture of *fun* precisely because she's aware that it exists, but she can't seem to find any: "Oh, let's have fun." Before the word could gain worldwide adoption, American *fun* would have to be attainable without effort. Or at least seem as easy to come by as being American it-self.

The American birthplace of Global English *fun* proved to be California, which went on to supply the world with concepts of *fun* that translated more readily than any particular kind of fun defined by Jack Kerouac and other resident Beat poets. There was Hollywood, where *fun* was packaged in the form of films and TV shows. Nearby was Disneyland, which opened its gates in 1955, and where phrases like *family fun* would gain literal traction via such amusement park diversions as Mr. Toad's Wild Ride. The 1960s then delivered a new lifestyle option of mythological proportions: *fun in the sun*, readily had on the beaches of Malibu and Santa Cruz. With *fun times* in such high demand, *fun* was franchised as an adjective as well as a noun. Surfing (often in a Jack O'Neill wet suit) was suddenly among the most fun things one could take up on the shores of the Pacific Ocean. Other activities included skateboarding, hula hooping, Frisbee tossing, and volleyball playing.

At the same time, San Francisco and its environs delivered airbrushed impressions of hippies on pot or peyote, or on magic mushrooms and their synthesized twin, LSD, plus a whole dopeload of other experimental drugs. All while flower children at least appeared to be experiencing fun dancing naked in Californian rain or hitchhiking barefoot to a commune in Topanga Canyon.

The Poppy State also supplied the free world with a massive dose of addiction-forming pop tunes, all reinforcing and elevating the fun factor of life on America's West Coast. Those with access to a record player or a tuned-in radio station could repicture themselves starring in a more fun version of their dreary lives, with recorded music supplying the fun-augmenting soundtrack. There was the infectious refrain in the Beach Boys' 1964 hit tune "Fun, Fun, Fun": "And we'll have fun, fun, fun now that Daddy took the T-Bird away." *Fun* would never again seem quite so spontaneously abundant in the region's pop music. By the end of 1971, the Canada-born but Malibu-entrenched Joni Mitchell had already reframed the sun-and-fun mood of a changed nation. In the song "All I Want," from her masterpiece album *Blue*, came the yearning "I want to have fun, I want to shine like the sun." California *fun* seemed to be in the process of becoming an object of nostalgia.

Just in time, in the same year, the phrase *Silicon Valley* was coined to capture the rising computer industry in Santa Clara Valley. From the valley town of Sunnyvale, a new company, Atari, released a video game called Pong. While sun was no longer a natural partner of fun, fun on its own was still to be had, indoors. Fun poured out of screens, and eventually from multiplayer video games and entire virtual worlds, like Second Life, launched in 2003. By then, *surfing* was just over ten years old in its second life as a verb for browsing the (notably water-free) internet. And music-loaded iPods, enjoyed on beaches and pretty much anywhere else, had just begun to put sunscreen back in the story of Made-in-California (or at least Designed-in-California) *fun*.

Post-American fun, manufactured and had around the world, has developed into a global species of delight. Young speakers of Vietnamese use *fun* in Global English phrases like "have fun with game," and Greenlandic teenagers in Nuuk seek fun by break-dancing. It's no surprise, then, that much of the world is now discovering that it's not only useful to speak English, it's also fun. In every major language, and in lots of less-spoken ones, heavily hit websites exhort the visitor to "Have fun learning English!" or to pick up English "the fun way." Notably less popular are those sites beckoning English-speakers to find fun with their own forays into foreign tongues. But as the attractions of multilingualism grow among the world's monolingual populations, more fun may yet be harvested from languages other than English.★

I can vouch personally for the fun part (if not the fast) of a book called *Learn Russian the Fast and Fun Way*. In lesson 2, English-speakers discover that *работает* (pronounced roBOtaet), which shares a common Indo-European root with *robot*, means "it (or he or she) works." (Actually, one first learns to say *Не работает*, pronounced "NEE-EH roBOtaet," and meaning "it doesn't work." Judging from the lesson, the phrase serves visitors well following their efforts to use showers, lamps, and TVs in Moscow hotel rooms.) Now, that is fun. (And funny.)

★One fine reason to learn a new language is that it's "good for the brain." Scientists have recently shown that language learning improves memory.

5

LINGUA FRANCA AND ENGLISH

lingua franca Any language serving as a medium between different nations etc. whose own languages are not the same; a system of
communication providing mutual understanding.[1]

To this point in our exploration of Global English, we've viewed
the language from two perspectives. One has given us a wide-angle
view of Ænglisc as it's evolved, out of its deep roots in Proto-Indo-
European, through "fire-new" terms both borrowed and native and,
from British through to American English, into a language of global
scale. Another has focused on specific words: their changed meanings, their roots, and some of the reasons behind their globalization.
This has given us a chance to zoom in on Global English, and to
discover in more intimate detail how its culture is taking form.

Both approaches, the aerial shots and the close-ups, have shown
in different ways how English has spread out to become a shared
language of planetary scope. This situation is unprecedented in
world history. Never until now has there been a single, default

common tongue the human population uses for potential species-wide conversation. But this doesn't mean that the world hasn't seen shared languages of broad sweep in the past. Indeed, many have served speakers who don't share a native tongue, and many still do. Let's now look at Global English from a third standpoint and ask how it compares with other prominent lingua francas past and present.

When a boy welcomes a native Dutch-speaking journalist to the hideout zone of Subcomandante Marcos in the Lacandon jungle of Chiapas, Mexico, the lingua franca is Spanish. The Maya boy is educated in Spanish at school, even though he speaks a Maya language at home, in his hamlet on a bank of the Usumacinta River. For her part, the Dutch reporter learned Spanish in order to broaden her employment opportunities after she attended journalism school in her native city, Utrecht. Spanish isn't the native language of either speaker, but is for over 300 million people in more than twenty countries.

By contrast, a Portuguese-speaking whaler in search of provisions among Inupiaq Eskimos on the northern coast of what is now Alaska was more likely, one hundred twenty years ago, to use a hodgepodge lingua franca employing Inupiaq and some Portuguese words, but also English and even Hawaiian—tongues of those who had previous contact with speakers of Inupiaq. This pidgin, or simplified language combining elements of more than one language, was spoken in no school or home, but it provided enough mutual understanding for the visitor and native to converse with each other before carrying on with their lives in other languages.

Aside from the elemental need to communicate, there are other reasons to have recourse to a specific lingua franca. When people speak multiple languages, their choice of a common one is at times a matter of prestige or of convention. German and Spanish violinists discussing how most exquisitely to entertain their sovereign in Vienna would have spoken in Italian, a language prized in Europe's Habsburg capital for its aesthetic supremacy. In the same era, German- and Spanish-speaking diplomats meeting officials in the Russian court of Catherine the Great would have been hard-pressed to employ any language other than French, Europe's lingua franca for ambassadors and envoys over hundreds of years, and a language richly equipped to address delicate and solemn issues of mutual interest to leaders of diverse countries. (It's no accident that French supplied to English both *ambassador* and *envoy* and, indeed, most of the other words in that last sentence. It's difficult to conduct or even talk about diplomatic matters without using words from French!)

Among the lingua francas of the historical era, the most renowned and well documented is Latin. Should we see Latin as a language whose story ended with the arrival of the modern era? The question is important, because our view of Latin conditions our view of the evolution of English as a distinct yet also spectacularly widespread lingua franca. Both languages were initially spoken by small populations but became formidable and prestigious in multiple spheres of activity, and for large populations. In many ways, the fate of Latin could herald that of English. So what actually happened to Latin? And what does its record suggest for the future of English?

Initially spoken by a relatively small community in Latium in the seventh century BC, Latin later spread via its speakers' military conquests, eventually to become the common tongue of a vast empire. Indeed, so successful was Latin that it supplanted all its ancient linguistic cousins—other Italic languages once spoken on the so-called Italic Peninsula: Faliscan, Oscan, Umbrian, and South Picene. In the western provinces of the Roman Empire, Latin was used by native and nonnative speakers alike for tax collecting, commerce, entertainment, rituals, and ceremonies, and in the all-important Roman military. Even after the Roman Empire's collapse in the fifth century AD, Latin continued to thrive as the lingua franca of the Christian Church, whose sphere of influence largely mapped onto the same western European territory that had been absorbed into the Latin-speaking Roman Empire. By this time, Saint Jerome had translated the Bible from Ancient Greek and Hebrew, as well as Aramaic and Old Latin, into one linguistically consistent sacred text in Medieval Latin, further solidifying the centrality of the language throughout the Christian Middle Ages.

Like the Roman Empire, the Church was governed from Rome. For roughly another thousand years in western Europe, Latin would continue to prevail as the must-know language of the learned, a common tongue not only for men and women of the cloth, but also for students, teachers, and thinkers. Even to this day, Latin remains a persistent language in Western education. While it's certainly possible to get by without it, those who study Latin acquire a broad historical perspective through a language that endured for thousands of years; gain insights into its relationship to their own native tongues; and incidentally obtain direct knowledge of many words and concepts that continue to dominate in areas as diverse as the natural sciences and theology.

Altogether, Latin in its different forms has been spoken by varying populations for over twenty-five hundred years. Remarkably too, Latin remains an unbroken, functioning lingua franca among small pockets of conservative Catholics and in Vatican City, the tiny state from which their Church is governed. Nonetheless, by most standards, it is now considered "dead," a language that, while employed, is no longer actively evolving in step with our times (even if Vatican City does boast an ATM that operates in Latin).*

Before the expansion of the Roman Empire, inhabitants of an extensive area of western and central Europe, including large parts of contemporary Portugal, Spain, and France, spoke Celtic languages, cousins of Modern Irish. However, people in these areas of the empire for the most part came to adopt Latin as their mother tongue. For some five hundred years, as the Roman Empire held sway, expansive networks of roads, bridges, and aqueducts fluidly connected Latin-speakers to one another. These arteries facilitated the flow of military personnel, messengers, merchants, and travelers, and fueled the vitality of their common language. In spite of great distances and considerable geographical obstacles, Latin circulated across much of western Europe, with the result that its speakers belonged to an integrated—and evolving—linguistic community.

With the demise of the Roman Empire, populations covering most of the large area from the southern tip of Spain and reaching up into northern Europe, those very populations that had given up their previous native languages in favor of Latin continued to use a much-changed spoken variety of Latin as their first language. But with the empire's retreat, Latin was no longer a medium interconnecting its former, far-flung provinces. Busy imperial traffic, which had focused on maintaining the empire as an integral body, was supplanted by Christian traffic, which had different objectives.

Over several centuries, Latin evolved into a lingua franca tying the Church to scholars and universities, and to sovereigns and their courts. By then, vernacular languages, such as Italian and French, were in use among the lay populations. And by the fourteenth

---

*As delightful as a Latin-speaking ATM may be, it would probably still eat your card after the third presentation of "*Hic PIN invalidus est.*"

century, Latin was further isolated to the spheres in which it preserved a vibrant literature: religion and learning. Save in this ecclesiastical and scholarly archipelago, among scientists and doctors, and in the conservative and highly scripted language of religious practice, Latin became a language of books, one to read and write but rarely to speak.

With these significant obstructions in the flow and use of Latin, most of its early medieval speakers were relatively cut off from one another. And even if there had been cause for plenty of Latin-speaking movement along all of the old roads and bridges leading to Rome, there was no longer an empire to maintain them. Natural boundaries, such as the Pyrenees Mountains, became cultural and linguistic barriers, forming subpopulations of speakers whose contact with one another became more vital than contact with those beyond their own horizons.

Throughout the second half of the first millennium, former Latin speakers came to speak what were effectively new languages, all offshoots of Vulgar Latin. Unlike Classical Latin, Vulgar Latin was not standardized, so no rules governed its grammar or spelling. It was consequently freer to evolve in step with its communities of speakers, much the way English did over the centuries between 1066 and around 1350, when it was rarely used for writing. The so-called daughter tongues of Latin eventually emerged as distinct tongues in their own rights: Portuguese, Spanish, Catalan, Provençal, French, Italian, Rhaeto-Romance, and Romanian, among others. But even as these languages arose—at first they were only spoken, but beginning with French in the ninth century, they were written as well—Latin remained a living lingua franca used by special groups among speakers of the new Romance languages. That is, while Latin, through a process of fragmentation, diversified into a number of thriving and eventually widespread daughter languages, this development did not prevent Latin from also continuing down a distinct path of its own.

English, in its stature and spread, is often compared with Latin. Both languages have been regarded as extensions of superpowers, with English first notably proliferating under British rule, and later through America's heavy international presence. Both have also been spread by trade, as wider economic landscapes opened up to their speakers. But where the unbroken endurance of English has come from its plasticity, we've seen how Latin "survived" rather differently, by becoming an unregulated, unstandardized language, and thus by splintering into sublanguages. Had tools like the telephone or the internet, or less cumbersome and taxing modes of transportation, been available to speakers of Latin, we can imagine that even the fall of the Roman Empire might not have led to Latin's fragmentation. What would have happened had all roads led to Rome—electronically? It's tantalizing to consider how alternate technologies could have directed Latin (and its speakers) into an alternate future.

The British linguist Nicholas Ostler has surveyed major lingua francas in his book *Empires of the Word: A Language History of the World*. He divides them into two major groups. First are those that circulated chiefly over land, in regions undivided by oceans. These include Egyptian, Phoenician, Arabic, Chinese, Sanskrit, Greek, Latin, Persian, Turkish, and Swahili. Each of these languages has its own story to tell and became a lingua franca for specific reasons. For example, recall that Phoenician was spoken over three thousand years ago by people who traded throughout the Mediterranean. It became a common language, for commercial purposes only, for speakers of dozens of native languages who had dealings with the Phoenicians. Their crucial technology was that most powerful of all ancient linguistic tools: the phonetic alphabet, which speakers of Phoenician along lucrative trade routes used to record sounds of the language.

By contrast, ancient Sanskrit spread from what is currently India to eastern regions of Asia, and not through trade, but as a religious tongue. This early language, Vedic Sanskrit, was used to write the Vedas, sacred to Hindus and Buddhists.* Many other languages spread powerfully when their native speakers gained military dominance over people who adopted them, either as lingua francas or as new native tongues. Examples of languages that have proliferated courtesy of daunting, mobile military technology include Greek, Latin, Turkish, and Arabic. Incidentally, some linguists would add PIE to this group, with the view that the language, or some key fraction of its speakers, spread over vast territories through ascendancy built on such technological advances as the spoked chariot wheel and weapons forged of metal.†

If we trace the contours of some major lingua francas in world history, we can see that they have served as common tongues over impressively wide territories, and yet each nevertheless remained a lingua franca for speakers within specific spheres of activities or within specific regions of the world.

Ostler's second category features those languages that traveled across oceans to be shared by distant populations. Ostler observes that languages of this type belong to the modern era of exploration,

---

Vedas is the English plural form of the Sanskrit word *véda*, meaning "wisdom" or "insight." The word's root persists in English words meaning "know," as with *to wit*, and "see," as in *video*, from the Latin *vidēo*, meaning "I see."

†By the same token, others have proposed models whereby PIE was spread peacefully, via agriculture. It's interesting to note, though, that even the agricultural vision of the spread of Indo-European languages comes yoked to new technology, such as the plow, or a heavier wheel that didn't feature spokes, the block wheel. Some linguists have embraced a combination of peaceful and not-so-peaceful models, arguing that Indo-European languages most probably spread by multiple means.

colonialism, imperialism, and communism: all of these have greatly widened the territory of specific lingua francas.[2] Apart from Dutch and English, the most striking of these comparatively recent "by sea" languages are daughters of Latin—the Romance languages—and particularly those of the formidable modern maritime powers: Portuguese, Spanish, and French. Following this new kind of language proliferation, Romance languages are today native to some 800 million speakers worldwide and serve as lingua francas to a much wider population. If we consider the world picture again, this time looking solely at the Romance languages, we can see that they're spoken not only where Latin had gained a foothold in antiquity, but also in large areas across much of the planet.

One of the less-remembered offshoot "languages" of Latin was none other than Lingua Franca proper, which gave rise to the generic term we use today. *Lingua Franca*, from the Italian for "language of the Franks," did not refer to Franks per se, nor to any language spoken by them. Rather, *franca* was used in the sense of *franj* or *frenk*, words that populations of Arabic- and Turkish-speakers in the eastern Mediterranean had used (and continue in some communities to use to this day) to refer to those western Europeans who began showing up there, in large numbers, in the guises of medieval Crusaders. But Lingua Franca wasn't a standardized or codified language. The term was rather a catchall for a variety of pidgins spoken in the Levant. These pidgins resembled the one resorted to by our Portuguese-speaking whaler and his Inupiaq-speaking interlocutors: they were never spoken as mother tongues.

With Latin having been such a commanding and prestigious lingua franca, *Lingua Franca* arose in the eleventh century to refer to any of a very diverse set of spoken tongues that could be considered offshoots of Latin. The core of Lingua Franca was a language that Latin had fractured into: Italian. An interesting detail, especially given what we've seen about the loss of inflection in the history of English, is that the spoken languages referred to as Lingua Franca mainly used uninflected Italian: dropping inflection made Italian words easier for nonnative speakers to use. Depending on the native languages of people speaking them, the pidgins collectively referred to as *Lingua Franca* also integrated elements from Arabic, Turkish, Greek, Portuguese, and other native languages of the Mediterranean. While some of these were Indo-European, such as Greek and Portuguese, others, like Arabic and Turkish, each of which is from a distinct language family of its own, were not.

Employing words from Indo-European and non-Indo-European languages alike to facilitate trade and diplomacy, the "language of the Franks" helped to bridge East and West across the Mediterranean for nearly a thousand years. Note, however, that Lingua Franca never produced any literary treasure. The literary cultures of its speakers were forged in other languages: Italian, Arabic, Turkish, Portuguese, Greek, and others that variously added words to Lingua Franca.

An entirely different situation occurs with another lingua franca, one that also employs words from Indo-European languages but whose core is non-Indo-European: Swahili. Spoken in a large area of sub-Saharan East Africa, initially in coastal trading zones and on the influential island of Zanzibar, but later used inland as well, Swahili is a Bantu language from the widely dispersed Niger-Congo family of languages. In Tanzania and Kenya it's a national language, and it is widespread in Uganda. In a number of adjacent countries too, including the Democratic Republic of the Congo, Swahili is, for many speakers, a critical second or third language. For some, it can be an avenue to English. For example, students on East African campuses, employing Swahili as their lingua franca, more often learn English than those who don't know Swahili. (As so often elsewhere in the world, knowledge of a regional lingua franca eases acquisition of the global one.)

Unlike Lingua Franca, Swahili has its own literary tradition and has been adopted as a national language. Like English, Swahili is used by far more nonnative speakers than native speakers, and is gaining appeal among those whose less-spoken tongues, not used outside smaller communities, only take them so far. In this respect, Swahili resembles English. Over long periods, both languages absorbed nonnative words introduced by waves of foreign influence. But where we've seen that speakers of English were in contact with those of Scandinavian, French, Latin, and Greek, speakers of Swahili have, over time, traded with or been visited, joined, occupied, or colonized by speakers of Arabic, Portuguese, Italian, Gujarati, Hindi, and Persian. Through its manifold linguistic interactions, Swahili preserved its core Bantu vocabulary and grammar, much the way English remains Germanic in spite of its huge non-Germanic vocabulary.

For most people across the globe, a lingua franca is a powerful means to expand opportunity and to participate in a wider world. We've seen how a few languages and pidgins have, for diverse reasons, become lingua francas. But English is nonetheless categorically different.

Like all lingua francas, English is used by a population beyond that of its native speakers. It facilitates conversation and communication among people of varying tongues. It also resembles other "prestigious" lingua francas, such as Latin, French, Mandarin Chinese, and Swahili, in that it's been a language of literacy and governance, of cultural and international influence. Through specific words, we've looked at English in spotlighted close-ups; from the vantage point of its long history, we've also taken a full-body shot of the language. So let's now view English's unique lingua franca status in stereoscope.

Examinations of core samples extracted from the Global English lexicon tell us that the language serves as the dominant international lingua franca across a spectacular range of endeavor. French has served as a major lingua franca in diplomacy, the arts, law, education and research, fashion and luxury goods, and more. Lingua Franca itself was used primarily for trade. Sanskrit and Latin evolved into lingua francas of learned and religious communities. But English is the unrivaled common tongue, on a global scale, of higher education, science, health and medicine, aviation and maritime affairs, tourism, sports, media, diplomacy, intergovernmental and nongovernmental organizations, law, security, exploration, entertainment, trade and commerce, banking and finance, transportation, environmentalism, technology, and communications. These last two—technology and communications—have been central to the story of English's emergence as the first planetary lingua franca. Made-in-English innovations in these fields created the very channels that literally put global language on (or better, all over) the map. The list, seeming almost comprehensive, sparks the question, is there any global domain in which English *hasn't* taken on lingua franca status?★ Viewed in this light, the spread of English is not only geographically unprecedented; it has advanced into nearly every global arena of human interaction. It not only crosses borders, it is essentially border-free. Indeed, Global English is used by a wholly new kind of speech community.

While investigating the stories of Global English words, we've

---

★A notable realm of conversation missing from our list is religion. Then again, no one language can claim to be the world's sole sacred tongue. For those who oppose Global English, or the pursuits of its speakers, could religion, or sacred languages, serve as the most effective means to challenge the secular global world and "its" English?

also tracked the evolution of the language. And from this angle, we've seen a surprising picture: over the course of its first millennium, English was in no special position to become a lingua franca, let alone a global one. On the contrary, English looked primed for extinction at more than one juncture. And yet, as English continued to be spoken, we saw two major trends: the acquisition of new words and ideas, and even grammar, from diverse languages; and the loss of inflection, the shedding of special case endings and forms of words that contain grammatical information.

A natural question arises from even a cursory survey of both these facets of the language: is there anything about the nature of English that explains its global sweep?

The linguistically correct answer is that no language has any intrinsic capacity to become more widely spoken than another. Yet certain things about English have arguably favored its extensive adoption. Somewhat by chance, English has become increasingly uninflected. It is therefore easier for nonnatives to learn and use, at least on a functional level. Just as accidental is the fact that, for as long as it's been a written language, English has been recorded with a phonetic alphabet. Had another enduring writing system been employed, it's unlikely that English would have been so easily and widely picked up by nonnative speakers. Finally, English has never been academy-ruled. Officially sanctioned congresses of academicians don't convene in or under the auspices of either of the language's two main globalizing nations, the United Kingdom or the United States, to define, let alone regulate, a correct use or future path of English (as is done in one form or another for Chinese, French, Portuguese, Spanish, Swahili, and many others).

But what about the less accidental, "internal" features of English that could explain its globalization? Here we have less to go on, particularly considering the language from its earliest phase, as

Old English.* Yet over the course of its evolution, English proved
to be a language of vast and highly diverse lexical heritage, elastic
grammar, varying word orders, significant phonetic changes, and
profoundly disturbing spelling conventions. If any single feature of
the language should, by all rational measures, have stopped English
from gaining global lingua franca standing, it is surely spelling. Yet
even this hasn't stopped English from being crowned Lingua Franca
Prom Queen by multitudes of Earth's speakers.

Is the world in the thrall of Global English? Or is it in love with
the world to which English grants access? For the moment, these
two things are indivisible. It's simply impossible to get within range
of global opportunities and within hearing of global conversations
without resorting to the world's global language. Could another
language replace English as the planetary lingua franca? Given
that English is now solidly established, and that its uses and appeal continue to expand and change, it's unlikely to be supplanted
in the immediate future. Then again, speakers generally must use
language on a fluid and uninterrupted basis if it is to evolve in step
with their lives.† As we've seen, "fire-new" words need to be reforged
and tended to by entire communities of speakers, not just a handful of inspired poets or prolific monks or even screenwriters, media
personalities, and bloggers.

Latin, evolving over thousands of years, eventually forked into
diverse languages. Will English do the same, or will it continue to

*One could point to the fact that English, unlike Chinese, isn't a "tonal" language. And
that, unlike Zulu, it isn't a "click" language. Arguably, these languages are more difficult to
adopt as lingua francas because they rely on sounds that are generally harder for nonnative
speakers to replicate.
†A notable exception is Hebrew. In the third century AD, Classical Hebrew largely fell
silent save as a liturgical language. But from the late nineteenth century, it was revived as
Modern Hebrew, now the mother tongue of a large speech community. Hebrew has also
been the official language of Israel since the nation's founding in 1948.

draw on those adaptive strengths, however accidentally acquired, that explain its own sensational evolution to date? Both languages have had their means of "survival." On the vocabulary level alone, we've seen that Latin fragmented, while English absorbed. (While a single word in Vulgar Latin generally produced many in its daughter Romance languages, borrowed words were abundantly added to the native lexicon of English.) But we also saw that Latin's fracturing was a response to the breakup of its empire and the erosion of those critical networks of transportation that linked its speakers.

English is used in an altogether different world. The language depends for its global evolution not on engineering that takes it across high mountains and wide rivers, but on technologies and conditions that have redefined how linguistic communities form and, in all probability, how they will endure. Global English's "academy" is not an august body that convenes in some marbled hall at 10:00 a.m. on the first Tuesday of each month except holidays. Or an inherited rule book outlining standard usages and noting what's proper. Rather, it's the hundreds of millions of speakers and users, native and nonnative, who plug into English around the clock.

Lingua Franca, or rather any of a number of related pidgins descended from Latin, eventually became lingua franca, any language that speakers use as a common tongue. Could English someday give its name to a future language that follows where it has broken new linguistic ground? One wonders whether *English* could become *english*, "a planetary lingua franca" or "default common tongue of the human species." For now, the *english* of choice is Global English. Where Global English will go from here remains a huge question, one we'll take up in our next, and final, chapter.

Before we imagine the future of English and consider just how much it could and probably will change, let's take a final word tour of Global English. We'll trace most of the terms in this group back

Lingua Francas: From Latin to Global English[3]

The reach of the Roman Empire made Latin a valuable and prestigious language. Latin evolved into the Romance languages, today widely spoken. Strongly influenced by Latin and Romance languages, English is the world's most-spoken language. In the millennial era, English has defied national boundaries to become a global lingua franca.

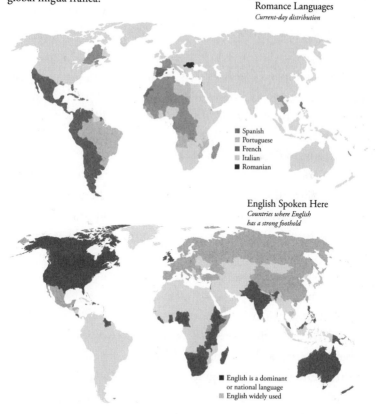

Romance Languages
Current-day distribution

■ Spanish
■ Portuguese
■ French
■ Italian
■ Romanian

English Spoken Here
Countries where English has a strong foothold

■ English is a dominant or national language
■ English widely used

to Latin, that starring lingua franca that produced so many others, including Lingua Franca. And we'll see how all these expressions, no matter how familiar to native English-speakers, look somewhat different when viewed through lingua franca glasses: *stress*, *SAT*, *relax*, *safari*, *deluxe*, *O.K.*

STRESS

Running late? How's that heart rate? Are you check-ing the clock's second hand again? Will you never cross those top three items off that urgent to-do list or catch up on messages and bills? If this sounds like you, welcome to the fellowship of the stressed out.

Things could be worse. Perhaps you've been experiencing panic attacks, nightmares, or insomnia. Have you lost or gained a lot of weight? Been abusing any substances? Hair falling out? If so, you may want to talk to your doctor about *stress*. It could be *chronic stress*, in which case you may benefit from some form of *stress management*. Or *acute episodic stress*, treatable with *antistress* therapies including medications.

Then again, you may be looking at *post-traumatic stress disorder* (PTSD), a condition caused by severely stressful events such as major injury, a close brush with death, the witnessing of a life-threatening event, changing residence, failing an important examination, divorcing, emigrating, or being fired from a job you've held for years. If one of these is the culprit *stressor*, more extreme approaches to *stress reduction* could be in order. According to the *Merck Manual of Medical Information*, you're not alone. Every person has a real chance of developing a stress-related health problem over the course of a lifetime.

Stress was borrowed by speakers of a slew of languages after World War II. In 1942, it was for the first time used in English to refer to physiologically damaging responses to stressful events.* This twisted up ideas previously conjured by *stress*, because the new meaning identified trouble coming not only from external incidents or conditions, but also from powerfully disturbing reactions to them. Yet, as with so many phenomena that eventually command a lot of human attention, these reactions were first observed in laboratory rats. In time, the postwar variant of *stress* was not to be a rodents-only experience. The term proved to be crucial for the diagnosis and treatment of minds and bodies of people. From the 1960s on, *stress* marched out of doctor's offices and hospitals and into homes, workplaces, and schools. It also marched into other languages.

By now, *stress*—the word as well as the state of mind and body it denotes—is put to use around the world. Somali immigrants are identified by relief workers as sufferers of *resettlement stress*, Iraqis endure the effects of *wartime stress*, and tsunami survivors in the South Seas experience *natural disaster stress*. Tokyo workers and students try to remain productive in spite of prevalent *sutoresu*, which, if you say it fast enough, will capture how the word *stress* comes out

*The language-changing concept of stress was introduced by Dr. Dwight J. Ingle.[1] As a eugenicist, Ingle subsequently also caused a lot of stress, notably by advocating sterilization of African Americans.

in Japanese.* Residents of Bogotá, Colombia, complain of *estrés* resulting from ongoing security problems throughout their nation. And in Paris, taxi drivers report that *le stress* peaks on days when traffic congestion caused by protest marches causes passengers to miss flights and trains. Where did so much stress come from? And why has *stress* gone global?

In the nineteenth century, speakers of German employed the phrase *Sturm und Drang* to capture the aesthetic potency of the era's new Romantic movement. That phrase was translated into English as "Storm and Stress," with *stress* referring to the adrenaline-churning effects produced by Romanticism's most absorbing literature, painting, and music. Some expressions of Romanticism were of such stress-inducing, life-and-death intensity that they led followers to be diagnosed with clusters of symptoms named after the artworks that caused them. Johann Wolfgang von Goethe's deliriously popular late-eighteenth-century novella *The Sorrows of Young Werther* set off a rash of cases of *Wertherfieber* or "Werther fever." The work's high Storm-and-Stress rating reportedly even led some readers to commit suicide in imitation of the consummate Romantic hero. Nowadays German-speakers are gripped by a different pair of words: *Die Stress und Das Burnout.* (That latter term, *burnout*, is none other than the Global English compound cousin of *stress*, its workplace sidekick.)

Stress has been at home in the English language since the early fourteenth century, when its speakers shortened a key word that had long been used by their French-speaking rulers: *destresse*, "distress." †

---

*Pre–Global English grandparents of the stressed Japanese would have been familiar with a more traditional but no less disagreeable sensation: *jūatsu*, or "heavy-pressure."

†The first attestation of *stress* in English dates from 1303. Robert Mannyng, a monk, employed the word to capture the forty years of hardship suffered by the Israelites of the Old Testament. Note that Mannyng spells the word as "stres": "Whan þey were yn wyldernes Forty wyntyr, yn hard stres."

The noun had come from the Vulgar Latin *districtia*, meaning "pressing tightly" or "restraining." Converging with *destresse* to influence the sense of *stress* in English was another word in French: *estrece*, meaning "narrowness" or "oppression." Related words in English include *strict*, *constrict*, and *restriction*. The Latin was in fact the past participle, "drawn tight," of the Latin verb *stringere*, "to draw tight." From the family of Latin verbs related to *stringere*, English gained words such as *stringent* and *prestige*.*

It would be tempting to blame early signs of *stress* on the Romans of antiquity, or to trace the word *stress* back to its Latin origins and leave it at that. But the roots of *stress* stretch beyond the peninsula of the Italic branch of the Indo-European language family. Indeed, the Proto-Indo-European root *streig-*, meaning "to stroke," or "to rub" or "to press," lies in the deep linguistic ancestry of *stress*.

Before it absorbed *distress*-related words from Latin via French, or borrowed from Latin any words to do with *strictness*, English had already inherited related words from its Germanic past. From the same Indo-European root, there was the Old English word *strīcan*, meaning "to stroke." This word evolved into the Modern English "to strike." Old English also had the noun *strica*, meaning "stroke" or "line," the source of the current English word *streak*. These native English words themselves go back to Indo-European roots, independent of Latin and the Romance languages.

In the majority of the most-spoken languages today, *stress* has

---

*In case you're wondering what "drawing tightly" has to do with *prestige*, the answer, in a word, is: blindfolding. While it developed into a high-status word, *prestige* is from a Classical Latin noun meaning "trick," or "illusion." That noun, *praestigia*, evolved from a verb that was used in the fixed phrase *praestringere oculōs*, literally meaning "to tightly bind the eyes," or "to blindfold," as in "to blind temporarily," and so "to dazzle the eyes."[2] From this concept, and the associated one of deceit, arose the notion of a pleasing illusion, and then of that hypothetically nonillusory quality that prestige seekers find in anything from jobs and diplomas and wristwatches to zip codes. And words.

become a loanword that readily captures particular experiences of the nerve-rattling kind, those common to people who inhabit the faster-paced millennial world—and who have identified the key source of their problems as their unsettling experience of that world. As coming generations of global denizens wrestle with new challenges, including persistent impressions that it's maddeningly impossible to keep up with daily demands on limited time and attention, *stress* is looking set to remain one of those top three words we're unlikely to be able to cross off the Global English to-know list.

SAT

Rachel can recarpet her studio apartment at a cost of $9.53 per square yard. Her floor area measures 17 feet 6⅖ inches by 9 feet 4⅜ inches. For one week only, Rachel has the opportunity to purchase carpet at a 15% discount.

"What did you get on your SATs?" If you've ever applied to a college in the United States, you probably took the much-dreaded examination administered by the College Board. The inescapable question about one's scores can be almost as aggravating as the test itself.

The SAT is particularly challenging for those test takers for whom English isn't a native or only language, and that group constitutes more than a quarter of the present 1.5 million high school seniors who take the exam annually. (The nonnative-English-speaking cohort is expected to grow. A decade ago, that fraction was only one-sixth.*) On top of the language factor, students who

---

*These figures are self-reported by high school seniors taking the exam. In 1999, 136,037 students chose not to respond to the question about their native language. In 2009, the test-taking year of a more forthright generation, only 49,604 chose no response.

take the test annually in over 170 countries and territories, from the Aaland Islands to Zimbabwe, must contend with often-strange concepts that show up on the test. As one would expect, notions that are alien to teenage nonnative speakers of English abound in the verbal sections of the exam. But plenty also lie in the so-called quantitative reasoning parts as well. There, individuals who are accustomed to, say, the metric system must also be conversant with the imperial system (now embattled even in the kingdom of its formerly eponymous empire, Britain) pretty much solely for the purpose of taking the American test. Questions routinely involve inches and feet, miles and yards, ounces and pounds, gallons and quarts.

Why are so many foreign nationals torturing themselves? One answer is an impressive number of schooling options: the United States is home to more than four thousand institutions of higher learning. Another factor is perceived quality. Comparing institutions on a global scale, by various yard- and metersticks, evaluators routinely fill many of the top two hundred spots on their lists with U.S. colleges and universities.

Besides the United Kingdom, other countries whose postsecondary institutions prominently appear in uppermost tiers across global rankings include Japan and France. In both nations, educators adhere to centralized curricula determined by ministries of education. With Japanese and French colleges geared toward national preparation, applicants typically master not only the national language but also a body of "national" knowledge, much of it acquired simply by rote. U.S. institutions in the aggregate employ a far broader array of teaching methodologies and resources. And with America's established melting-pot custom of educating its diverse population diversely (homeschoolers aren't indicted in the United States, and neither is the teacher at an Amish school employing scripture to instruct students in reading, writing, geography, and history; the national range of educational experiences is wide), its colleges are better equipped to take on students who were schooled abroad or who don't have a native command of English.

As the utility and prestige of the planetary lingua franca rise, so has the value of a degree from the world's fountainhead of Global English. In academic year 1985–86, 343,000 foreign nationals were officially enrolled in U.S. institutions of higher learning.[1] That count has since nearly doubled. And it's slated to continue climbing—the U.S. Department of Commerce has identified education as one of the country's most lucrative "exports" in the service sector.* And why not advance policies to raise nonnational enrollment rates, if U.S. institutions can attract foreign currency as well as foreign minds? Either would be a terrible thing to waste.

So what does *SAT* spell, apart from anxiety? For a long time, *SAT* was an abbreviation for *Scholastic Aptitude Test*. The first cohort to sit down and fill in its blanks, in 1926, comprised some eight thousand young adults. In 1990 closer to 1.6 million seniors were sharpening up no. 2 pencils to select answers. By then, the word *aptitude*, implying that students were being tested for natural fitness or inborn talent, would no longer do. The politics of *aptitude* had made the test's name, along with standardized testing in general, controversial. *Assessment* was trotted out to replace *Aptitude*, though it did little more than render the word *Test* blandly redundant. For a few years, *SAT* would abbreviate a hypothetically less offensive but indisputably more awkward name for the examination: *Scholastic Assessment Test*.

Whether the *A* stood for *Aptitude* or *Assessment*, all three words

---

*For example, in the academic year 2006–2007, 582,984 foreign nationals were officially enrolled in institutions of higher learning in the United States. The Department of Commerce rated the sum "export" value of these educational services at $14.5 billion.

captured by *SAT* had been either directly or indirectly borrowed from Latin. Hardly surprising, since Latin had its impressive second wind as the lingua franca of scholarship. No accident, either, that *verbal, literacy, pencil, study, curriculum, globe, campus, college, university, computer,* and *education* are among the thousands of classroom terms that English had, directly or via French, reassembled from words made in Latin. Even in colonial America, Latin preserved its prestigious status as a distinctive language of the learned.★ The Latinate character of *SAT* aptly, if tacitly, declared American English indebtedness to educational concepts forged in Latin.

> *At 3:17 p.m., Rachel takes a stroll to reflect on the advantages of purchasing floor covering at the discounted price. Advancing at an average speed of 2.88 miles per hour, Rachel walks a path measuring 1,220 yards.*

SAT mutated yet again in 1993, the very year that English secured firm footing as lingua franca of the World Wide Web. While the College Board continued to call its examination the *SAT,* it declared that the three letters no longer abbreviated anything. They would thereafter officially serve as a mere placeholder for the concept (and proxy for the stress provocation) of the test. This step suggested that the most important resource for the exchange of ideas, and the surest to offer the most promising and profitable transnational education, was no longer anglicized Latin but rather

---

★Instead of taking any test resembling the SAT, some young men applying to college in the colonial era were rather tested for their skills in classical languages: "Harvard, founded in 1636, had set the following admission standards in 1642: '*When any schollar is able to read Tully [Cicero] or such like classicall Latine Authore ex tempore, & make and speake true Latin in verse and prose, and decline perfectly the paradigmes of Nounes and Verbes in the Greek tongue, then may hee bee admitted into the Colledge, nor shall any claim admission before such qualifications.*' Once admitted, students were forbidden use of English within the college precincts."[2]

rebranded English. Such rebranding caught the spirit of the age that would see Federal Express become FedEx, the international ad agency J. Walter Thompson become JWT, and a host of periodicals reducing their titles to alphabetic sequences, or a mere letter: *GQ, HG, FMR, AD*, and *W*.★

Similar exercises in educational test branding produced the *SAT Reasoning Test*. *Aptitude* was class- and culture-bound, and therefore biased, but ostensibly, *reasoning* is not. *Assessment Test* was redundant, but a *T* that used to mean *Test*, followed by a *Test* that does mean "test," presumably isn't. The new phrase managed to be stranger than any preceding it. As *SAT* harkened back to its old abbreviation, millions naturally found themselves recalling it, and so thinking of the new test as the "Scholastic Assessment Test Reasoning Test." What self-respecting exam corrector, no matter how exhausted, wouldn't bolt upright to yank out a red pen and mark *that* phrase as rife with errors?

Decades of verbal surgery performed on *SAT* have made it an unsettling linguistic artifact to behold. It's neither abbreviation nor acronym. Could it be a word? Certainly not as the past tense of *sit*. It's not a phrase. Is it language of any kind? Or is *SAT* now closer to a logo or cipher—or a mysterious cluster of runes, recognized for their hieratic significance, but otherwise illegible? As the alphabetic

---

★Most English-speakers arguably have to think for a moment, or consult a source, to determine that 3M once stood for "Minnesota Mining and Manufacturing Company," or that IBM still stands for "International Business Machines." Over the course of the twentieth century, America grew increasingly fluent in what could be called "ticker tape English." But whatever their degree of detachment from phrases in Modern English, or degree of attachment to specific entities, corporate or not, certain strings of letters, such as FBI, URL, LSD, SEC, SUV, TB, VIP, AAA, ABC, CNN, omg, lol, WMD, WWW, and even OED, have by now gained the independent status of what could be called English elements rather than words. After all, while it won't be found in the *OED* (which gives the etymology as uncertain beyond the Latin *elementum*), one oft-proposed source of *element* is the sequence of letters *L-M-N*, from that elemental tool, the Latin alphabet.

symbol for a rite of initiation into education in English, *SAT* may not be classifiable as a *part* of speech, but it is likely a harbinger of new *kinds* of speech evolving in Global English. Kinds not yet seen on the SAT Reasoning Test.

Welcome to the SAT experience. Exasperating, yes. And we haven't even addressed college applications themselves. But if handsome SAT scores gain you admission to the college of your choice, you may not care that the test's label is ungrammatical, redundant, or politically dated. Or that it's meaning-free. Time to brush up, then, on metric conversions of feet, inches, pounds, and pints. And if you're taking the test in Buenos Aires or Moscow or Melbourne, you may want to sort out what Americans mean by a cup or a ton or a degree Fahrenheit. (You'll also want to spell *Fahrenheit* correctly if you're using the word in the test's writing section. Not that *Fahrenheit* is any harder to get right than *Celsius*, SAT English for what many foreign nationals think of as *Centigrade*.) Perhaps America's mixed use of both metric and imperial systems is a symptom of its attractively diverse standards in the field of education.★

Further, as English gains lingua franca status on campuses even in locations where it isn't a first tongue, more and more seekers of an education in the language, including Americans, will find themselves exempt from the SAT ordeal. As the Brussels-based Academic Cooperation Association (the ACA) notes, European programs of study taught in English have tripled since 2003 and now number

---

★Too bad America's thinking isn't as flexible when it comes to the SAT. There is the other multiple-choice exam, the ACT, which offers four short tests in English, mathematics, reading, science, and one optional writing section. Given that both standardized tests are arguably defective as measures of students' strengths and weaknesses, it may be little comfort that more institutions are now giving applicants the option of choosing one over the other exam. In any case, the ACT has followed in the footsteps of the SAT. *ACT* had previously stood for *American College Testing Assessment* (even though one would expect that to be abbreviated *ACTA*). But, from 1996, *ACT* would stand for nothing.

nearly twenty-five hundred. The association sums up the new position of English in a telling note: "Emperor Charles V was quoted as saying 'I speak Spanish to God, Italian to women, French to men, and German to my dog.' Today, he would probably add 'and English to academics.' "[3]

On reflection, Rachel decides not to carpet her living room. In fact, she's resolved to stick with her job as a New Accounts Customer Liaison Representative in the financial service sector for 6 more months, sell her studio apartment, move to the Netherlands, and pursue a bachelor's degree in management at Erasmus University Rotterdam. She won't be taking the SAT. In fact, the only test Rachel could be required to take is one demonstrating that she is (like 95% of the Dutch population) competent in English, the lingua franca employed for her degree-granting course of study in Holland.

A. Rachel is smart; she can't afford the carpeting and may as well leave the country.

B. Why is there a higher percentage of English-speakers in Holland than there is in the USA?

C. The guy my parents paid $200 an hour for SAT tutoring said there would be no carpeting questions on this test.

D. Where can I apply for a degree program offered on an Erasmus U. campus in Europe?

E. All of the above.

Please use a #2 pencil to fill in completely the circle corresponding to your answer:

A. ◯ (A)

B. ◯ (B)

C. ◯ (C)
D. ◯ (D)
E. ◯ (E)

STOP!

THIS IS THE LAST QUESTION FOR THIS SECTION OF THE SAT REASONING TEST. DO NOT TURN THIS PAGE UNTIL INSTRUCTED TO DO SO BY YOUR EXAMINER.

RELAX

What makes you relax? If you're not sure, consider how others have recently answered this big global culture question. Internet threads abound on the subject in languages from Armenian to Zulu. Here's a sampling of translated replies from around the world:

Riding my bike into the forest, listening to music, sleep, movies (mostly thrillers), a good historical novel, bathing, drumming, gambling, strolling in a park, long conversations with friends, a glass of wine, a beautiful landscape, sex, traveling, stargazing, paying bills, a sauna, planting flowers, dancing, skydiving, talking on the phone, cooking empanadas, playing electric guitar, people watching, reading old magazines, writing in my journal, drawing, massage, gaming, daydreaming, watching soccer matches on TV with friends, bodysurfing, attending a sumo wrestling match, singing in choir, yoga, collecting things made of blue glass, bridge night, cruising bars, writing letters of complaint, reading bedtime stories to my sons, drinking vodka, sunbathing, just hanging out, cleaning my car, flirting, doing crossword puzzles, fishing alone, surfing the net, shopping for shoes, smoking pot, knitting, beekeeping, kayaking, solving math problems, braiding my sister's hair, truffle hunting.

Not so long ago, *relaxing* in English was less about doing than about not doing, or doing less. Increasingly, it's rather about activity, or at least about activity other than the usual. Something relaxing. How did this happen?

During the Industrial Revolution, English-speakers divided life into *business* and *pleasure*. In the global era, they've divided life yet again, only this time into *stress* and *relaxation*. But these two sets of words and concepts, much as they have redrawn their speakers' lifestyle maps, don't overlap as much as you'd expect. After all, you can be stressed *or* relaxed while conducting business. And the same goes for being in pleasure mode. *Pleasure* can involve an activity as stressful as motorcycle racing, or one as relaxing as visualizing the shadows of gliding clouds.

Other languages naturally have their own words for states of being and activities that are entertaining or diverting, or that bring sensations of restorative fulfillment or restfulness. Some languages are abundantly supplied with terms for enjoyment of everyday life. Italian is one. Its phrases such as *la dolce far niente*, meaning literally "the sweet doing nothing," or "pleasing idleness," as opposed to sitting around bored out of one's skull or fidgeting nervously for lack of anything worthwhile to do, would seem to make Italian a good candidate for immunity to the Global English word *relax*. But even Italian has zealously adopted *relax* to refer to lifestyle options, idyllic vacation rentals, hotel facilities, and downtime with friends. What's going on here?

Let's go way back and look at the deepest known layers of the word *relax*. Its Proto-Indo-European root has been solidly reconstructed from three distinct branches of Indo-European languages—Hellenic, Italic, and Germanic—as *(s)lēg- meaning "to be slack" or "to be languid." The Germanic stem, *slak-, underlies the Old English word slæc or "loose," the direct ancestor of Modern English slack, slacken, and the word for that work-avoiding creature revived in America's 1990s, the slacker. But even as English inherited words for ideas of being "loose," it also adapted, from the French of England's medieval conquerors, another word that had come down from the same PIE root to flourish in Latin and the Romance languages: relaxer, meaning "to liberate," "to acquit," "to pardon," and, in medical terms, "to loosen." The French word comes from Latin relaxare, "to loosen," or "to lighten." This Latin verb was built on the adjective laxus, meaning "loose," an Indo-European cousin word of English's native slack.

English-speakers initially used relax much as the French had. But while its concepts in French were restricted to notions medical and physical, or penal (as with "the loosening of a muscle," or "the liberating of prisoners"), relax in Early Modern English gradually also came to mean "to calm someone (else) down" and then "to cease one's (own) efforts"; and later, in reflexive phrases like "he relaxes himself," it meant "to make oneself less tense." But at this stage—we haven't yet moved beyond 1800, our working start date for Late Modern English—relax had a ways to go before it would signify unwinding to vocalists like Enya, Ireland's New Age siren.

In the wake of the French Revolution of 1789, English-speakers of a less austere European era relaxed at once physically and socially "into a smile," or "into conversation," or "in the company" of others. And in the early twentieth century, with concepts of the unconscious mind much discussed in Europe and the United States, such social uses of the word took a new turn. Relax continued to refer to conduct in the outward and social world, but it was also used to talk about a far more intimate one, the self. The first attestation of *relax* in this sense, from 1907, was penned by the American psychologist William James: "To relax, to say to ourselves 'Peace! Be still!' is sometimes a great achievement of inner work."[1] As the new century unfolded, English-speakers would seek to "become less tense" in this more invisible (if newly labor-intensive) way, in mind and spirit as well as body.

Relax had taken this new direction just ahead of the arrival of *stress* in its sense of inner and psychological as opposed to external forms of oppression and constriction. Perfect timing. Stressed people and their doctors would have a fresh option at their disposal to cope with the relentless tense-making stimuli of life in the era of mass production, burgeoning cities, noisy automobiles and buses and subways, distracting advertisements on billboards and over radio waves, and flashing neon lights: *to relax*.

And thanks to the mushrooming postwar appeal of yoga, meditation, and other Eastern approaches to health that were increasingly to seize the attention of westerners, *relax* also took on the sense of "to let the mind go," even "to refrain actively and deliberately from paying attention to *anything*." *Relax* had gone from being about giving up control of things like rules and bowel muscles (perhaps with some help from a *laxative*) to being about striving to do something quite particular: *nothing*.

By the end of the twentieth century, *relax* had changed yet again. And this time, multibillion-dollar activities would be in play. *Relaxation* then naturally gained the attention of entrepreneurs catering to seekers of inner peace. Out of the relaxation movement arose relaxing music; relaxing spa retreats and facials and massages; the relaxation response; relaxation medication; relaxation techniques and exercises; and relaxing vacations and destinations and accommodations. One was urged to find time to relax; look at relaxing colors; think relaxing thoughts; take relaxing drives; play relaxing sports; wear relaxing clothes; read relaxing poems; adjust dials to relaxing radio frequencies; fall into relaxing sleep; sip relaxing tea; burn relaxing incense; put one's body into relaxing yoga postures; and, if humanly possible, work a relaxing job. A few hundred years earlier, that would have been strictly impossible, since *relaxation* simply meant being in a state of *not working*.

By the time *relax* had taken this surprising turn in English, nothing in French resembled it. Postwar French then adopted *relax* in its least relaxing, imperative form: *relax!* With that command, French put the word to work, and in quite a variety of ways.★

Like speakers of French, speakers of other languages around the world discovered that they too were bereft of any adequate term to convey the new mix of ideas captured by *relax*. The word was a natural for global borrowing. No self-respecting upscale São Paulo residential building omits from its glossy prospectus, featuring lap pool, sundeck, gym, and fully equipped gourmet kitchen, the *sala de relax*, or "relaxation room." In Hungary, serenity hounds are drawn to the *relax apartman* and *relax studio*, the "quiet apartment" and "quiet studio." In Japan, there is *relax esute*, "relax esthetics," encompassing treatments such as facials and massages. There are also *relax stay* spas and retreats, *Relax Herb* cough drops, *Midnight Relax* bath oils, and *U Relax* computer technology.

Relax is also a prized term in Vietnamese, as when supermodel Thanh Hang tells curious fans, "*Shopping là m·ôt cách relax*," or "Shopping is one way to relax."[2] Speakers of Icelandic shop for

---

★In French there's the feminine noun, *relaxation*, meaning "relaxation." There's also the adverb, *relax*, as in *vivre relax* or "to live worry-free." And there's the adjective, which comes in both masculine and feminine forms: *une soirée relaxe* is "a relaxing evening" and *un coin relax* is "a relaxing corner," but *un coin relaxe* is a "relaxation corner," as in "area." And then there's *le relax* on its own, meaning a chair intended to enhance relaxation, a French variation on the La-Z-Boy, the latter designed in 1928 to provide America's weary workers of the mass production era with what its inventors described as "nature's way of relaxing."[3]

stuttbuxur relax, literally "short pants relax," or "casual shorts." And if you use your iPod to relax, you can listen to Relax FM radio broadcasting in Russian from Moscow while you check into the Hotel Relax in the Paharganj neighborhood of downtown New Delhi.

But there are also new avenues of opportunity to enjoy free time in the global world. In the United States, for example, there is Robots and Relax Com, Inc. Its specialty? "Robots and robotic appliances, tools and equipment that mow the lawn and vacuum the home while you relax."

SAFARI

No other word globalized by English evokes the mix of pleasure and peril that surrounds *safari*. It has been diffused worldwide in steps, first by speakers of British English, then by speakers of the American variety. Let's go on a verbal safari to see where this rare specimen of Global English leads.

In 1843 an obsessive Lutheran missionary, Johann Ludwig Krapf, a native of Tübingen, Germany, set out from his post in Abyssinia for the coast of East Africa. Reaching the islands of Lamu and Zanzibar, Krapf settled in Mombasa and lived among the Swahili.★ He might have thought of himself being *on safari* as he journeyed to Africa by boat, but he had yet to encounter the Bantu

---

★In Swahili, Swahili is called *Kiswahili*. Krapf himself uses both terms to refer to the language, and both are now recognized in Standard English. I've chosen to use *Swahili*, much in the same way I'm more comfortable referring to French as French rather than *Français*, or to Spanish as Spanish rather than *Español*. But calling Swahili *Kiswahili* wouldn't be as weird as either of my Romance examples since the terms for the Bantu language operate on nearly equal footing. In Swahili, the *ki-* prefix is used to designate inanimate objects and to mean "in the style of." Attached to *Swahili*, it means "the language spoken by" the Swahili.

term for traveling and sailing. Krapf's linguistic resources were kaleidoscopic: he'd mastered Ancient Greek, Latin, Hebrew, Arabic, and English. On arrival in Africa, he set about studying more languages. He was zealously intent on his mission: to spread the gospel.[1] To that end, he translated sections of the New Testament into a number of African tongues, including Swahili. The reverend's work on these little-known idioms resulted in books, some written and published in Latin or German but many in English, including his *Dictionary of the Suahili Language*, the fruit of Krapf's groundbreaking study of Swahili vocabulary and grammar.★

As Krapf had occasion to observe while studying Swahili, its speakers had, over time, borrowed many words from other tongues with which they'd come into contact. And by the time Krapf's dictionary was published in London, in 1882, Swahili had added new European languages to its long list of foreign contacts, including Krapf's native German and the English of other newcomers to East Africa.†

Krapf's book about Swahili was based on research he had conducted from 1844 through the 1850s, a period when European exploration of interior Africa began to explode.‡ Under the entry *sáfiri*, later standardized as *safari*, he notes that the word, translated

---

★One of Krapf's earlier dictionaries, which he'd been working on in a manuscript, was devoured by white ants in East Africa. Another was published, along with a study of Swahili grammar, in 1850, in Germany, for a more limited readership.

†Among English words to enter Modern Swahili was *doctor*, to which an *i* was added to form the Swahili noun *daktari*. (This practitioner of Western medicine is different from the traditional healer, termed a *mganga* in Swahili.) And from the English *spark*, speakers of northern dialects of Swahili use the word *spaki* to mean "electricity." (Those speaking southern dialects use the native Swahili word *umeme*, meaning "lightning.")

‡Like certain other missionaries, including the Scotsman David Livingstone, Krapf distinguished himself as an early explorer of Africa. He and fellow missionary Johannes Rebmann are thought to have been the first Europeans to see Mount Kilimanjaro and Mount Kenya. Unlike Dr. Livingstone, however, Krapf never gave up his missionary work to become a full-time explorer.

as a verb but also used as a noun, means "to travel or set out on a journey, to start, to sail."[2] Like many nonnative terms embraced by speakers of Swahili, *safari* was borrowed from Arabic, in which *safara* means "to travel." Krapf's early definition suggests that there was nothing especially adventure-driven about *safari* as used by mid-nineteenth-century speakers of Swahili, for whom it had, matter-of-factly, to do with travel, or with instigating a trip or an action. Swahili-speakers still use *safari* in this sense, whether for a trip made by airplane to study for a year in Edinburgh, or for one involving a bus ride to visit an aunt in a village thirty miles away.

English-speakers began to use *safari* with reference to their own travels in the later nineteenth century, and then only in African circumstances that required careful planning, cumbersome caravans, and often significant numbers of bearers and attendants. Moreover, the earliest westerners making journeys into Africa's interior weren't on short trips. They were hunters, scientists, and explorers for whom a *safari* was an ambitious enterprise, one that required special equipment, clothing, and provisions, not to mention experience and nerve.

Then too, the safari naturally presented Africa's visitors with sights yet unseen by their compatriots. By the end of Queen Victoria's reign, the word *safari* had begun to evoke in the minds of her subjects engravings of storied hunting grounds along the Cape of Good Hope; watercolors presenting the curious spectacle of a Masai warrior posing stiffly beside an acacia in his regional "costume"; pen-and-ink depictions of jungle lilies previously unknown to European botanists; or drawings of big cats paying surprise visits to men making camp for the night.

The "great white hunters" of the prewar era, such as the Englishman Frederick Selous and the American president Teddy

Roosevelt, added to *safari* a mystique that persisted long after the big game hunt became nearly extinct. Thanks in no small measure to the narratives of Ernest Hemingway and Isak Dinesen, the pre-war aura that had engulfed the *safari* endured for decades. Meryl Streep and Robert Redford, in the film adaptation of Dinesen's *Out of Africa*, did their parts to romanticize old safari ideas, and to at-tract fresh attention to *safari* as a powerful marketing term. Travel outfits got in on the game too, packaging "exotic" itineraries that promised unforgettable safaris.

A latecomer to the *safari* mania who nonetheless boldly put the word to work as a brand was that American icon of rugged indi-vidualism Ralph Lauren. He even launched a fragrance called Sa-fari, proof that, by 1990, the loanword from Swahili had journeyed far from its literal, earlier meanings. (After all, the stinky smells experienced on a veritable safari hardly suggest aromas you'd set out to trap in a bottle.) As the century waned, the glamorous old-style *safari*, which could be defined as "traveling by caravan to rough it near wildlife in Africa, but not without access to a porcelain tea set," had been replaced by the peppy new-style *safari*, "nature travel anywhere, so long as it involves unconventional transport and a modicum of hazard offset by pampering."

The ideal new-style safari also offered plenty of opportunities to record the journey. Recent decades have updated the early sa-fari image repertoire to Kodachrome, videotape, and pixel-packed digital snaps, all to be seen on animal-lover blogs, YouTube clips (heavy on the lion-attack genre), and glossy brochures. There are now kayak safaris to observe polar bears along mountainous coasts of Norway's arctic Spitzberg. (Which counts as a dual safari if you opt for the dogsled ride to the kayak pier.) And if escaping the cold is a priority, there's a Brazilian canoe safari to observe birds on the Pagodão River, a tributary of the Amazon. Or a jeep safari into the

Gobi Desert of China, where you may be lucky enough to glimpse the indigenous snow leopard.

There's also Snow Leopard, an operating system. It's indigenous not to the Gobi but to Cupertino, California, where employees of Apple Inc. unleash it into hardware. This species of leopard bounds onto computer desktops outfitted with its manufacturer's proprietary passport to internet travel, the search engine called Safari. Unlike places immortalized in the lyrics of the Beach Boys' hit tune "Surfin' Safari," which extols the joys of safariing by surfboard "from Hawaii to the shores of Peru," Cupertino, while a pleasant township, does not cause dazzling nature imagery to leap to mind. But in the era of virtual surfing, that's precisely the point. Whatever browser they're employing, people world-wide use the web to *go on Safari* without packing a bag, or getting dirty, or hot, or wet, or cold, or too lost. And at minimal expense.

Safari isn't the only word that's been substantially transformed by the computer age. Consider these: *window, word, field, desktop, document, system, utility, preview, tool, application, quit,* and *mouse.* And who would have predicted two decades ago that *sleep* could be used to refer to a mechanical state of affairs that was neither *on* nor *off*? *Safari* has fast joined cyberspeak. In fact, there are now far more people daily traveling on Safari than there are native speakers of Swahili.

Safari, a word to watch in decades ahead, belongs to a special, relatively new class of Global English artifacts: non-Indo-European in origin, embraced across rapidly changing spheres of activity (travel, communication, information technology), and poised for significant transformation. In coming years, as virtual, extraterrestrial, and other senses of the word gain global ground, English-users will likely take *safari* on new adventures in meaning.

GOING ON MANENO?
While many Swahili-speakers go on Safari online, they also have the option of going on *Maneno*, Swahili for "words," "talk," or "matters." Designed to serve sub-Saharan Africa, Maneno is a multilingual communications platform that works with the region's major lingua francas: Swahili, Lingala, Zulu, English, Spanish, Portuguese, and French.

DELUXE

Back in the old preglobal days, the material world was your oyster *de luxe*—if you could afford what *de luxe* promised: "greater prestige, excellence galore, and a lot more expense." In Global English, the language of choice for the world's most avid consumers, *deluxe* now means other things. And having kept up with the times, it neatly illustrates how speakers of English collectively reassemble word parts passed down to them from lingua francas of the past.

Deluxe still carries more than a whiff of opulence from that sophisticated lingua franca in which it was last substantially transformed: French. But for most Global English users, the stronger smell exuded by *deluxe* is American. It can range from the guilty-pleasure aroma of the *cheeseburger deluxe*, to the fond hope that a little extra quality (or at least the appearance of it) can be had for money. Redefined by its Global English-speakers, *deluxe* has come a long way over the last two-thousand-plus years.

Deluxe evolved out of earlier ideas associated with the word *luxury*. But it was only with the rise of consumer culture, and the Industrial Revolution, that luxuriousness gained respectable and desirable associations. Before then, *luxury* and its word cousins were in bad odor, tainted by negative meanings acquired across centuries. In the Middle Ages, the French noun *luxure* meant "over-abundance" or "debauchery" and was associated with the deadly sins. French had borrowed the word from Medieval Latin, in which *luxuria* was sometimes personified as Lust or Gluttony or Greed. But even before the Christian era, *luxuria* had been a favorite term to describe despicable excesses, notably of certain Roman emperors.

Writing in the second century AD, the biographer Suetonius employed the word *luxuria* to characterize the degenerate behavior of Emperor Nero, whose habits he said included traveling with a thousand carriages pulled by mules shod with silver, and entertaining in his wildly extravagant palace, which he had overlaid with gold and fitted with pipes to spray perfume on his guests. In the sexual exploits department, Suetonius's Nero surpassed himself in *luxuria*: "He so prostituted his own chastity that after defiling almost every part of his body, he at last devised a kind of game, in which, covered with the skin of some wild animal, he was let loose from a cage and attacked the private parts of men and women, who were bound to stakes."[1] Only after reading Suetonius does one realize how jejune were the excesses decried on *Lifestyles of the Rich and Famous*.

But long before Robin Leach stalked the airwaves, when Modern English first borrowed *de luxe* from French, its classical and Christian connotations had faded. French's adjectival phrase, meaning "of luxury," already encapsulated the idea of something not exactly obscene but extravagant and rarefied, prized precisely *because* it was over the top. Painter Eugène Delacroix caught the French feel of the term in an 1849 diary entry describing décor in a house where he had dined: "The *luxe* is arresting: rooms wrapped in magnificent silk, including the ceiling. Sumptuous silver services, music during dinner."[2] British English would initially use the phrase in its French sense, but American English soon retooled it as the simple adjective *deluxe* and gave the operative element, *luxe*, its updated, global-era meanings.

With American repackaging of their phrase, French merchants and service providers are happy to advertise and sell *deluxe* silks, *deluxe* silver services, *deluxe* meals and entertainment, *deluxe* real estate and interior design, not to mention *deluxe* diaries in which you can make your own notes about any luxurious dinner parties you may attend. And in spite of all this, *deluxe* is officially not recognized as a French word.* How can this be?

The theoretical absence of *deluxe* in France stems from a major difference between French and English. Beginning in 1635, under King Louis XIII, French became an Academy-ruled language. The sovereign then established the Académie Française, or "French Academy," as a means to standardize or "fix" (the Academy itself uses the verb *fixer*) the French language as it was to be used by all speakers throughout the kingdom of France. A number of learned sages—to this day referred to as "the Immortals"—were appointed to gather and sort out the formidable problem of defining the French language, determining its grammar as well as its vocabulary.

Why is this history of interest to makers of Global English? One key reason is that France sought to accomplish something that England never set as an objective: actively to shape a single national language so that subjects (and later citizens) would themselves form a more cohesive—and governable—population. Before the French Academy existed, dozens of distinct patois and dialects were spoken throughout France, the great variations among them crying out for

---

*Nor is the word recognized as any different from the adjectival phrase *de luxe* in the *Oxford English Dictionary*. American dictionaries usually tilt in the other direction, giving the concept as a one-word adjective, *deluxe*, and noting the French adjectival phrase from which it arose. Global English dictionaries could well take into account the differences between *de luxe* and *deluxe*, and acknowledge the even simpler variant *delux*.

regularization.[3] And while efforts arose in the Early Modern period to standardize English via dictionaries and school curricula, English was not, in the end, to be restrained by any single institution or authoritative body.

As a result of its academy-free status, English took a very different path from French, which, at least in France, has for nearly four hundred years been a language harnessed to some extent by the determinations of its academicians. And they, the Immortals, have decided that there's no reason to adopt the anglicized, indeed Americanized, adjective *deluxe*, when the existing adjectival phrase *de luxe*, "of luxury," has served France, and its French, perfectly well.

Still, French-speakers worldwide, including those in Belgium, Switzerland, Canada, and even in France and its territories, from New Caledonia to Guadeloupe, find that there are moments when the un-French *deluxe* is undeniably *le mot juste*. The Global English word is simply de rigueur for speaking the language of targeted consumers in the world's global market.★ Thanks to the influence of American usages attaching the word to more mundane items, whether diner food or nail polish or Alamo rental cars, *deluxe* in all its spellings and senses is now a Global English qualifier of plenty of things that are unlikely to cause jaws to drop in astonishment, or clergymen to rail. Or even bank accounts to be drained and credit cards maxed.

The difference between *de luxe* and *deluxe* may seem trivial, but

---

★At the same time, even savagely enthusiastic adopters of Global English *deluxe* would agree that certain boundaries should be respected. For example, the quintessentially French luxury item, champagne, is only in gauche instances redundantly characterized as deluxe. Incidentally, for the late French critic Roland Barthes, the key to champagne's luxuriousness would be in the evanescent lifting of its bubbles. "As for foam, it is well known that it signifies luxury. To begin with, it appears to lack any usefulness." Barthes finds the same quality at work in the suds and froths produced by shampoos and modern cleansers. Sadly, he neglected to say whether this "light and vertical" subclass of things *de luxe* could explain how speakers of English came to use *shampoo* as a slang word for champagne.[4]

such seemingly minor shifts often drive the evolution of words and meanings. Gradually yet forcefully, speakers give the slightly different, unofficial word a fresh twist of meaning. *Deluxe* carries, in the narrow context in which it finds its widest everyday usage, a clear and concise denotative sense: "accompanied by a slice of tomato, a leaf of iceberg lettuce, fries, and a pickle." The fries may be "french," but the platter is international.★

O.K.

O.K. ranks as the world's favorite American loan-word. Or loan letters, depending on how you spell it. Even in "dictionary English," no single spelling rules over others as correct or superior. There's *ok*, *O.K.*, *okay*, *OK*, *o.k.*, *okeh*, *Ok*, *'kay*, and any of the funky variations on the expressions that show up as *okie dokie*, or *okee dokee*, or even *hokee-doke*. And if you don't have time to bother with any of these, there's also the text-message variation, *K*.

The utility of *OK* is captured by its much-loved flexibility on several fronts, not just spelling. (And since *OK* is *okay* with it, I'll use a variety of *o.k.* spellings freely and interchangeably in these comments on *O.K.*) *Okeh* is also laid-back about stress: you're welcome to emphasize it as you please: *O-kay*, *o-KAY*, or *O-KAY*. Pronunciation is loose as well. People saying and hearing *o.k.* know what

---

★In French, french fries are called *pommes frites*, literally "apples fried." For short, people just called them *frites*, turning the old plural adjective describing the plural noun *pommes*, "apples," into a plural noun meaning "the fried ones." *Pommes* itself is a shortening of *pommes de terre*, literally "apples from soil," as in "earth apples," French for "potatoes." So, if you were a French chef creating a dish of "fried apples," you'd probably not call them *pommes frites*, unless you were eager to surprise the person who ordered them. One way French gets around this dilemma is by specifying the type of apple that will be served fried, so *pommes sauvages frites* is clearly "fried wild apples" and *not* "french fries."

they mean, and it works even across major cultural and linguistic divides. Is an inscrutable Iranian mechanic saying "*dorost shod*" as he repacks his tools and looks up from the motorcycle battery that died on you ten kilometers down the dirt road from the Goosfand Sara base camp of Mount Damavand? Damn. Unless you've been brushing up on your Persian, you're probably still holding your breath. But when the same mechanic puts his thoughts in Global English with sounds resembling "gho-khay," you know you'll be on your way once again.

The simple clarity of *O.K.*'s meaning is often conveyed with backup affirmation of okayness in the form of a gesture, although the traditional American one—an *O* formed by forefinger and thumb, with remaining fingers standing erect beside it—does not travel as smoothly as the verbal *ok*. In some places, the American *OK* gesture is obscene, akin to flipping someone the bird. A thumbs-up generally provides more reliable coverage as an *ok* hand sign in Italy, where some believe it has conveyed approval at least since ancient audience members used it to cast their opinions on deserved fates of gladiators. Older Italians in particular will be happier to see a thumbs-up, since the *OK* hand gesture resembles one that was quite offensive in less global times. But even the thumbs-up has its caution zones. (You'd want to think twice about using it to communicate with your Mount Damavand motorcycle repairman, since Iran is one of those countries where a thumbs-up suggests to many inhabitants something a lot less friendly than *O.K.*)

The prewar observer of words H. L. Mencken said of *O.K.* that it was one of the "American masterpieces"—words formed of a few humble letters, like COD or PDQ★ Mencken noted the surpris-

---

★And since *O.K.* was to be the most successful of these, we often now forget the meanings of the others that Mencken admired: *COD* = "Collect (or Cash) On Delivery," and *PDQ* = "Pretty Damn Quick."

ing endurance of *ok*, and its phenomenal popularity in foreign languages across the world, as far away as continental Europe and Asia. As an American, he was also impressed by a British view of his compatriots' fondness for such abbreviations: "Life, they say, is short and the pace is quick; brevity, therefore, is not only the soul of wit, but the essence of business as well. This trait of the American character is discernible in every department of the national life and thought—even slang being curtailed at times."[1] With the global adoption of *Ok*, a crucial fraction of that matter-of-fact and easy-going "American character" now belongs to the world. In planet-wide Global English, *okay* captures clear and congenial concepts, from "yes," and "I agree," to "got it," "no problem," "sure," "all is fine," "you may proceed," and "your motorcycle battery is working again."

As one may expect from an expression of such elemental components and multiple accepted spellings, the origins of *okay* present a subject of lively debate. But of course that's o.k. in the land of *O.K.*'s origins, where differences of opinion lie at the very political heart of the word's popularization. Few would contest that the globally embraced *OK* first gained wide usage in America in 1840, when Martin Van Buren's presidential reelection campaign enthusiastically deployed it on a national audience.[2] The letters were made to stand for the candidate's nickname, Old Kinderhook, the latter word being for his birthplace in New York, and the former referring to the relatively aged Van Buren himself. (He was fifty-seven at the time, well beyond life expectancy for the era; even so, Old Kinderhook went on to become Much Older Kinderhook, living to age seventy-nine.) "Vote for OK" became the big Democratic campaign slogan, and by the time Van Buren had gained victory in specific districts, "OK!" was exclaimed as shorthand for "OK has won!" But while his run for reelection made it a household expression throughout the United States—all twenty-six of them—*ok* was in fact used as an abbreviation before Van Buren's Democratic campaign was under way. (History note: "OK" lost his campaign for reelection.)

In certain circles on the East Coast, and notably in Boston, it became fashionable in the busy and, for some, clubby industrial world of the late 1830s, to employ shortcuts for common phrases, like NG for "no go," much in the spirit that *np* now serves in text messaging as a quick and fun way to convey "no problem."

In time, abbreviators of the 1830s discovered that there was even more amusement to be obtained by using letters for phrases spelled wrongly. The new NG became KG, for "know go." And O.K. then arose for "oll korrect," the deliberately incorrect spelling of "all correct."[3] Was this then juvenile and now globally indispensable innovation inspired by other words and phrases that were in the air, such as the *okeh* that Choctaw Indians used for "it is," or the *waw-kay* that meant "yes" in Wolof, a language that African-American slaves introduced into the American word pool? Perhaps.★ In the American spirit of inclusiveness, lots of alternative ancestors for *okay* have been proposed since Mencken offered eleven potential etymologies for *O.K.* in 1919. Many are naturally from American English, but others that have been floated apart from Choctaw and Wolof include Scots, Finnish, German, Russian, Greek, French, Occitan, and even Old English and Latin.

★Wolof is a national language in Senegal and a lingua franca in parts of West Africa. One scholar has suggested that Wolof is also the source of certain "Americanisms," in fact Africanisms that have entered mainstream American English. For example, he suggests that *honky* is from Wolof *hong*, meaning "pink," or "red." And that *jive* is from the Wolof *jev*, "to talk disparagingly." *Dig* appears to be from *dega*, "understand." Similarly, *cat* is used by some speakers of American English in its Wolofian sense of "person." Another nonstandard word, *fuzz*, for "police," presents a curious case because it means "horse." But it was purportedly used by Wolof-speaking slaves in the United States with reference to mounted plantation overseers.[4]

Whatever the *okay*like words then used across the land and which could have conditioned America so fully to embrace the new expression, *o.k.* is now commonly used by speakers of hundreds of languages. Some discovered *OK* through direct contact with the United States, as when a seaman laying a transatlantic cable in 1869 reported from his ship, *"Tout est O.K. à bord"* or "All is O.K. on board," the first attested use of *O.K.* in French. The Frenchman, reporting from a French ship named *Le great Eastern*—it had been *The Great Eastern* before it was purchased and relaunched—was so pleased with his American *O.K.* that he used it twice in the same communication. After relating how the cable was laid out to Duxbury, Massachusetts, he finished with *"Tout était O.K.,"* or "All was O.K." [5]

Foreign languages that hadn't absorbed *okay* by the end of the nineteenth century would have their own opportunities to fall in love with America's upbeat, can-do word through new avenues of contact. Over the next hundred years, *ok* went global thanks to its use by stars in popular films and radio shows; by U.S. Air Force pilots and military troops; by worshipped astronauts on TV; and, of course, in technology, with *o.k.* being a favorite global label for digitalized options on such everyday items as ATMs, cell phones, portable and stationary credit card machines, and computer operating systems. By now, *O.K.* looks and sounds *oll korrect* pretty much anywhere on language-using Earth.*

---

*Another thing that looks okay is the health of scholarship on the history and possible sources of *O.K.* Could a Department of OK Studies soon be in the works on one of the world's English-speaking campuses?

6

FUTURE GLOBAL ENGLISH SPOKEN HERE

"Hello! Fred Hanson?"

"Yes."

"This is Rachel Lopez with the Beijing CarbonCredit Yínháng, in the Minneapolis fēnháng."

"Oh, right! I sent three e-requests to open a zhànghù."

"I apologize for the delay. The jīnglǐ for online applicants was out last week."

Could you find yourself in a similar conversation in the foreseeable future? At first glance, it may seem improbable. But I invite you to put on your magic glasses and take another look.

Over the centuries, the porousness of English has enabled it to absorb many thousands of new words from other languages. Where academy-led languages, such as French, have walled out influence from foreign tongues, English, academy-free, has borrowed so many terms that those now far outnumber its native ones. English has even taken on whole batches of foreign words from particular spheres of activities. Ancient Greek supplied English with sets of words to do with ideas and philosophy, including *logic*, *essence*, *aesthetics*, *theory*, and *practice*, as well as *idea* and *philosophy*. And while these are terms for big and abstract concepts, balancing them are clusters of words enlisted for precise action, as with those in the English ballet lexicon. Here, English borrowed a group of linked terms from French, the language in which ballet was pursued and from which it gained international status: *jeté*, *pas de deux*, *pirouette*, and of course *ballet* itself are all from French. In certain settings of the American West, architectural discussions don't advance far without plenty of words that entered English via colonial Spanish, such as *patio*, *hacienda*, *plaza*, and *adobe*.

Just as English has, in the past, pulled in whole bundles of words from other languages, its global incarnation is set to do the same. As new speakers use English in new ways, and to talk about unprecedented matters, whether local or planetary, English is likely to be altered by an array of languages that haven't had significant influences on it in the past. But just how different is Global English likely to become?

Let's start with the most basic element of spoken English: the word.

Where English has previously taken on new vocabulary serving groups as diverse as axe-wielding Germanic warriors of Britannia and automobilists commuting in the American Midwest, Global English is now gaining words that serve life—and whole new clusters of speakers—in the global era. Given the demands and opportunities that are sure to face Earth's population in coming generations, we can expect the Global English lexicon to explode in areas addressing critical spheres of common planetary concern such as communications, technology, education, health, migration, human rights, law, finance, climate change, security, and perhaps most vitally in coming decades, new sources of energy. Matters of vast reach and involvement will undoubtedly require speakers of the planet's most commonly used language to absorb, coin, and diffuse lots of new words, as much to speak about as to shape, and adapt to, life on global-era Earth.

Consider current English terms for banking. In its financial sense, we saw how *bank* arose in northern Italy just when Romance languages were giving fresh life and meaning to words inherited from Latin. Little wonder that many words of "banking English" have been passed down to us as part of a verbal package deal, linked aspects of a finance culture whose terms chiefly stem from Latin: *percent, principal, capital, profit, investment, amount, account, activity, balance, credit,* and, alas, *debt.* For hundreds of years from the Early Modern period to the present, most English banking language has consequently had a Latinate ring to it. But in recent years, global economic turmoil has rocked the foundations of financial services that were established in, and for, the era of Christopher Columbus.

Have words like *bank* run their course? Other nouns for related institutions preceded it, and more are sure to follow. Unlike such natural things as *star, moon, tree, water,* and *earth,* whose English roots run deep through time, those to do with banking have, across the ages, been more volatile, susceptible to the shifting cultures of finance. What's more, plenty of current banking terms now produce confusion or unwelcome associations. If those financial practices that the world inherited from medieval Italy fail to adapt to global economic realities, and if the vocabularies linked to them fail to refer to emerging concepts that work better, English-speakers will naturally use fresh batches of words and phrases. And they'll adopt these new terms from whichever language(s) gain decisive global sway in this sphere.

Were *bank* to become bankrupt of meaning in coming years, which languages do you think are most likely to inject fresh sets of more useful words into English? One solid guess would be Mandarin Chinese, the national language spoken by people whose country plays an ever-larger role on the global economic stage. Chinese is also one of few major languages that haven't borrowed any version of the word *bank* (from English, Italian, or French) to refer to their own brands of financial institutions. Instead of *bank*, Mandarin-speakers say *yínháng*, literally "silver" + "profession."★ Where English has the idea of a "branch office," Mandarin has a *fēnháng*. The notion of an "account" is akin to the concept of a *zhànghù*. And the "manager" (or entities we've become habituated to refer to with such phrases as "customer service representative supervisor") is embodied somewhat differently by the *jīnglǐ*.† Would native English-speakers be taken aback at the thought of employing Chinese terms for

---

★The Chinese compound "silver profession" was formed on the basis of another compound word for a native type of bank in the late nineteenth century to capture a concept of "bank" that had been introduced to China by the British. In 1865 British banks were established in Hong Kong and Shanghai to fund trade with China. In 1949 Maoist China nationalized all mainland banks. Since that time, while banks in the People's Republic of China have changed to accommodate combinations of different kinds of ownership, they are centralized and chiefly owned by the national government.

†Note that *yínháng* and other Chinese terms are represented here in the Latin alphabet, but with special markings to indicate tones. Modern Mandarin, a tonal language, employs four distinct tones, or "pitch contours." In English, change of pitch can at times play an important role. For example, I ask you, "Would you like to invest in a sharkproof wet suit?" You would perhaps reply, "No." But say I report, "Jack was bitten by a shark while testing the 'sharkproof' wet suit!" You would likely use pitch to express shock in your response: "No!" However, in Chinese, pitches are used to convey meanings of words and sometimes grammatical information as well. Tonal languages are arguably more difficult than English for nonnative speakers to learn. Thus, even though native speakers of Chinese far outnumber native speakers of English, English could nevertheless remain more adoptable as a worldwide lingua franca. For the purposes of illustrating Chinese loanwords, I include the markings that Chinese-speakers use to indicate tones. But were these words borrowed by Global English, their special tones would probably not be borrowed with them. So we'll suppose that these Chinese words would simply be said as they'd most easily be read by most speakers of English: without attention to matters tonal.

things they have become used to calling by other (often surreally cumbersome) names? Very possibly. But if new words, and the somewhat different things and ideas they refer to, were to reduce the probability of personal or professional ruin, most people would quickly wrap their tongues around a few sounds and syllables that seem, as did the vast majority of English words current today, odd or even alien when first appearing in English.

Through every phase of its development, the English vocabulary has been altered by words that speakers needed as they carried on their lives. Often, new words aren't required, but are adopted anyway. For example, we saw how speakers of Old English had the native word *heaven* but nonetheless borrowed the word *sky* from Scandinavian to refer to "the heavens" differently. English-speakers can often choose among such alternate ways to refer to similar concepts, and to savor the distinct flavors these afford, the varying accents that they place even on experience. You may prefer to announce that you can be found reading on a *patio* instead of in a *courtyard*. Or to blog not about an exquisite dancer's *sauté* but about her *leap*. In the future, you could tell a friend you need to drop by a *yínháng*, rather than a *bank*.★ In this imagined future, a *yínháng* whose capital is derived from carbon emissions credits, rather than property mortgages, would be substantively different from a bank, and a better place to stow your hard-earned savings.

There is another good reason to guess that Chinese words could play a significant role in the future of English: Chinese speakers of English are slated to outnumber native speakers of the language by the time a child born in 2010 graduates from high school. History

★Speakers of some languages already have such a choice. In Vietnamese, for instance, the formal expression for "bank" is *ngân hàng*, from the Chinese *yínháng*. Yet many Vietnamese-speakers still say *nhà băng*, borrowing a word for "bank" that had entered their language from the French: *banque*.

has taught us that when a critical mass of speakers adopts a new language and remains in unbroken contact with those for whom it is a mother tongue, the new group's native language can play a prominent role in the evolution of their adopted language. As we saw in the case of English, French-speakers drastically altered the course of Old English when they conquered England and ruled from London over several centuries. Had French not been mixed into English as it then was, much of the English vocabulary would not now be composed of words derived from French. Admittedly, it's a bit early to assess how electronic forms of conversation will alter speech, but the technologies enabling them, via fluid and constant interaction, may remind us of those ancient road- and waterways that maintained Latin as the Roman Empire's lingua franca. How will exchanges on the world's digital superhighways influence the evolution of English?

In the past, English has borrowed or adapted relatively few words from the languages of China. Some of these are *tea, yen* (as in "a craving"), *kowtow, gung ho,* and, more recently, *chi, wok,* and *feng shui.* Most familiar are those adapted from the culinary sphere, to refer to dishes initially purveyed by Chinese immigrants, mainly from Canton, and hence from Cantonese: *chop suey, bok choy, dim sum, wonton.* But the paucity of Chinese words in English to date can be partly explained by the fact that dominant languages of China are not Indo-European, and have been written using non-alphabetic systems that make borrowing far more difficult. Other factors contributing to the minimal influence of Chinese on English have been China's physical remoteness from core English-speaking populations and, in certain periods, the country's deliberate isolation. Until recently, only small numbers of Chinese-speakers have had occasion to import English words into Chinese or to add Chinese words to the vocabulary of English. Along with shifts in

China's politics and its openness to foreigners, the advent of internet technology, and the growing acceptance of the Latin alphabet (in tandem with traditional characters such as 银行, the Chinese ideograms for "yín" + "háng," meaning "silver" + "profession," as in "bank"), have in recent decades painted a new picture for Chinese-speakers.★ They are increasingly at home in the Latin alphabet, and they are joining the English-speaking community in significant numbers.

As millions and millions of speakers enter the Global English–speaking community from China, which Chinese words can we expect to start hearing and seeing? We've considered a few from the realm of banking, and have imagined these being borrowed directly. Now let's imagine Chinese entering English indirectly, much the way we saw certain Latin terms enter English via French. How would this work? Consider the Korean term *gosu*, meaning "master," or "expert of the highest level," often in the context of martial arts. While the Korean alphabet is not related to the Latin alphabet, or even to the Phoenician, it is phonetic. The syllables "go" and "su" are, reading left to right, represented by 고수. *Gosu* is in fact the Korean pronunciation of the Chinese compound *gaoshou*. Written 高手 in Chinese, the two terms in the compound *gao shou* mean "upper" + "hand." *Gaoshou* therefore carries a hierarchical spin in

---

★Whether Chinese proves a net borrower or lender of words, its future will likely be influenced a good deal by the extent to which Chinese-speakers embrace a phonetic script. In general, the permeability of vocabularies between speakers of languages is vastly increased when their writing systems overlap. In 1979, China officially added the Pinyin alphabet, based on the Latin alphabet, to its existing nonalphabetic writing options. But for the time being, most Chinese nationals continue to use only ideograms. (It's interesting to remember that, of the world's nine most-spoken languages, Chinese is the only one to employ a nonalphabetic writing system.) In his book *The Languages of China*, S. Robert Ramsey examines China's periodic efforts during the twentieth century to introduce alphabetic writing. He also gives an account of the colorful early-twentieth-century Swedish linguist Bernhard Karlgren who, in his early twenties, found ways to reconstruct what he called Ancient Chinese in spite of barriers posed by the lack of a phonetic writing system.[1]

Chinese: expertise is tantamount to stature. English—particularly as a major cultural tool of rising numbers of native Chinese-speakers—could conceivably borrow *gaoshou* from Chinese to refer to an expert of the Chinese "upper hand" variety. But what if English borrowed the Chinese term indirectly, via Korean? If Korean were the language in which *gaoshou* were "last substantially transformed," we would expect the adopted concept to be closer to the one *gosu* carries in Korean. And we'd expect its English sense to be colored by the sphere of activity in which borrowing takes place.

As it happens, Korean-speakers in the multiplayer gaming community have used *gosu* to designate a player of exceptional skill. And who's been playing games like Starcraft and World of Warcraft with the speakers of Korean who introduced *gosu* into this electronic arena? English-speakers, generally young ones. Having already become familiar to some speakers of English, *gosu* could be diffused to more, and eventually become a standard word in Global English. Might the gaming community be the portal through which *gosu* enters other spheres of English? If so, gamers could put their own stamp on it for future English use. Perhaps *gosu* will come to refer to any "expert" one encounters in virtual reality. Or to the person of greatest skill in contexts involving planetwide competition.

Does English really need another word for "expert," or a single word for "best player out there" or "person of tremendous authority"? We know from past examples that new words can enter English even if they seem initially to be little more than another way of saying something that can already be conveyed. From its Germanic roots, English inherited the word *smell*, but it also borrowed words of related meaning derived from French, Latin, and Ancient Greek, including *fragrance, perfume, bouquet, scent, odor, aroma*, and the related concept of the *pheromone*.

Consider that, in the late 1960s, thanks largely to the Beatles' appearances with Maharishi Mahesh Yogi, a large number of English-speakers were introduced to the Hindi term *guru*. While one could simply have called this person a "teacher" or "spiritual guide," *guru* nonetheless gained currency in English to capture the then highly distinctive concept of a Hindu master of disciples' spiritual pursuits. *Guru* later won appeal as a word for all manner of valued individuals. Click and Clack became radio gurus of things automotive; Dr. Phil, the TV guru of relationship advice; and Warren Buffet, America's revered investment guru. With *guru*, one can see how quickly a foreign word can be retreaded once it circulates in one nation's English, and becomes a specimen of America's not-that-spiritual culture. Of course, you can still use the word *guru* to refer to an "actual" guru, say the Indian spiritual leader behind your favorite yoga technique. But however counterintuitive it may seem, the word is now more likely to be used to describe people who will never set foot in an ashram, and are completely oblivious to the existence of sacred texts written in the ancient Indian language Sanskrit.

Which Chinese words are positioned to become the new *guru*s of Global English? Could Global English-speakers eventually say *băoxiăn* to refer to something resembling "insurance" for global travel or medical emergencies? Or *lăoshī* to designate the "school-teacher" who prepares students to succeed in a world of greater Chinese influence? Or how about *nánpéngyou* as the Global English for "boyfriend"? Of course, no one can predict which foreign words will enter Global English. And no one can divine how their meanings will be forged anew. But if we did have a crystal ball, it would surely show us English-speakers, especially nonnative ones at first, and those in contact with them, adding significant numbers of foreign words to English. Native speakers as well could be motivated to adopt new words for terms that have become strained, provocative, or tainted, including words that we would normally think of as referring to "the same thing." Fresh words can change not only how we refer to things, but also how we think about and experience them.

Which words have you had just about enough of? Which make you cringe or require you to throw out air quotation marks every time you use them? Or just bug you because they don't quite say what you mean? *Relationship, single, commitment, dating. Sex.* Or a word that some now find more user-friendly than *sex*, even though it produces its own brand of awkwardness for suggesting that *sex* is somehow to be avoided: *sexuality.* How about *ethnic preference?* Or *gender?* I suspect some people would welcome other ways to say (and think of) *fat, diet, weight loss, baldness, graying, potbelly,* and *dandruff. Eczema* is a word that seems uglier than the condition it designates. I'd be happy to lose it, even if it meant having to adopt a word that's harder to spell. And while we're at it, will we want less stigmatized ways to say *blended family* or *broken home?* Are we ready to do away with the para-death-like ring of *retired?* Or the weirdness factor of *adolescent?* Lexical replenishment could also be due for *amazing, passionate, intense,* and *great,* which have lost punch from overuse. Everyone's dissatisfied with at least some terms in current English.

With foreign speakers and users of English now outnumbering native speakers by more than six to one, and with that ratio projected to widen in coming decades, Chinese but also Japanese, Korean, Portuguese, Bengali, Russian, and other languages, including English's close cousins German, French, and Spanish, will possibly alter vocabulary to the point that current English words will look as foreign to future Global English-speakers as Old English looks today: *"Forþon nū mīn hyge hweorfeð."* ★

Arabic is among those languages likely to supply English with more words and phrases in coming years. Along with Chinese, Spanish, English, and Hindi, Arabic is one of the world's five most-spoken native languages. Of these, Arabic also happens to be the language that has lately seen the fastest growth on the internet—that key global crossroads where speakers of so many languages encounter and use English, by a wide margin the most popular language for internet users. In less than ten years, Arabic-speakers increased their internet use by well over 1,000 percent, a growth rate rivaled only by speakers of Russian.

In the past, Arabic words entered English more readily than those from the languages of China. One likely reason for this is that Arabic employs a phonetic alphabet, a distant cousin of English's Latin one. (To read Chinese well, one must learn to recognize and memorize thousands of ideograms. To begin sounding out Arabic, one needs little more than a day to learn its alphabet.) Another reason that there's been borrowing from Arabic is that important works by medieval scholars of the Arab world were translated into Latin and other languages, and disseminated in manuscripts across western Europe. Thanks to then relatively fluid channels of exchange among the literate clergy, English adopted Arabic terms particularly from fields of mathematics, natural sciences, and philosophy. A few examples are *algebra*, *alkali*, *zero*, *zenith*, and *nadir*.

Later, Arabian *coffee* and *cotton* were also imported into the British Isles, along with words that were anglicized. Other English

★"And yet my spirit soars." These words are from the tremendous poem *The Seafarer*. As the passage continues, "The mind of the speaker leaves his body and ranges like a bird over land and sea."[2]

words influenced by (and not necessarily originally from) Arabic include *sugar, candy,* and *sorbet.* These no longer sound imported. Nor do they even look imported, although had they been transliterated more or less directly from Arabic today, we might rather have been saying and seeing: *sukkar, qandi,* and *sharbaat.* Since the rise of the Palestinian-Israeli conflict, however, and especially since the terrorist attacks of September 11, 2001, words directly imported from Arabic have sounded less sweet to many native speakers of English. Some terms in Arabic have come attached to little-understood religious matters—or to disturbing political issues. Words such as *mujahedin, madrassa, fatwa, Sharia,* and *jihad,* not to forget *Muslim* and *Islam* themselves, can trigger strong emotions.

But Arabic could contribute words to other spheres of life, especially as Global English-speakers wrestle with new approaches to energy, architecture, engineering, and farming. Perhaps Global English will adopt the Arabic word *qanāt.* It refers to an ingenious method of subterranean irrigation that exploits gravity to create arable land far beyond water sources, typically in desert environments. Arabic may also inject fresh terms into journalism, the arts, and entertainment, including cinema and TV, with Doha, Cairo, Beirut, and other cities of the Arab world playing roles in these areas. For the sake of illustration, let's imagine that the global fashion scene were to be infused with words employing Arabic.

We saw that *burqini* has already been coined in English to refer to a bathing suit whose "body veil" or *burqa*like qualities make it an ideal choice for Muslim women adhering to strict interpretations of Islamic law, or *Sharia,* which prohibits exposure of all but a few spots of mature female flesh. Let's imagine more influence from the desert-contoured vocabularies and cultures of Arabs, especially as wider populations seek protection from the elements. A global take on the unisex *galabiya,* a loose-fitting outer garment, designed to protect wearers from the sun as well as sand and wind, might conceivably gain popularity among UV-shunning followers of fashion outside the Sahara and the Arabian Peninsula. So too could clothing traditional to Muslim India and Pakistan, such as the *salvar* (long pants) *kameez* (long-sleeved top) ensemble, again worn by men and women.* Unlikely though this may sound, we can nonetheless hear the kind of conversation it would lead to between salesperson and shopper:

> "Welcome!"
> "Hi. I'm shopping for a beach holiday."
> "We have the new galabiyajean ensemble by Karima Khan!"
> "Hmm . . . and burqinis?"
> "Sharkproof?"
> "Yes. And how about a T-kameez?"
> "With vintage logos? We have 'Out of Vietnam' and 'Coca-Cola.' "
> "I'm more into modern fashion. Do you have anything with the original green and silver Beijing CarbonCredit Yínháng symbol?"

Granted, this conversation may not be unfolding in your neighborhood just now. Or soon. Or ever. But in such a mocked-up dialogue, we glean the curious interplays of English and unrelated languages that have already become commonplace in many parts of the world. Could this aspect of the Global English phenomenon become second nature even to native speakers of English?

Remember *shampoo*? It was no less exotic than *kameez* when it greeted English in its early forms. By now it sounds as everyday

Salvar is a word of Persian origin, also spelled *shalwar*, *shulwar*, and other ways. *Kameez* is of uncertain origin. One view is that it comes from an Arabic word for "shirt." The more widely accepted etymology suggests that *kameez* is an Indo-European word and related to the French *chemise*.

as *soap* (probably of non-Indo-European origin, so surely no less a novelty in its own time). And while English has so far not absorbed much from unrelated languages, like Arabic, one need only think of words like *amen* and *alleluia,* or for that matter *bikini, cola, tycoon, kayak, canoe, zombie,* or *artichoke,* to be reminded that even words from unrelated languages have become as familiar as *skill, knife, ugly, cookie, rap, ski, reindeer, schmooze,* and *kindergarten*—all borrowed from Germanic tongues closely related to English.

We've been looking at an extraordinary dual movement of words. We've seen English absorb them from myriad other tongues that preceded or influenced it, and noted how English words have been dispersed to a planetwide community. Along the way, we've observed periods of dramatic vocabulary explosion when English-speakers are in contact with other languages. These historical episodes introduce elements of foreign languages into the daily life of English-speakers, with the result that the English vocabulary has ballooned and evolved alongside something larger and more difficult to measure: the shape of English, the way it puts the world together, its magic glasses.

So let's shift gears and picture how English is likely to change more profoundly than in its vocabulary alone. This level of change is akin to one we imagined earlier in surgical orders of difference: an organ transplant rather than a series of Botox injections. And speaking of orders of difference, let's call these possible changes to English general forecasts, not precise predictions. No one is saying that, at 4:47 a.m. on January 7, 2024, Persian syntax will alter Global English discussions concerning airport and seaport security. Rather, we're forecasting that English is going to be altered by foreign languages. And we're going to picture specific but imagined examples, to capture how change could happen. We'll also try to get some answers to the question, if English is to be transformed in the near future as much as it was in previous remarkable periods of its evolution, what would that degree of variation be? How different would current English become?

Of course, there is no sure method available to project how any language will evolve. Significant change to the course of a language can arise from even a single event. It could be a mass migration: say, climatic conditions prompt 40 percent of the world's desert population to move toward its poles (or vice versa). Another generator of sudden and profound language permutation could be a major conflict, or a regime change. Or a far-reaching technological surprise. Imagine the internet being irreversibly jammed by terrorists or blocked by governments hostile to global interaction. Any occurrence of such magnitude could drastically alter Global English's evolution. As we've seen with English's past, sensational shifts occur as a result of curve balls and spanners in the works, and not of business as usual. So we'll want also to consider some possibilities brought about by wild cards dealt to the language. But first, it's irresistible to make a few guesses of the more conservative variety.

A reasonable premise is that the aspects of English that have changed most in previous eras will remain those most given to change in the future. And those that have been relatively unchanged since the early days of English are, it would be sound to postulate, those most likely to remain constant over coming generations as well. So where does this put us?

Let's start with that major piece of language "surgery" that we've already looked at: grammar. We saw how English shed its grammatical complexity to become a less-inflected language. Recall that in current English, "rose" stays *rose*, and "nose" stays *nose*, unless you're adding an *s* to form a plural or a possessive. But in Old English, "nose" could be: *nosu*, *nosa*, or *nosum*. It was also feminine, one of three genders of nouns that English-speakers used. An example of a masculine noun is *scip*, meaning "ship." In Old English, grammar would determine whether someone would use that word as *scip, scipes, scipe, scipu, scipa,* or *scipum*. Now, to say "*the* nose" or "*the* ship" in Old English, you would select one of the following words, depending on the gender and grammatical function of the noun it would specify (and this chart doesn't even show all the optional forms):

Case	Masculine	Neuter	Feminine	Plural (all genders)
Nominative	se	þæt	sēo	þā
Genitive	þæs	þæs	þære	þāra
Dative	þām	þām	þære	þǣm
Accusative	þone	þæt	þā	þā
Instrumental	þ̄y, þon	þ̄y, þon		

All these are captured today by one little Modern English word: *the*.

What a huge step that was. We don't have to think about a noun's gender or its grammatical functions: *the* works all *the* time. *The* guitar sounds wonderful. Paul and his friend spoke about *the* jeep breakdown. Alaya was two days into *the* journey to see a doctor. What if a condor landed on *the* bicycle racks? No one returns via *the* Batcave! What a fine word *the* is. English became far easier for nonnative speakers to learn because of it.

How much simpler and sleeker can a language become? None, right?

Let's zero in on *the*. It's a one-size-fits-all definite article, referring to a particular object: *the* thing. It's distinct from its one-size-fits-all associate, the indefinite article, *a*, referring to some object, but none in particular: *a* thing.

Native speakers of English get this *a*-versus-*the* distinction without having to think about it, and so do native speakers of most Indo-European languages. But for many, including those whose mother tongues are Chinese, Japanese, and even Russian and Polish and other Slavic languages, articles are mysterious and confusing because their own languages simply don't have them. If I say to a Russian friend, "I'll take the bus to meet you at the concert," he will—if he's not a fluid speaker of English—wonder or ask, "Which bus?" He already knows which concert: it's *the* concert we're going to attend. And because I said *the* bus, he could naturally infer that I mean an individual, specific bus. "The bus that goes to the rock club," I may say, meaning not *a* bus, but a bus service or line. Yuri, however, is unlikely to hear the difference between "the bus" and "a bus," or "some bus," or even "any bus in town." And in fact, he's got a point: I don't mean a specific bus. *The* is letting me down: the definite article is being used in an indefinite sense.

If I ask my Chinese houseguest to pick up "a bag of rice" while she's out, Minghua may ask, "Which kind?" I could say "the brown rice," meaning "as opposed to wild rice or Basmati rice or whatever other kinds are in the store." If I say "a brown rice," it may suggest that there's more than one kind of brown rice to choose from and that I'd like her to select one.

These very subtle differences between *the* and *a* can drive nonnative English-speakers mildly insane, because articles often suggest specific information that others can find difficult to tease out. To speakers whose languages do not employ articles, it would be clearer and simpler to say, "I will take bus to meet you at concert." Or to ask someone to "pick up bag of rice." Those of us who grew up speaking English would likely find this a big, disconcerting step. But note that, in these instances, no critical meaning would be lost by giving up articles, and shedding them could reduce confusion when we're speaking Global English. Dropping articles would further be supported by the fact that the vast majority of nonnative speakers are comfortable—and frequently speak—without them. In fact, plenty of people using Global English as a lingua franca have already found themselves dropping articles, and they're doing it intuitively, aware that they're making more sense. If a change simplifies without reducing clarity, or clarifies without adding complication, it's a strong candidate for adoption.

Like other languages that have expanded their user bases, English has already benefited from some organ transplanting. More major procedures are likely to be performed on Global English in decades ahead. The number of non-article-using English-speakers is poised to explode in coming generations both in absolute terms and as a percentage of all English-speakers. Will English articles be abandoned? Or could articles be dropped in specific instances, perhaps particularly in spheres where non-article-using languages gain most influence? Let's return to our fictional Beijing CarbonCredit Yínháng. If words from Mandarin Chinese do stream into financial sectors, we could also see, piggybacking on the vocabulary influx, a grammatical shift toward article-free English. Consider the banking dialogue again. This time, grammar changes with new vocabulary, much the way English has been altered before, by Old Norse and French:

"Hello! Fred Hanson?"

"Yes."

"Rachel Lopez, with Beijing CarbonCredit Yínháng, Minneapolis fēnháng."

"Oh, right! I sent three e-requests to open zhànghù."

"I apologize for delay. Jīnglǐ for online applicants was out last week."

But consider how that exchange would look if it were altered not by the deletion of articles but by another approach, one also familiar to a large number of incoming English-users: native speakers of Arabic. In Arabic, articles exist but not as they do in English. Instead, to convey the idea of *the*, Arabic puts *al-* immediately before the word. Without its *al-*, the noun is, by default, indefinite. So how does this work? If I want to say "a desert" using Arabic grammar, I simply say the word for "desert": *ṣaḥrā'*. (And if that word reminds you of *the* Sahara, that's no accident. *Sahara* is from the plural form of this word, so means "deserts" in Arabic.) When I say *ṣaḥrā'* on its own, it's bound to be an indefinite noun, so it's clear that I mean "a desert." But if I want to say "the desert," I say *al-ṣaḥrā'*.

English-speakers are already familiar with the Arabic article *al* because it's incorporated into the phrases *al jazeera* ("the island"), *al qaeda* ("the base" or "the foundation"), and even *Alhambra* (adapted from *al-ḥamrā'*, meaning "the red one.") And that hidden *al* in Alhambra is familiar in other English words taken from Arabic, such as *alcove*, *alkali*, and *algebra*.★ Arabic's *al* can be harder to recognize when its "l" sound has been lost in transmission. An example here is none other than *artichoke*, from *al-kharshūf*, meaning "the artichoke" in Arabic. (The signature Arabic *al* is a lot easier to spot in the Spanish word for the edible thistle: *alcachofa*.)

Pretty straightforward so far. But this brings us to an unfamiliar side of the definite article in Arabic. Let's put it under a microscope and see whether it strikes us as a credible candidate for adoption in Global English.

In English, we only need to use *the* once in a group of linked

---

★These are all words that, were they borrowed by English today, would likely be split up and put into the Latin alphabet following current practices of transliteration, as seen in *al-qaeda* and *al-jazeera*. Were they written *al-hamra*, *al-qubba*, *al-qily*, and *al-jabr*, "Alhambra," "alcove," "alkali," and "algebra" would look a lot more foreign.

words to understand that it covers all of them. For instance, if I say "the big, glorious red fortress," you understand that the definite article captures ideas about the bigness and gloriousness and redness of the fortress as well as that of the fortress itself. All the concepts behind the adjectives are automatically attached to the noun specified by *the*. But in Arabic, this set of relationships remains murky unless we put an *al-* not only in front of *fortress*, but also in front of all the words that describe it, those we want to include in the idea of *this* fortress. The Arabic for my English phrase would (grammatically) add up to "*al-fortress, al-big, al-glorious, al-red.*"★

Now let's do some Global English algebra. We'll add some elements that would be more familiar to speakers of Arabic and see whether this would increase or reduce clarity. Take another look at our shopper heading for a beach holiday. This time, instead of nouns with zero articles, we've got something more familiar to speakers of Arabic:

> *"Welcome!"*
>
> *"Hi. I'm shopping for beach holiday."*
>
> *"We have the-galabiyajean the-new the-ensemble by Karima Khan!"*
>
> *"Hmm . . . and burqinis?"*
>
> *"The-sharkproof?"*
>
> *"Yes. And how about T-kameez?"*
>
> *"With the-logos the-vintage? We have 'Out of Vietnam' and 'Coca-Cola.'"*
>
> *"I'm more into the-fashion the-modern. Do you have anything with the-Beijing the-CarbonCredit the-Yínháng the-original the-green and the-silver?"*

★A fuller name for the Alhambra is *al-Qal'a al-ḥamrā'*, or "the-Fortress the-Red," or more simply "The Red Fortress." Or, for short, "the-Red," captured by the familiar word *Alhambra*.

You're thinking, *No way?* So am I. It's unlikely that Global English-speakers will adopt this approach. This is not because Chinese-speakers will have greater numbers or greater pull than Arabic speakers; both are engaged with Global English and are in positions to influence its evolution. But our intuitive reading tells us the Chinese approach to the problem of English articles is more likely to find traction because it simplifies, while the approach seen in Arabic would complicate mutual understanding.

This said, there's no reason to expect that influence on Global English will follow some strictly rational or democratic one-influence-unit-per-capita course, or even one that's predominantly one thing or another. Consider that a major population of new Global English-speakers in years ahead now claims another Indo-European language as a native tongue. If you total up the English-using native speakers of Hindi, Bengali, Spanish, Portuguese, German, French, Italian, and so on, numbers suggest that many changes in the offing for Global English will be introduced by other Indo-European languages. But there are additional factors at play.

If we consider the large number of Mandarin-speakers, and the already significant participation of Japanese- and Korean-speakers in global exchanges, we'd want to account for potential influence from these languages. Especially in areas where their speakers are likely to play more vocal roles, such as in financial sectors, manufacturing, technology, and alternative energy. Timing is likely to be a significant issue as well. Speakers of certain Asian languages, having already begun to enter Global English conversations, are poised to influence the course of the shared language over coming generations. If Mandarin-speakers provide impetus for English to let go of articles before nouns, for example, Global English probably wouldn't regain more elaborate use of articles later on, even if an article-rich language were, in the future, to become the most-spoken native language of Global English users.

There is also a question of local variation. Global English as used in the Far East has already taken on its own regional peculiarities. With over fifty independent languages officially spoken in the People's Republic of China, English is used by some Chinese as a lingua franca within their own country. And English, diffused throughout India when the country was part of the British Empire, has remained an official language since 1947, when India declared independence from the United Kingdom. While the vast majority of Indians speak one of many other languages at home, English has long served them as a national lingua franca. And, as in China, English in India is spoken as a language of prestige.

English is also the most important language of governance for the European Union, which has grown to include more than two dozen nations. English serves members of the EU across its borders, but even emails between ministers from Austria and Germany—though German is the native language of both—are written in an English with European-tailored traits. English is one of five official lingua francas recognized by the African Union, which includes every African nation save Morocco. Arabic-speakers could likewise have their own reasons to develop an arabicized Global English for use across their multilingual borders. While Arabic itself is one of the world's most enduring and effective lingua francas—it is today the native language of over 250 million people, and its nonnative speakers are nearly as numerous—Arabic alone does not offer access to discussions unfolding on a global scale.★

So while the *al-* approach to nouns in Arabic strikes us as un-

★With the worldwide Muslim population estimated to be close to 1.5 billion, a much higher figure would be captured by the number of people who read, recite, or quote the Qur'an in Arabic.

wieldy for Global English, it could be used in specific regions, or in discussions with those regions. For instance, an exchange about opening a new account could employ Arabic elements for clarification. Rachel Lopez represents an outfit based in Beijing. She is in Minneapolis when she calls Fred Hanson. Let's say he's applying for the account from his office in Qatar. Speaking to a potential client in the Middle East, Rachel may see fit to employ Arabic articles to emphasize her location:

> "Rachel Lopez, with Beijing CarbonCredit Yínháng, in al-fēnháng al-American in Minneapolis."

English has in the past demonstrated flexibility when it comes to grammar. One vivid early alteration we looked at accommodated speakers of Old English with words to distinguish between *him* and *them*. Ænglisc then adopted Scandinavian grammar, taking on the linguistic ancestors of *they*, *their*, and *them* to supplement an Old English pronoun repertoire. Following our method, then, English pronouns, having been altered by a foreign language in the past, ought to be receptive to such profound changes in the future.

Keep in mind too that English pronouns have been wobbly for decades. For instance, *he*, *his*, and *him* have long been used in so-called Standard English to refer to a hypothetical person of unknown gender, as in "If someone needs help, please give it to him." Since the 1970s, and the women's rights movement, at least some English-speakers have taken extra steps to avoid using *him* in this way. Instead, one hears alternatives like "give it to him or her." Or even "give it to them," a solution that saves its speaker from having to say "him" to refer to a person who could be female. But it's also a solution that stirs up fresh grammatical noise. What, for example, are we to make of "If you love someone, set them free." *Them?*

The form English borrowed from Scandinavian to refer to males and/or females in the plural so as not to confuse *them* with the single male *him* has, weirdly, found new life as a pronoun referring to a hypothetical person of either sex. Further, *them* can carry the idea that one is trying actively to avoid using *him* to refer to what may in fact be a *her*. Thus, English has recently gained a new kind of uncertainty surrounding *they*, *them*, and *their*. Many so-called native English words, like *water*, *stone*, *earth*, and *star* but also *ship*, *nose*, and *ring*—those that we can trace back to Old English—have remained largely unchanged for some fifteen hundred years, even if they were once packaged into the language with more grammatical complexity. Unlike those words whose forms and meanings remain stable, pronouns have been turbulent. So we can guess that they will remain open to alteration—and improvement in the eyes of their next users—as Modern English becomes Global English.

Which of the major languages interacting with English is likely to become the new Scandinavian, and to pass on to English an updated pronoun thread for "the individual of unspecified gender" to replace *he*, *his*, *him*; *they*, *their*, *them*; or *he or she*, *his or her*, *him or her*? Could we end up contracting phrases like *him or her* into *himmer*, or *his and her* into *hisher*? And would that last candidate be pronounced "HIZer"? Or would the legions of global users of written English, their ears less attuned to native pronunciation of English, eventually have everyone saying "HISHer"?

Or could another approach prevail? Mandarin uses one word for *he/him*, *she/her*, and *it*: *tā*. (For *they* and *them*, *tā* becomes *tāmen*.) Could English eventually adopt *tā* to refer to someone who could be male or female? "*If person needs help, please give it to tā.*" Mandarin speakers may find this clearer, but whether such change is in store for English depends on whether any Mandarin-speaker would have occasion to introduce it, and whether English-speakers in general would embrace it as an enhancement to their common tongue.

Speakers of the major non-English languages are in positions to exert influence on the evolution of Global English purely on the basis of their numbers. That is, if many millions of new English-speakers find a choice between *the* and *a* troubling because nothing in their native language resembles it, their refashioning of English could present alternatives that other speakers would naturally adopt as well, not least to avoid being sidelined when the world is engaged in its most encompassing conversations. Let's take a look at a few more of these possible problem spots and see how they could, cumulatively, help English on its course into a new historical phase.

Enormous populations of nonnative speakers of English are flummoxed by a single letter: *s*. Since its earliest days, English has shifted a lot in how it treats plurals and possessives, and indeed verbs. (Note that six words end in *s* in that last sentence: one possessive, two verbs, and three nouns!) The result has been a confounding proliferation of *s*'s. Look at how *-s* performs multiple roles in Modern English: the English as a Second Language teacher says the word *bridge*. The class repeats it. Then she adds an *-s*. Some students hear this as a plural: "*bridges* span rivers." Some hear the possessive: "the *bridge's* span is one kilometer." Others hear the present indicative, third person: "she *bridges* a gap." Without a context to clarify, each of these interpretations is reasonable and right. So far, everyone is earning an A+ in our ESL classroom. But in about ten minutes, 90 percent of the class is struggling to make sense of sentences employing more than one of these different kinds of *s*'s.

How might nonnative speakers remedy the *s* trouble in English? One step could be to drop the *-s*. Or at least drop some uses of it. Consider the verbal form of *-s*. English has already lost all other inflection used to form verbs in the present. A single no-*s* form is used *almost* across the board: "I bridge, you bridge, we bridge, they bridge." So why not "he bridge" and "she bridge" and "it bridge" as well? No meaning would be lost by letting go of -*s* in this instance. We could also get by without the plural -*s*. Mandarin does. If confusion arises, there's the option of adopting another ending, say Arabic's -*in*, as in the plural word *assassin*, meaning "assassins" in Arabic. If that option were taken up, the Global English for "assassin" would be *assassinin* or, to better reflect Arabic pronunciation of the plural ending, *assassineen*. But most words wouldn't look so strange: *wordeen, glasseen, sharkeen, Batsignaleen, artichokeen*.* Or there's the route taken by Bahasa Indonesia, a lingua franca to more than 160 million people. It offers a simple way to make plurals: given twice, nouns are literally "pluralized." So the plural for *sheep*? *Sheep sheep*. And for *bike*? *Bike bike*.

With plural -*s* and third-person verbal -*s* out of the picture, the -*s* ending could be reserved for possessives alone: *Rachel's application to Erasmus University. Alaya's first toy doll.* Sentences would be easier for our ESL class, and for all other nonnative speakers of English, to understand: *Mrs. Greider say bookeen are Freddy's*, or *Lǎoshī say book are Freddy's*. Or, *Teacher say book book Freddy's*. What a relief to most of the world's *speakereen* not to have to disentangle the three senses of English's three -*s* -*s*.

Also crying out for global simplification is the ambiguous second-person pronoun: *you*. Native speakers of many other languages don't see how one word can possibly double for such critically distinct notions as *you* (singular) and *you* (plural). "I love *you*." In this last sentence, I could be talking to someone I'm about to

---

*A lateral advantage to these no-*s* approaches is that dastardly irregular plurals would no longer cause distress, or even hesitation: *Pokémoneen, sheepeen, gooseen, phenomenoneen, indexeen, criterioneen, childeen, tootheen*. So much for trick noun questions on future Global English SATs.

kiss ardently at the Little White Chapel Tunnel of Vows in downtown Las Vegas. Or to my parents. (If they're still speaking to me after hearing about the drive-thru wedding.) In Shakespeare's time I would have said "I love *thee*" to my new spouse, and "I love *you*" to my parents. And I would have had other pronouns at my disposal to speak of *you* as a subject rather than an object of my affection: *thou* for my Las Vegas honeybunch, and *ye* for the dismayed parents.

The vanishing of these forms of *you* presents a stark case of grammatical "leveling," the loss of inflection that has characterized the modernization of English. But while such streamlining can facilitate the language's spread, it can also forfeit clarity. And in lots of contexts that presents problems. Native English-speakers have grown accustomed to grappling with the consequences of this critical case of inflection deprivation. Only genuine American Southerners feel entitled to say *y'all*, and even the most overindulged teenager gets looked at askance for addressing his grandparents as *you guys*. Regional innovations, such as *yous*, *yinz*, and *you-uns*, may work just fine for the lucky speech communities of Boston, Pittsburgh, or Appalachia, where many use these forms to say *you* when addressing more than one local individual. But these versions of plural *you* aren't guaranteed to make conversation smoother in other places, and are sometimes frowned upon even in Boston, Pittsburgh, and Appalachia as "incorrect" English. As for other words that have come to the rescue since plural *you* went AWOL, there are *folks* and *dudes*. These are great, as far as they go, but of course they're not even pronouns. Rather, they're nouns that some people resort to when the absence of a plural *you* in English seems to have left them no other choice.

Such awkward things get into language, even though no one in his or her or *tä*'s right mind would have foreseen it. Plural *you* is yet another piece of English grammar that's been altered more than once over the centuries. So, you guys, what if English inclined toward the Mandarin ending *-men* to forge a plural *you*? This may initially look like cause for a new wave of gender bafflement. But in Chinese, the added syllable turns a single pronoun into a plural one. *Wǒ* is "I," but *wǒmen* is "we." *Ní* is "you," so *nímen* is "y'all." Could Chinese influence on English deliver *youmen*? French offers another approach. *Tu* is "you" in the singular, and *vous* is the plural form. Could English-speakers keep *you* for the singular second-person pronoun, and borrow *vous*, or a more phonetically driven spelling like *voo* or *vou*, for the plural? Here's a six-year-old using our imagined Global English: *"OK, voo* [Alaya and Naira] *can play with my Pokémoneen!"* And a *gosu* at a trade fair hyping a financial service product: *"Energy zhànghù zhànghù free at Shanghai Yínháng, if you-men register with online jīnglǐ."*

And now for a final possible change in the grammar zone: the verb *to be*. Imagine you tell a friend that analysts expect major hiring freezes in the public education sector just as you are applying for jobs as a high school English teacher. Your friend says, "I am optimistic." This afternoon? Since birth? Is she talking about her immediate impression or rather her immutable state? Most of the Romance languages take a different tack in this situation. Spanish, like Portuguese, employs two verbs for "to be." *Ser* conveys permanence; *estar* covers temporally bound, flucuating conditions. An example of *ser* would be *Soy de California*, meaning *"I am* from California" (and that would be true no matter what else I'm doing today). An example of *estar* is *Estoy en California*, meaning *"I am* in California" (for the moment, but not perpetually). So, if your friend were speaking Spanish and replied, *"Estoy optimista,"* you'd know that, while she may not by nature view the world through rose-colored glasses, and may even be a grump by disposition, her outlook on your job prospects is positive.

Given the advantages of the Spanish approach, and enough influential Spanish-speakers injecting their extra "to be" into Global English, we could eventually hear *to be* reserved for enduring states, and something like *to esbe* cropping up around more fleeting conditions. Widespread adoption, of course, would depend on the distinction's being thought by speakers in general to be worth the trouble of expanding English's options. Then a dialogue like the following wouldn't be out of the question at the immigration desk of an international airport:

> *"Occupation?"*
> *"Cyberterror security gosu at Wall Street Carbon Yínháng, Singapore fēnháng."*
> *"You hold more than one passport?"*
> *"No, I am Spanish. One passport. Al-passport al-Spanish only."*
> *"Purpose of visit?"*
> *"Business. Esam here in Berlin for conference."*

There are other grammar hot spots in English, but we've covered enough ground to see the kinds of paths likely to lead to linguistic change. We'll see what all of this adds up to in a moment.

What about something as habitual, and hardwired, as word order? Could this also alter? Such significant transformation has been an absorbing aspect of English, particularly from the time it lost much of its earlier grammatical complexity. Certainly, word order is critical in Modern English. Recall the famous example: *The dog bit the man.* This utterance means something totally different from *The man bit the dog.* In Old English, word endings conveyed which creature is doing the biting and which is being bitten, so there was built-in flexibility for word order. Inflection telling us "dog-subject bites man-object" allows words to be switched around without confusion: "man-object bites dog-subject." Alerted that *the man* is the object of the verb, we can hold him in mind as the recipient of a bite made by a subject we know will be revealed next: "dog."

By the time English evolved into Middle English, loss of inflection meant that nouns no longer contained much grammatical information. On its own, the word *man* could be a subject or an object, or even an indirect object (as in "The dog fetched *the man* a bone"). To compensate for this loss of information that inflection had provided, word order became critically important. If *the man* appears after the verb *bite*, we know he's not the one doing the biting: *The dog bit the man*. Indeed, having lost so much inflection, Modern English relies heavily on word order to convey grammatical information. And it doesn't much like having its conventional word order upset.

Back to Rachel and Fred. She tells him, *"For apologize I delay. Out for last jīnglĭ online was week applicants."* We recognize that English is somehow involved, but also that a fundamental breakdown in syntax has made Rachel's speech bewildering. Certain sequences of words are rigid in English, and one quickly runs into trouble when reordering them. For example, one can say "You have gorgeous roses in your garden" and "The roses in your garden are gorgeous." But if I say "You have roses gorgeous in your garden," you may be too puzzled by my English to hear a compliment to your horticultural skill.★

English does welcome some variations on its default syntax, as

---

★Note that I can say "I like my roses gorgeous," because in this case a few important words have been left out. A more complete version of that sentence would be "I like my roses to be gorgeous."

when foreign words or phrases come into the language with their own principles of order. Consider a word that English absorbed from Irish: *galore*. In Irish, the adjectival phrase *go leór*, meaning "enough," comes after the words it modifies. When English adopted *galore*, it preserved the very un-English syntax attached to the word in Irish. We say "gorgeous roses" and "abundant roses," yet "roses galore" does not grate on the ear. Nor does "roses aplenty." When we use constructions like "burqinis galore" or "nánpéngyous aplenty," we're making use of Irish syntax.

Something similar is going on with phrases like *secretary general* and *heir apparent*. English would normally express such ideas using its native word order: "general secretary," "apparent heir." How did these phrases get turned around? The answer is that their syntax had already been fixed by conventional usage when they passed into English from French, whose adjectives typically follow rather than precede nouns. The French syntax of *attorney general* now sounds perfectly natural. Switching this phrase to something more "English"—"general attorney"—would be as odd as cheering about "galore roses." French usage had locked in place the words of certain phrases, so English received them as a unit: *president-elect*. What's become very "English" is, precisely, the mix of word orders embedded in the language.

Some incoming word orders could initially seem peculiar, or even outlandish, compared to those absorbed so far from Indo-European languages like Irish or French. As growing numbers of nonnative speakers of Global English bend English around their own word orders, at least a few could gain wide usage. With fresh input from Arabic speakers, English could, in the future, see sentences that resemble this one: *"The roses, the ones in garden-yours, gorgeous."* Or, with sufficient influence of Japanese-speakers, the following could in time appear unremarkable: *"I that Japan-from cell phone broke."*

Even influence from other Indo-European languages could have a distinct impact on Global English word order. Will French be as influential in the future as it's been in the past? English could adopt the Gallic approach to indirect pronouns for statements like *"The dog him gave the bone."* How about syntax from a more distant Indo-European relative, Persian? Our Spanish cyberterror expert, arriving for that conference in Berlin, might by now have received a message that reads, *"I from San Francisco many documents about cyberthreats, most dangerous ones, to you yesterday sent. Question: you them received have?"* Far-fetched as that last hypothetical reworking of syntax looks and sounds, it still makes sense; native English-speakers would have no trouble answering, and neither would the Spaniard, an old hand with Global English. In contrast, King Ælfred himself, sent through a time warp and landing in the middle of a reading by Chaucer at the court of Richard II, would have had a lot more difficulty understanding what he heard. (While everyone around him is laughing at Chaucer's description of the Prioress's fussy "Frenchness," our royal native speaker of Old English is probably using his best lingua franca, Latin, to ask someone which language the storyteller is speaking.)

Seldom in its history has the English language been subjected to significant efforts to "cleanse" it, or keep it free of foreign influence. Even when such a project was loosely attempted, as with the Inkhorn Controversy, it was a hopeless case: English had simply always been an evolving mixture of "foreign" tongues. We've seen how writers and speakers of English have generally remained open to nonnative influences. In certain cases, there have even been deliberate, sometimes zealous, efforts to introduce new words into English, with some of these proving lexically productive. That is, plenty of words that initially looked preposterous eventually "stuck" and were passed down to subsequent generations for whom they became invaluable. What would life in English be like without *universe, skeleton, energy, algebra, tea, shampoo,* or *assessment* and *test*? Indeed, over all phases of its evolution, English has seen its vocabulary, grammar, word order, pronunciation, and spelling altered as its speakers took up alternatives introduced by influential foreign languages.

Now for the elephant in the room, or perhaps the *hulafint een thrume* or the *glehllawfoont n tah eloom*: spelling. The untamed mix of ways to write similar sounds perplexes English-users galore, native as well as adoptive. Anyone who's survived beyond fourth grade in an English-language classroom can recall the supreme frustration of trying to master spellings of words like *caught* and *lot*, or *three* and *be*, or, for that matter, *be* and *bee*. Forget *knee* and *night, sleigh* and *slay, high* and *dry*. Spelling and pronunciation are famously at odds, and have been ever since early medieval monks yoked English to the Latin alphabet, which they modified to capture the sounds of a Germanic tongue.

Some of the seemingly irrational diversity of ways to wed the sounds of English to Roman letters can be attributed to its layers of diverse linguistic influence. Inconsistent spelling and unpredictable pronunciation have been costs that English has paid for the privilege of gaining foreign words and ideas. Until the so-called Age of the Dictionaries, in the seventeenth and eighteenth centuries, when English spelling and usage were harnessed and standardized, spelling was much looser, even zanier than today.

Consider that when we write the name of the leading dramatist in the English language, the spelling is deemed incorrect if it's not *Shakespeare*. In his own day, the Bard's surname was spelled twenty different ways, including *Shakespear, Shackespeare, Shaxspere,* and even *Shagspere*. The spellings of almost all English words were once equally unfixed. For instance, since the concept of England existed, the word has been spelled dozens of ways: *Ænglaland*, *Engelande*, *Enkelonde*, *Yngelond*, and *Inglant* are just a few of them. No one version was more right or wrong than another. Attempts to standardize English were largely arbitrary, shaped by conventions in the places where English was most influentially studied, recorded, and "tamed" by rules and guidelines. And unlike similar processes undertaken for Romance languages, especially French, standardization of English has never sought, at least not for long, to be comprehensive or consistent. And so, even in the twenty-first century, anyone hoping to master reading and writing English must set aside plenty of time to learn—largely by rote memory—standard spellings that seem to be as closely guided by pronunciation as the former planet Pluto is by Play-Doh.

Are we going to see spelling alter with the rising use of Global English? Following our basic approach of looking into the past for glimpses of the future, the answer looks to be yes. English spelling has changed tremendously over the centuries and even now differs somewhat in the United States, Britain, Australia, Singapore, and India. Global speakers too have already begun to use spellings of their own and show no signs of letting up. Don't be surprised if, in time, you receive a greeting resembling this one: *"Vilkum tu Behjing KharbunKhredeet Yinhang ahnlayin sirvees."* Look weird? Or *weyard*? Or even *hweyiard*? How about *khweehart*? Or *wuiãdo*? Such alternative spellings are wrong in English. But one or more of them may become current and perfectly proper in Global English, depending on which letters of the alphabet can best help the palates of planetary speakers make the sounds that most will recognize. If such spelling change strikes you as exaggerated, consider how rapidly orthography has come to serve text messaging. Who now bothers to text such a sentence as "I will see you for dinner tonight at 7!"

when "*wll c U 4 dnnr 2nit @ 7*" is perfectly legible txt mssg Englsh? *Webster's Dictionary* may have yet to catch up with these alternative spellings, but that doesn't make them any less functional, recognized, and real in the texting world, an increasingly large subset of *the* world.★

Another stunning possibility on the spelling front could be introduced by Semitic languages. Like English, Arabic and Hebrew employ phonetic alphabets. Indeed, we saw how Phoenician, an early Semitic language, was the first to employ a powerful phonetic alphabet, which was passed down in adapted forms to many of the world's languages. Like the Phoenician, the Arabic and Hebrew alphabets differ from the Latin alphabet that's used for English in that they generally do not record the sounds of vowels. Rather, they focus on consonants, leaving readers to add missing vowel sounds when uttering the words aloud. Why would this approach be of any special value to Global English? For one, vowels are notoriously unstable building blocks of any language's pronunciation. Even populations living side by side can adopt markedly different accents, most audibly in their pronunciations of vowels. (Think of the contrasting vowels of native English-speakers simply among the boroughs of New York City.)

As English goes global, the meteoric rise in variations on accents is a natural outcome, and pronunciations of vowels will only become even more sensationally diverse. Already, Brazilians—aficionados of Global English almost as much as of soccer or *futebol*—are compelled to transliterate "pickup" as *picape* and "knockout" as *nocaute*,

★Other languages have gone in similar directions. One concise double example: a lone *c* in text-message French = *c'est*, "it is," and notably in Brazilian Portuguese = *você*, "you." In both languages, the letter of the alphabet and spoken versions of the term it replaces are pronounced the same way: "say." Global English-users worldwide just as casually participate in remaking day-to-day language.

and not just to get rid of the *ks* that look strange to them, but also to nail the foreign vowel sounds. Much Global English seems set to be used for reading and writing rather than speaking. For these purposes too, vowel-free text could very well work as it does now in txt mssgs. Unspoken English is sure to remain a key forum of Global English usage, and to be an important factor in its evolution. But even where Global English continues to be spoken, it could gain from adopting a Semitic approach to its alphabet. Why insert vowels if they don't capture sounds that speakers are actually making? Or that, in some instances, they are even able to make? Just as English-speakers can struggle mightily to pronounce the idiosyncratic *u* in the French word *aperçu*, nonnative speakers of English run into trouble trying to capture "standardized" vowel sounds in words like *sought, mother, book,* or *half.*

These consonant-emphasizing alphabets do have the option of using symbols resembling commas and apostrophes in order to signal the presence (and not the precise pronunciation) of vowels. Readers, pronouncing vowels in diverse ways, are thus free to insert their own pronunciations. So this writing system has a built-in appeal for writers and readers spread over vast areas—say, the entire planet—across which such variations range widely, even wildly.

Seriously now, if you say *tomayto* and I say *tomahto*, should we really have to call the whole thing off?

A passage from a book aimed at improving one's sex life might reasonably read like this in Global English:

Vrtl rlty hs chngd xprnc 'f snslty 'n sphr 'f rmnc. Nw, mny cpl hv dflty mntn'ng hlthy physcl rpprt wth prtnr. Sx 's oftn splntd by vrtl rltnshp, whch cn dstry hmn afctn nd'd t' dvlp mngfl sx lf. Rschr fnd tht gvn chc btw 'rl sx 'nd vrtl gm'ng, yng mn r 68% mr lkly t' chs tchnlgcl stmltn 'vr physcl plsr xcpt 'n crcmstnc—

We've taken stock of some big ingredients sure to be modified in future English: new words, altered grammar, varied word orders, revised spelling. It sounds like a lot, but these elements of English have all changed in the past.

English will surely also develop along less foreseeable tracks as its users refashion it in new circumstances and ways of life—those forming Global English culture. Some of these will likely be driven by necessity, others by wild-card factors.

Let's start with necessity. Who isn't a bit thrown when the airline's automated voice-activated reservations system takes itself for a human? "*Hel-lo! My name is Cas-ey. Please hold,*" says Hal's chipper, although still identifiably robotic, kid sister. "*I am work-ing on your res-er-va-tion. Now.*" (Eerie computer Muzak in background.) And Casey is nothing compared to, say, Ichek, the robot that (who?) will soon be calmly announcing "his" or "her," or "*tā*'s" intention to X-ray strip-search you before allowing you to proceed to the gate for your flight.

How do we think and talk about—and to—these language-using, personality-claiming machines? The ones we'll be seeing a lot more of in years ahead?

A less-spoken language happens to offer a solution. Swahili is attuned to diverse kinds of animacy, even to degrees of animacy. This African language therefore comes equipped with an approach that could help English adapt to a world of not-quite-human creatures.

From its Bantu roots, Swahili inherited a special prefix to distinguish among nouns. Ellen Contini-Morava, a leading authority on noun classifications in Swahili, argues that this prefix distinguishes nouns that early speakers of Bantu perceived as falling into gray areas, or in-between zones. Nouns of this type are characterized by vitality but not by the same kind of animacy that Swahili-speakers assign to humans or animals. (Swahili has other prefixes for classes of nouns designating humans and animals, but also inanimate objects and abstract ideas.) This special prefix, *m-* or *mu-* in the singular, is associated with plant life and natural forces, such as fire and wind.* For example, the Swahili word for "tree" is *mti*. Similarly, "fire" is *moto*, and "sound" is *mlio*. While these last two are inanimate, certain of their properties, such as motion, resemble those of living creatures. Other nouns in this *m-* class are parts of organisms, as in the word for "heart," *moyo*.† With this in mind, let's perform Swahili heart surgery on English.

In a world increasingly reliant on innovations in robotics, artificial intelligence, and biotechnology, could Swahili lend to English its *m-* prefix to capture entities that are at once biological and man-made? Or humanlike but robotic? For example, could a car smart enough to avoid running over your neighbor's child, a "cerebral" car

---

*In Swahili, this prefix is clearly marked as special only in its plural form, *mi-*, because in the singular *m-/mu-* it overlaps with another noun prefix. Nonetheless, the idea of a gray area class of nouns exists in both singular and plural forms. In any case, since we are imagining that English borrows only the prefix concerning objects or life-forms of in-between status, and not the entire Swahili grammatical system of noun classifications, this detail need not worry us. That is, we're supposing that other prefixes of Bantu origin would play no role in future Global English.

†Even as English now rarely distinguishes among types of nouns, we've seen how Old English was a different story: nouns were grouped into three genders. In Swahili, the noun plays an even more elaborate role. In the late nineteenth century, J. L. Krapf noted: "South-East African languages have a tendency to forming separate families, or classes of nouns, which govern the whole grammatical edifice; therefore the noun has the precedence, and all the other parts of speech are, as it were, its dependents, or camp-followers. Every noun belongs to a particular class, and this classification is recognized by the various initial forms [such as *m-/mu-*], which put the noun's grammatical monarchy or chieftaincy upon the verb, the adjective, and all the other parts of speech."[3] As had Sir William Jones with regard to the roots of Indo-European languages, Krapf imagined that "The true cause of this peculiarity must lie in the deeper recesses of the South-East African mind, which distinguishes between animate and inanimate, between rational and irrational beings, between men and brutes, and between life and death." Today, linguistic reconstructions allow access to that world of the Proto-Bantu-speaker. Contini-Morava has studied the Swahili noun classification system in the context of its roots in Proto-Bantu.[4]

outfitted with a microprocessor that simulates and "improves on" the human brain, be referred to using some combination of *m+car*? Such advanced machine "brains" are now being developed in high-tech labs around the world. How would Global English-speakers pronounce a car that runs with one? Is *mcar* just too un-English?* Or would English-speakers potentially modify it to *m'car*? Or *mucar*? Or *emcar*?

It's not difficult to picture English adopting a device like the Swahili *m-* and putting it to use in inventive ways. One reason it's not so incredible a possibility is English's predisposition, seen earlier, to compounding. Putting words, or key parts of words, together to form new words, as with *moonshine* or *daylight*, *crossroads* or *earthquake*, but also *linebacker*, *lemonade*, and *jump-start*, comes naturally to speakers of English. And recently they've taken heavily to compounding with prefixes in ways that bear some resemblance to Swahili: *i-banking*, *X-Men*, *K-cars*, and of course all the higher-tech compounds like *e-commerce* and *email*.

Before leaving you with some future-leaning Global English that puts all our imagined elements together, I want to introduce a possibility in the wild-card category, and from a disparate, not widely spoken language. Wild cards are bound to be in play as English is increasingly used in border-free environments.

Let's imagine how speakers of Global English could embrace a nonnative suffix, one that could prove useful, even vital, to them in the years ahead. Consider that the world is adjusting to new

---

*One shudders to think what our anti-inkhornian Professor Cheke would have made of such a word entering his native language. Or even of the proposal that its addition to the English lexicon be entertained. Then again, robot engineers wouldn't have advanced far had Cheke had his way; a huge percentage of the terms used in their field are not native to English. And, as we know, *robot* is one of them.

thinking about a whole host of issues including energy, space, land, water, air, and ideas of what's most planet-friendly and even most beautiful. Not long ago, Americans widely considered a big house, rooms aplenty, energy-consuming appliances and gadgets, plus a multicar garage filled with fancy gas-burning cars to be worth striving for. Increasingly, perceptions of these things have shifted from admiration to concern and even to disapproval. Smaller, less energy-consuming items are now often equated with "better." Can we imagine a word part that would allow Global English-speakers to refer to a house or a car or a machine or a bank or anything else in terms that equate its bigness with its unwanted impact on their global community?

Now, let's imagine that no suitable component is offered by one of the major languages most likely to influence the immediate future of English: of course not, because these "big" languages are typically averse to small-is-beautiful thinking. Their very success has afforded them this way of seeing the world. An oft-neglected or marginalized language would be more likely to provide us a new building block. All that's needed is a single, strong-voiced person, say an activist, political leader, or celebrity whose access to English-using populations is assured through global channels such as the internet, TV, radio, or other media. We're going to suppose that the agent of our wild-card shift is a Basque activist.

Basque is a mysterious language. It's spoken by fewer than seven hundred thousand people in southern France and northern Spain, in and around the Pyrenees Mountains. Although surrounded by Indo-European languages, Basque appears to be related to none of them. In fact, many experts believe it is, like Korean, an isolate language, akin to no other known tongue. While it has absorbed a good many words from Latin daughter languages, especially Spanish, its presence in Europe may predate the spread of

Indo-European into this area. Yet its influence on other languages has been minimal, in great part because the Basques have been pressured to assimilate to the cultures whose nations their territory bridges, and have not enjoyed the kinds of platforms of influence held by speakers of their neighbors' languages.* Whether this balance is fair is not our immediate concern; the point is that global language and communications networks are remarkably equipped to step over borders of all kinds, including natural, national, and linguistic ones.

Basque's very isolation provides it with a highly distinctive set of magic glasses. One example of a Basque way of seeing the world is embodied in the suffix *-tzar*. (The colloquial version is simply *-zar*.) By adding *-tzar*, the Basque-speaker inflates the idea captured by a word, saying it's larger than usual. More to our point, the ending can carry a pejorative sense, as in "big = bad." The late Dutch linguist Rudolf P. G. de Rijk, who devoted his life to study of the language, notes that in Basque there is "a commonly felt association of big size with big nuisance."[5] One can see how a language sandwiched between two of imperial swagger, such as French and Spanish, could have its own outlook on something as fundamental as proportion. Dr. de Rijk gives interesting examples of how the *-tzar* ending works to correlate size with trouble. Let's see how meanings slide when the suffix bonds with common words:

*The European Union recognizes state languages as those officially employed across an entire country, and it grants official status to certain regional languages as well, including Basque. But while such official status promotes use of regional languages in certain contexts, in practice their speakers often strive to preserve the linguistic integrity of their communities. This is especially the case when their communities are relatively small. In Spain, three regional languages are recognized by the European Union: Catalan is spoken by 9 percent, Galician by 5 percent, and Basque by only 1 percent of the Spanish population according to the 2005 survey conducted by the European Commission.

buru—head   *burutzar*—large head, pighead

gizon—man   *gizatzar*—big man, brute

andre—lady   *andretzar*—tramp, prostitute

suge—snake   *sugetzar*—large snake, slick operator

arrain—fish   *arraintzar*—huge fish, sea monster

Suppose that our Basque activist, competent in English, elected to editorialize on a blog. On this blog, a large house might become a *housetzar*, and an SUV could morph into a *cartzar*. A plane with a low passenger-mile/fuel ratio could be reconceived as a *jetzar*, and a country with an overloud political voice might be termed a *nationtzar*. Adopting the Basque suffix, Global English could now and again don Basque-speakers' glasses, whose unique optical properties bring size into a different focus.

Let's go back to Rachel and Fred, and see what happens when a number of these imagined linguistic changes occur together.

FRED: *Hello?*

RACHEL: *Mister Hanson, Rachel Lopez here. Esam with jīnglĭ.*

FRED: *Youmen have documenteen for zhànghú-mine?*

RACHEL: *Yes, in five hour al-zhàng hú al-deluxe open will be.*

FRED: *OK! Also I made application for loan loan.*

JĪNGLĬ: *Wŏmen see file, but purpose not given.*

FRED: *For business purchase, night-security parking m'guard. And personal, sharkproof scubagear.*

Now that we've tried out some near-future Global English, let's jump ahead one generation and put even more changes into the fictional mix. We'll say that Rachel's Dutch-born daughter, Kaatje, is conversing in cyberspace with Mrs. Greider's great-grandson. They've met on a site for Paris-lovers. Kaatje has recently visited the Eiffel Tower with her boyfriend (whom she thinks of as her *nánpéngyou*, even though she doesn't speak Chinese and neither does he) and is passing on her travel tips.

> "We had m'gosu tour."
>
> "Level 1 + 2?"
>
> "No, 2 only. Nánpéngyou-mine tired eswas."
>
> "M'it good?"
>
> "OK, m'gosutzar broke after 15 minute!"
>
> "Weeart! French make best tourist roboteen. Youmen visit level 3?"
>
> "Yes, al-panorama al-glamour al-omg-most there! But no snack . . . we very want did sugar crêpe crêpe."
>
> "Yínhángmachine on-Tower was?"
>
> "No cash, infrared epay system all place Paris now-is. Sine-off lol I-must. Bon voyage, and hi to Effl Twr if voo see tā!"
>
> "Thanxbye!"

There's cause for excitement among English-speakers. We happen to be living through one of the most extraordinary periods in the history of the language. Or of any known language.

Were Shakespeare alive, he would no doubt marvel at the verbal riches pouring into English, and at the cultural riches attached to them, the real and conceptual cousins of wheels and plows, alphabets, and printing presses. He would now witness thousands of fire-new terms flowing generously into the lexicon that he had augmented and renewed, and would probably recognize some kinships between the fast-growing English vocabulary of his world and of ours.★

Should English consist only of words that have found their ways into dictionaries? English-language dictionaries arose partly in reaction to the masses of new words surging into (and being dragged out of their coffins, or native habitats, by) English during the Renaissance. We're standing in one of those word showers now. Dictionary makers may take a while to pan for words and determine their value. By then, too, the moment of English's significant transformation may have passed. Until now, new words and ideas have entered Global English chiefly from English itself. But other languages, even some as unrelated to English as those we've touched on, could well supply a greater share of them as a distinctive population—a worldwide one—reassembles English yet again.

Global English is a new kind of lingua franca, but it's also the language of a new kind of culture. What is global culture like? What could it become within a generation? Once-new technologies, such as the wheel and the plow, moved, along with Indo-European languages and cultures, toward distant locales across the Eurasian landmass at an average rate of about one kilometer per year. Ideas and words now whip clear around the world in nanoseconds. And rising technologies remake the lives not of clusters of cultures over

---

★A final thought experiment: were Shakespeare to travel through time and retune his ears to Global English, which of its speakers would most inspire him to create a new character, say a Don Adriano de Armado of the twenty-first century? Would it be jet-setting *yínháng* deal doers? International bankers? SAT tutors? Bloggers? The *gosu*s of massive multiplayer games? Or would it be nonhumans, like Casey and Ichek, whose speaking roles are growing in "conversational" Global English? What would the Bard make, when first booking with National Rail, of being asked by a computerized voice whether he's traveling from London to Stratford-upon-Avon on a "business inclusive" ticket? For that matter, what would the Bard make of the extraordinary journey taken by the word *business* since he'd last employed it in his plays?

English Profileration on the Internet

Although it is the native language of only 330 million people, English is the dominant language on the internet in part because it is understood globally.

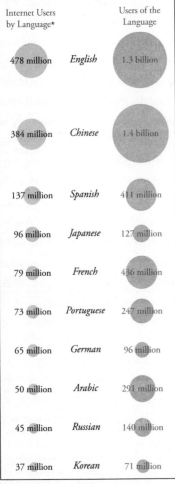

Internet Users by Language*		Users of the Language
478 million	*English*	1.3 billion
384 million	*Chinese*	1.4 billion
137 million	*Spanish*	411 million
96 million	*Japanese*	127 million
79 million	*French*	436 million
73 million	*Portuguese*	247 million
65 million	*German*	96 million
50 million	*Arabic*	291 million
45 million	*Russian*	140 million
37 million	*Korean*	71 million

eons, but of large fractions of the human species, and in far less than a generation.

At the same time, the mobility of populations (through ordinary travel and relocations, but also large-scale emigration and immigration) is projected to skyrocket. Throughout time, the movements of people and their languages have reshaped linguistic landscapes of wide regions. Speakers of Proto-Indo-European and its daughter languages are early examples of this important phenomenon. In our era, large population shifts could play a similarly influential role in the evolution of Global English. Could such shifts also replace English with another language?

For multivalent historical reasons, the phenomenon of a single common tongue has arisen for the most part organically within the global community that has begun to speak it. Many of Earth's English-using

*The data underlying this graphic is from Internet World Stats, www.internetworldstats.com, as accessed on December 31, 2009.

inhabitants, well over a quarter of the planet's population, apparently need and want to be on the same linguistic page. Their widespread lingua franca has raised legitimate concerns about the futures of nonglobal languages and cultures, but it has also become the golden arrow in a vast community's quiver, the only language to date that's in a position to address matters of planetwide interest. What tool could be more powerful than language as this large fraction of humanity collectively forges its future?

If English remains the planet's common tongue, can we expect it to change more rapidly in coming generations than it did a thousand years ago? Or five hundred years ago? While rates of linguistic change are in principle unpredictable, the unprecedented number and kinds of interactions among English-speakers of diverse native languages suggest not merely that English is in the process of being significantly transformed yet again, but that it's changing in ways that no language ever has.

There's obviously a limit to how much a language can be reordered in its nuts and bolts and yet remain itself. If, having gone from a face-lift to heart surgery, we were now to advance to a brain transplant, to what extent would we still be involved with the same patient? Helpful as it can be to think of a language as an organism, or as the "daughter" of another, we've mainly been considering English as an integrated and evolving set of tools used by communities of speakers that also evolve. How any language works as a constantly redesigned tool kit depends on how its speakers put it to use, and how the innovations that they introduce eventually furnish them with what looks like a brand-new supply of instruments. But how "new" has English become over the centuries?

Many current speakers of English would be suspicious if someone presented them with *Lāgon þā ōðre fȳnd on þām fȳre* and asserted that it was English.[6] But if we read the sentence aloud, and use *th* sounds where the letters þ and ð appear, we can hear each native English word in more familiar terms, literally "Lay the others, fiends, on the fire." In this line about fallen angels from a passage about hell, we see and hear deep connections between Old and Modern English. But religious discourse in any language is typically conservative. It alters less freely than does speech about secular matters, such as paying a visit to the Eiffel Tower, setting up a bank account, parking a car, or going on Safari to search for the best family holiday package.

Scant Old English remains in this sentence from the White House website page about Homeland Security: "The President supports efforts to develop and deploy technology to maximize port security without causing economic disruption, and enhancing the security of key transportation networks—including surface, air, and maritime networks—that connect our nation and the world."[7] Apart from verbal "connective tissue," like articles and prepositions, the governmental statement contains mainly "borrowed words." Indeed, English has changed over the course of eventful centuries and influential contacts with speakers of other languages. Large numbers of words made in French and Latin have equipped speakers of English to talk about and see the world differently.

English made its first appearances in a form that has, with hindsight, been named Old English. *Beowulf* was composed in the highly inflected English of this period. The next major phase was Middle English, the very French-influenced language spoken from the eleventh through the fifteenth centuries and recrowned with literary prestige thanks to Geoffrey Chaucer's works. Next came Early Modern English, whose native speakers included Shakespeare. Around 1800, his English evolved into the Late Modern English of such diverse speakers as Seamus Heaney, Donna Summer, and

Arnold Schwarzenegger. Given the new uses and users of English, however, today a distinct phase of the language is under way, Global English. And it comes tied to its own culture, one that we've glimpsed through telling specimens of its vocabulary.

We've seen through the lenses of specific word tools, from *hello* and *blog* to *lol* and *OK*, that an important facet of Global English culture is taken up with communication. Commerce and trade are also key: *Made in China, credit card, business, bank.* So are science, technology, and mass production; *robot* and *bikini* are examples along with those byproducts of automotive English reflected in words like *parking, STOP,* and *taxi!* Global English culture has also shaped perceptions of inner life and leisure with words like *fun, stress,* and *relax.* Are there words and ideas that you'd like to see added to (or subtracted from) the first global culture tool kit?

Perhaps you have creative proposals for new words, or ideas from other languages you think would serve Global English well. Now is the time to introduce them, and to see whether they'll be taken up by others. As the window for decisive change opens wide, there are and will be heightened opportunities to remake English. Word authorities, power wielders, conventional-wisdom providers, and defenders of the Queen's English are naturally going to be speaking and writing English as well, and influencing the course of their language's future. Editors of *The Chicago Manual of Style* and formulators of the SAT and ACT also have their roles to play, as do TV news anchors, radio personalities, Hollywood stars, and White House speechwriters. But none of them will be dictating which words and phrases and pronouns and more will ultimately gain wider use in Global English, the first work in progress to be crafted by a planetary speech community.

The global era is all about rolling up sleeves, stepping in, and changing what once appeared to be "natural," what might once have simply been accepted as given. Global times have taken us in a new direction: increasingly, humans take the initiative to change—and improve— the hands that they've been dealt. Language is one of those hands, perhaps the most important of all, as language is the medium through which we all experience and engage with the world we cohabit.

As we step into a historical era marked by English's transition into Global English, there is much to think about—and to act on. How do we nurture the particularities that make each living language a cultural treasure? Which languages are putting their marks on conversations of the future? How will a growing common language allow humans to partake of life in a wider world, to surmount obstacles of global scope, and to find solace in continuities with the past? And does Paul's friend still think that English lacks a decent pair of magic glasses?

BYE

Parting is a delicate moment in most cultures, and in their languages. It can be a strange transition, to go from speaking with someone to not. In the end, though, even solitude finds itself accompanied by the self-expanding stuff of language: a thought, a recollection, a determination, a hope. One may offer promises to meet again soon. Or wish wellness. Or good things to come. Or ask that peace go with the person whose company has been kept. In Marshallese, the language of Bikini Atoll, *hello* and *bye* alike are conveyed in the word *iokwe*, which also means *love*.* In English, the expression *bye* was once similarly fulsome: *God be with you*. Yet since the times when such complete wishes were commonly bestowed by speakers of English, its cultures have operated on faster metabolisms. It's as if the English language has itself become pressed for time, and has adapted its parting expressions accordingly. It may be a sorry state of linguistic and cultural affairs, but at the same time, *bye* sums up in a word the elastic side of a language that has changed in astonishing ways since

---

*In a playful folk etymology, speakers of Marshallese have given *iokwe* new meaning as a compound word because it sounds like *iia* + *kwe*, "rainbow" and "you." In this sense, *iokwe* is heard as "you are a rainbow" or "you are like a rainbow."

its emergence nearly fifteen hundred years ago. Viewed in an optimistic light, *bye* encapsulates the possibility that English will soon, and yet again, be significantly transformed—this time, to fulfill the unknowable needs of a community of speakers who have already begun to reshape the language into *their* English.

BYE FROM THE PAST AND INTO THE FUTURE

Old English	*God þē mid sīe*	King Ælfred? (unattested)
Middle English	*And God be with yow*	Geoffrey Chaucer
Early Modern English	*God b'wy*	William Shakespeare
Late Modern English	*good-bye*	Charles Dickens
Later Modern English	*bye*	Bret Easton Ellis
Global English	?	?

ACKNOWLEDGMENTS

One word that didn't make the final cut for discussion in this book is *teamwork,* but I can't think of a better one to introduce acknowledgments. The first definition given by the *Oxford English Dictionary* is "work done with a team of beasts." While no team of this kind was hitched to my project, there was the odd horse or camel, and I thank each of them for conveying me to patches of the English-using world. The dictionary's final definition is "work done by persons working as a team, i.e. with concerted effort."

It's now a great pleasure to turn to the humans. Agents Eric Lupfer and Suzanne Gluck were my dynamic duo at William Morris Endeavor Entertainment in midtown Manhattan. A few blocks away, in the Touchstone division of Simon & Schuster, the inspiring editor Lauren Spiegel and publisher Stacy Creamer came equipped with a formidable team of their own, including production editor Martha Schwartz and publicist Jessica Roth. Illustrator Mary Rhinelander worked with us from Providence, Rhode Island, and graphic designer Kris Goodfellow from Redlands, California. My "outside reader" was Jess Taylor, whose perspective came from São Paulo in Brazil.

For reactions to the work in progress—and indeed, for crash courses in their areas of expertise, from Indo-European linguistics to American diplomacy—I'm indebted to Jeffrey Bourns, Glenn Davis, Mathew Horsman, Richard Sieburth, and Daniel Simpson. Equally vital was Christopher Jennings, without whom many facts would have gone unchecked. As for my sometime coauthor Alan Riding, no one better knows my atrocious writing habits, or more kindly reminds me that they can be overcome. Errors, stupidities, bad transitions, excess commas, and opaque sentences are my own contributions.

A few people fall into a special category. Without them, this project wouldn't have taken flight as it did. Thank you Melissa Franklin, Gwyneth Horder-Payton, Matthew Lloyd, Jessica Marshall, Susan Morrison, Gregory Nagy, Bruce Nichols, Sydney Picasso, Megan Reid, and Sylvie Robin. My multilingual son Jordan Tucker (French, English, Japanese) and niece Naira Mar (English, Spanish, Dutch) gave me the stamina to complete a book about the one language they have in common.

For their varied forms of support, allow me to salute the Radcliffe Institute for Advanced Study; my 40 Concord office mates; the staff of Harvard's Widener Library; the International School of Boston; Galerie Thaddaeus Ropac; and, for providing a desk and a relatively quiet place to complete editing in their office, the police of Carbonara di Po in Mantua, Italy.

Bedouin purveyors of "tea" and "blanket" on an icy summit, a linguist conducting fieldwork in the Arctic, a record producer in Ethiopia, a Lithuanian diplomat, a Korean newspaper editor, and other speakers of diverse languages I thank by location for their generous words: Bogotá; La Paz; São Paulo; Rio de Janeiro; Oaxaca; the Lacandon forest; Nouméa, New Caledonia; Tokyo; Sendai; Kyoto; Hong Kong; Rui'an; Beijing; Hanoi; Seoul; Bangkok; Bartang Valley, Tajikistan; Tehran; Calcutta; Bombay; Istanbul; London; Oxford; Amsterdam; Paris; Geneva in both Switzerland and

France; Vezzi San Filippo; Rome; Salzburg; Split; Mostar; Krasnodar; Kaunas; Abu Dhabi; Tel Aviv; Sinai; Cairo; Addis Ababa; Nairobi; Johannesburg; Marrakech; Boa Vista, Cape Verde Islands; Vancouver; Montreal; Honolulu; Kotzebue, Alaska; Washington, DC; Philadelphia; Pittsburgh; Atlanta; New York; Hempstead; Brooklyn; Highlands, New Jersey; New Orleans; Charlottesville, Virginia; Concord, New Hampshire; Boston; Cambridge; Watertown; Amherst; Minneapolis; Los Angeles; Newhall; San Francisco; Stanford; and Santa Cruz.

NOTES

For standard definitions of words, etymologies, and attestations, I have generally relied on a handful of authoritative reference works. *The Oxford English Dictionary* in its online version was my basic source for discussion of English words. For Indo-European roots, and the English words employing them, I consulted *The American Heritage Dictionary of Indo-European Roots.* Some additional definitions of words and roots from specific branches of the Indo-European language family are from Carl Darling Buck, *A Dictionary of Selected Synonyms in the Principal Indo-European Languages: A Contribution to the History of Ideas* (1949; repr., Chicago: University of Chicago Press, 1988). For definitions, etymologies, and attestations of words in French, my source was *Le Trésor de la Langue Française informatisé,* an online dictionary of the Centre National de Ressources Textuelles et Lexicales. Translations from the French dictionary are mine.

ABBREVIATIONS

DIR *The American Heritage Dictionary of Indo-European Roots,* edited and revised by Calvert Watkins (Boston: Houghton Mifflin, 2000).

OED *Oxford English Dictionary,* www.oed.com (unless otherwise noted, from 2nd ed., 1989, last accessed on April 26, 2010).

TFLi *Le Trésor de la Langue Française informatisé,* http://atilf.atilf.fr/tlf.htm (unless otherwise noted, last accessed on May 5, 2010).

INTRODUCTION: MAGIC GLASSES

1. *Beowulf: A New Verse Translation,* trans. Seamus Heaney (New York: Farrar, Straus, and Giroux, 2000), 3. Note that the Old English text of the poem reproduced in this edition is based on *Beowulf, with the Finnesburg Fragment,* 3rd ed., eds. C. L. Wrenn and W. F. Bolton (Exeter, UK: University of Exeter Press, 1988).

HELLO?

1. For a description of the first telephone convention, and the use of *hello* on attendees' name tags, see Allen Koenigsberg, "The First 'Hello!' Thomas Edison, the Phonograph and the Telephone—Part 2," *Antique Phonograph Monthly* 8, no.6. (1987) (accessed February 1, 2010). I would like to thank Mr. Koenigsberg for elaborating on this, and other details of telephone history, in an interview—a phone interview of course—on February 1, 2010.

2. "hallo," *OED*.

3. Mark Twain, "A Telephonic Conversation," *Atlantic Monthly,* June 1880, 841.

4. Joe Strickland's letter to his Uncle Ben, dated "Septr. aidenth, 1000-ate-100 & 27," appears in the *United States' Telegraph,* September 25, 1827, 3.

1. GLOBAL ENGLISH

1. Claude Hagège, *L'Enfant aux deux langues* (Paris: Editions Odile Jacob, 1996), 272.

2. Data for this chart were extracted from diverse sources and dates, as aggregated on Wikipedia (http://en.wikipedia.org/wiki/List_of_countries_by_English-speaking_population, accessed May 27, 2010). Included in this chart are only those countries for which Wikipedia data could be confirmed. For more details on sources, see Wikipedia commentary and references. Data was drawn from national census records for: Australia (2001), Canada (2001), India (2001), Ireland (2006), Mexico (2005), New Zealand (2006), Philippines (2000), Russia (2002), United States (2000); data for Austria, Belgium, Denmark, France, Germany, Greece, Italy, Netherlands, Poland, Romania, Spain, Sweden, Turkey: "Europeans and Their Languages," *Special Eurobarometer* 243, Wave 64.3 (Brussels: European Commission, 2005), http://ec.europa.eu/public_opinion/archives/ebs/ebs_243_en.pdf; data for Cameroon, Malaysia, Pakistan, Sierra Leone, South Africa, Tanzania, United Kingdom, Zimbabwe: David Crystal, *The Cambridge Encyclopedia of the English Language,* 2nd ed. (Cambridge, UK: Cambridge University Press, 2003), 109; data for China (mainland only): Jian Yang, "Learners and Users of English in China," *English Today* 22 (2006): 3–10; data for Nigeria: Kelechukwu Uchechukwu Ihemere, "A Basic Description and Analytic Treatment of Noun Classes in Nigerian Pidgin," *Nordic Journal of African Studies* 15 (2006): 297.

3. Manfred B. Steger, *Globalization: A Very Short Introduction,* 2nd ed. (2003; repr. Oxford: Oxford University Press, 2009), 82. Tallies of living languages differ widely depending on how evaluators delineate one language from another. For instance, the French linguist Claude Hagège proposed in 2000 that we consider Earth home only to some 5,000 languages. To show how little this figure tells us about populations of speakers, however, he noted that "90 percent of the planet's languages are spoken by about 5 percent of the worldwide population." Claude Hagège, *On the Death and Life of Languages,* trans. Jody Gladding (New Haven: Yale University Press, 2009), 173.

4. For a highly readable consideration of those famous "words for snow," from first mention of them in 1911 to recent reexaminations by linguists, see Larry Kaplan, "Inuit Snow Terms: How Many and What does it Mean?," 2003, www.uaf.edu/anlc/snow.html (accessed May 1, 2010).

5. *Dictionary of Quotations,* 3rd ed. (Hertfordshire, UK: Wordsworth Editions, 1998), 79.

6. Robert McCrum, Robert MacNeil, and William Cran, *The Story of English,* 3rd rev. ed. (New York: Penguin, 2002), 9.

ROBOT

1. Karel Čapek's account of the origin of *robot* was published in *Lidove noviny* on December 24, 1933. It corrected the claim, published in the *Oxford English Dictionary,* that he had himself created the word. See http://capek.misto .cz/english/robot.html, article translated by Norma Comrada (accessed October 20, 2009).

2. Carl Darling Buck, *A Dictionary of Selected Synonyms in the Principal Indo-European Languages: A Contribution to the History of Ideas* (1949; repr., Chicago: University of Chicago Press, 1988), 540.

3. In Danville, Virginia, the review by James W. Dean ran in the daily newspaper *The Bee* on October 16, 1922, under the eye-catching title, " 'Machine-Made Men' Stalk on Broadway in 'R.U.R.' " www.paleofuture .com/blog/2007/5/16/the-robot-is-a-terrible-creature-1922.html (accessed April 28, 2010).

4. Bohuslava R. Bradbrook, *Karel Čapek: In Pursuit of Truth, Tolerance, and Trust* (Brighton, UK: Sussex Academic Press, 1998), 50.

SHAMPOO

1. *Hobson-Jobson: The Anglo-Indian Dictionary,* eds. Sir Henry Yule and A. C. Burnell (1886; repr., Hertfordshire, UK: Wordsworth Editions, 1996), 821.

2. Mahomet authored numerous letters describing his early life. Michael H. Fisher has edited and introduced these with a broader biographical sketch in *The Travels of Dean Mahomet: An Eighteenth-Century Journey Through India* (Berkeley: University of California Press, 1997). While Mahomet spelled his name both as *Mahomet* and *Mahomed,* I follow Fisher in using the former unless referring to a specific instance where the latter was employed.

3. John V. Shoemaker, "The Practice of Shampooing," *Medical Bulletin: A Monthly Journal of Medicine and Surgery* 20, no. 3 (1898): 47.

4. Note that the *OED* gives the etymology of the verb *shampoo* as only probably from Hindi but proposes no alternative.

JAZZ

1. Tom Piazza notes that, after Monk said "Jazz is freedom," he crucially added, "You think about that." In Piazza's view, those who have thought about the equation seem to conclude that "Jazz represents pure individual freedom (a lack of limits), and since any effort at definition represents some sort of limitation, *jazz* is the one word in the language for which, by definition, no definition exists"; Tom Piazza, *Blues Up and Down: Jazz in Our Time* (New York: St. Martin's Press, 1997), 181. Piazza's book, a collection of articles and reviews spanning three decades, is presented under the aegis of the indefinable: "no two people will agree on a definition for the word jazz." He proposes that this is because it "disguises deeper and more urgent concerns. Into the word *jazz,* whether we like it or not, are plugged long, heavy-duty cables connecting to issues of race, the individual and the group in a democracy, the role of the arts in a commercial culture, the relationship of so-called 'high art' to so-called 'popular art,' the question of whether there is such a thing as progress in the arts, and on and on" (page ix).

2. H. L. Mencken, *The American Language,* 4th ed. (1919; repr., New York: Knopf, 1957), 189–90.

3. Garvin Bushell as told to Mark Tucker, *Jazz from the Beginning* (1988; repr., New York: Da Capo Press, 1998), 13.

4. "jazz," *OED,* draft revision, March 2010.

5. In 2003, George A. Thompson Jr. uncovered the *Jazz ball* citation in the *Los Angeles Times,* April 2, 1912.

6. Ernest J. Hopkins's definition from "In Praise of 'Jazz,' a Futurist Word Which Has Just Joined the Language," in the *San Francisco Bulletin,* April 5, 1913.

7. For an account of Kelly's role and the spread of the word *jazz,* see Ben Zimmer, " 'Jazz': A Tale of Three Cities," *Word Routes,* Visual Thesaurus, June 8, 2009, www.visualthesaurus.com/cm/wordroutes (accessed November 12, 2009).

8. *Random House Historical Dictionary of American Slang,* Vol. 2, ed. J. E. Lighter (New York: Random House, 1997), 259.

COCKTAIL

1. "cocktail," *OED,* draft revision, December 2005.

2. For the complete list of words and phrases, see "The Drinker's Dictionary," in Benjamin Franklin, *Writings* (New York: Viking, 1987), 267–70.

3. "cocktail," *OED,* entry from 1803, draft revision, December 2005.

MADE IN CHINA

1. "make," *OED,* draft revision, March 2010.

2. Hunter S. Thompson, *The Proud Highway: Saga of a Desperate Southern Gentleman, 1955–1967,* ed. Douglas Brinkley (New York: Villard, 1997), 395.

3. "*bicyclette,*" and "*vélo,*" *TLFi,* 2009.

2. A FAMILY PICTURE OF ENGLISH

1. J. P. Mallory, *In Search of the Indo-Europeans: Language, Archaeology, and Myth* (New York: Thames and Hudson, 1989), 157.

2. See "Languages and Resurrection," in Claude Hagège, *On the Death and Life of Languages,* trans. Jody Gladding (New Haven: Yale University Press, 2009), 241–310.

3. For a succinct scholarly discussion of the central role played by "sound laws" in linguistic reconstruction, see Jay H. Jasanoff and Alan Nussbaum, "Word Games: The Linguistic Evidence in *Black Athena,*" in *Black Athena Revisited,* eds. Mary R. Lefkowitz and Guy MacLean Rogers (Chapel Hill: University of North Carolina Press, 1996), 180–82.

4. Here is a prime example of an Indo-Europeanist "in action" in a specific branch of the language family: Gregory Nagy, *Greek Mythology and Poetics*

(Ithaca, NY: Cornell University Press, 1990). For a short but engaging overview of Proto-Indo-European language and culture, see *DIR,* vii–xxxv. Other highly readable treatments of the subjects include Philip Baldi, *An Introduction to the Indo-European Languages* (Carbondale: Southern Illinois University Press, 1983) and J. P. Mallory, *In Search of the Indo-Europeans: Language, Archaeology and Myth.*

5. *DIR,* 56.
6. *DIR,* 89–90.

FILM

1. "film," *OED,* first attestation c. 1000.
2. William Shakespeare, *Hamlet,* ed. T.J.B. Spencer (repr.; London: Penguin Books, 1996), 119–20.

CREDIT CARD

1. Edward Bellamy, *Looking Backward: 2000–1887* (1888; repr., Harmondsworth, UK: Penguin Books, 1982), 118.
2. For a brief introduction to this phrase, see *DIR,* xxxii.

LOL

1. "lol" has not been included in the *OED* as of May 15, 2010.
2. For one consideration of "laugh," see the chapter "Interjections and Human Sounds," in J. P. Mallory and D. Q. Adams, *The Oxford Introduction to Proto-Indo-European and the Proto-Indo-European World* (Oxford: Oxford University Press, 2006), 359–63.
3. "Language and Culture Note," *DIR,* 42–43.

BLOG

1. Tim Berners-Lee's early proposal for the World Wide Web, referring to it as the *Mesh,* can be consulted on the web at www.w3.org/History/1989/proposal.html (accessed November 18, 2009).
2. "blog," *OED,* draft entry, March 2003.
3. William Safire, "Blog," *New York Times,* July 28, 2002, www.nytimes .com/2002/07/28/magazine/28ONLANGUAGE.html (accessed November 18, 2009).

DISCO

1. *"discothèque," TLFi*, 2009.
2. The *OED's* entry "disc, disk," traces the word's etymology back to the Greek *dískos* and no further, but see *DIR*, 14–15.

STAR

1. Durbin Feeling, *Cherokee-English Dictionary (Tsalagi-Yonega Didehlogwas-dohdi)*, ed. William Pulte (Telequah, OK: Cherokee Nation of Oklahoma, 1975), 220.
2. I am grateful to Indo-Europeanist Jeffrey Bourns for these reconstructions of the root for *star*, which he explained to me on February 13, 2010.
3. Complete lyrics, and a taped performance of the song, can be found at www .chinese-tools.com (accessed October 30, 2009).

3. MADE IN ÆNGLISC

1. For anyone eager to experience the language in more depth, there is a good book addressed to readers who wish to teach themselves Old English: Bruce Mitchell and Fred C. Robinson, *A Guide to Old English,* 7th ed. (1964; repr., Oxford: Blackwell, 2007). Following an introduction to the language, the book includes texts of major works in Old English such as *The Battle of Maldon*, *The Dream of the Rood*, *The Wanderer*, *The Seafarer*, and selections from *Beowulf.*
2. Word counts noted on the "Building English" map are given by Richard Hogg and David Denison, eds. *A History of the English Language* (Cambridge: Cambridge University Press, 2006), 2, citing the *OED.*

BUSINESS

1. That last sentence disobeys *business writing* rule number five: "Keep it short." Alicia Abell, *Business Grammar, Style & Usage* (Boston: Aspatore, 2003), 10.
2. Geoffrey Chaucer, *The Riverside Chaucer,* ed. Larry D. Benson (Boston: Houghton Mifflin, 1987), 28.
3. William Shakespeare, *Hamlet,* ed T. J. B. Spencer (repr., London: Penguin Books, 1996), 142.

PARKING

1. "parking," *OED*, draft revision, June 2008.
2. "park," *OED*, draft revision, March 2010.
3. For a chart showing PIE sounds known to have evolved into those used in the attested Indo-European branches of languages, as well as in the Germanic languages (including Old English), see *DIR*, 146–47.

T-SHIRT

1. But see the etymological note about "screw, n.1," *OED*.
2. For a seminal discussion of the phonetic alphabet and its importance in the global era, see Marshall McLuhan and Quentin Fiore *The Medium Is the Massage* (1967; repr., Berkeley, CA: Ginko Press, 2005).

FREE

1. The case for separate names for these languages is persuasively made by Aida Vidan in "Language as Process: Literary Norms and Everyday Reality of Bosnian/ Croatian/ Serbian," presented at the 11th International Conference on Minority Languages, Pécs, Hungary, July 5–6, 2007; http://icmll.law.ptc.hu/stuff/icml11abstracts.pdf. A version of this paper is under review for publication in the journal *Language and Society*.
2. "free," *OED*, draft revision, March 2010.

BANK

1. The *monty* appearing in the phrase *the full monty* has been proposed as a variant of the *monte* borrowed from Spanish and related to the Italian for "mound" or "hill" but also "pile." *Monte* in this sense is still used in Spanish-influenced English, mainly in the United States, for a gambling game involving stacks of cards, and is indeed etymologically related to the Italian *monte* meaning "hill" in that European capital of high-rolling gamblers, Monte Carlo. But for the *full monty*, the *OED* favors the explanation that it once referred to "the purchase of a complete three-piece suit" made by the tailor Montague Maurice Burton (1885–1952). *Monty* would thus have been a shortening of the tailor's first name, *Montague*. See *OED*, "full monty," draft entry, June 2001.
2. *The Code of Ḥammurabi, King of Babylon (About 2250 B.C.)*, ed., transliterated from the Akkadian, and trans. by Robert Francis Harper (Chicago: University of Chicago Press, 1904), 27.

STOP

1. The phrase *stop sign*, also Made in USA, is first attested only some years later, in 1934. "stop," *OED*.
2. "STOP," *TLFi*, 2009.

4. MADE IN ENGLYSSHE

1. William Shakespeare, *Love's Labor's Lost*, ed. John Kerrigan (repr., London: Penguin Books, 1996), I.i.176, p. 51.
2. Ibid., V.i.84–85, p. 106.
3. Vocabulary percentages, along with most examples of words in each category, appear in James Wilson Bright, *Bright's Old English Grammar & Reader*, 3rd ed., eds. Frederic G. Cassidy and Richard N. Ringler (1891; repr., New York: Holt, Rinehart and Winston, 1971), 4.
4. Jean-Paul Nerrière and David Hon, *Globish the World Over* (n.p.: The International Global Institute, 2009).
5. C. K. Ogden and I. A. Richards, *The Meaning of Meaning: A Study of the Influence of Language Upon Thought and of the Science of Symbolism* (1923; repr., San Diego: Harcourt Brace Jovanovich, 1989).
6. Word counts and percentages used in this time line are from these two sources: Richard Hogg and David Denison, eds., *A History of the English Language* (Cambridge: Cambridge University Press, 2006); Geoffrey Hughes, *A History of English Words* (Oxford: Blackwell, 2000).
7. Geoffrey Chaucer, *The Riverside Chaucer*, 3rd. ed., ed. Larry D. Benson (Boston: Houghton Mifflin, 1996), 25.
8. Thomas Wilson, *The Arte of Rhetorique*, ed. George Herbert Mair (1560; repr., Oxford: Clarendon Press, 1909), 163.
9. Sir John Cheke, letter to Sir Thomas Hoby, dated July 16, 1557, as cited by Hoby in his preface to *The Book of the Courtier by Count Baldassare Castiglione, Done into English by Sir Thomas Hoby Anno 1561*, ed. W. B. D. Henderson (London: J. M. Dent & Sons, 1928), 7.

CHECK

1. "check," *OED,* citation from c. 1440.
2. For a detailed overview of chess terms in Arabic, Persian, and Sanskrit, and of the history of chess in Islam and the Arabic-speaking world, see F. Rosenthal, "Shatrandj," in *Encyclopedia of Islam,* CD-ROM, v. 1.1, (Leiden, Netherlands: Brill, 2001).

PENTHOUSE

1. "penthouse," *OED,* draft revision, March 2010.
2. Carl Darling Buck, *A Dictionary of Selected Synonyms in the Principal Indo-European Languages: A Contribution to the History of Ideas* (1949; repr., Chicago: University of Chicago Press, 1988), 457.
3. "penthouse," *OED,* citation from 1892.
4. Architectural details of Condé Nast's penthouse, and the party he hosted on its terrace, are described in Christopher Gray, "1040 Park Avenue: A 1924 Apartment House That Repays Careful Study," *New York Times,* November 7, 1993, www.nytimes.com/1993/11/07/realestate/streetscapes -1040-park-avenue-a-1924-apartment-house-that-repays-careful-study .html?scp=4&sq=cond%C3%A9%20nast%20penthouse&st=cse (accessed October 30, 2009).

COOKIE

1. The document mentioning eight hundred "cockies" is cited in Sylvester Judd, *History of Hadley, Including the Early History of Hatfield, South Hadley, Amherst, and Granby, Massachusetts* (Northhampton, MA: Metcalf , 1863), 32.
2. "cookie," *OED,* first attestation c.1730.

JOB

1. GogoJobs.ru/cvandresumetips.htm (accessed May 5, 2010).
2. "job," *OED,* draft revision, March 2010.

5. LINGUA FRANCA AND ENGLISH

1. *The Oxford Dictionary of Foreign Words and Phrases,* ed. Jennifer Speake (Oxford: Oxford University Press, 1997), 233.
2. Nicholas Ostler, *Empires of the Word: A Language History of the World* (New York: HarperCollins, 2005).

3. Roman Empire in the fourth century, map by Sigurd Solberg Jakobsen; Romance Languages map as posted by the Académie Grenoble, www.ac -grenoble.fr; English Spoken Here map adapted from *Ethnologue: Languages of the World,* 16th ed., ed. M. Paul Lewis, www.ethnologue.com (Dallas, TX: SIL International, 2009), used by permission.

STRESS

1. Dwight J. Ingle, "Problems Relating to the Adrenal Cortex," *Endocrinology* 31, no. 4 (1942): 419–38.
2. "prestige," *OED,* draft revision, September 2009.

SAT

1. National Center for Education Statistics, U.S. Department of Education Sciences. Table 418, prepared July 2008, http://nces.ed.gov/programs/digest/ d09/tables/dt09_418.asp (accessed May 5, 2010).
2. Nicholas Ostler, *Ad Infinitvm: A Biography of Latin* (New York: Walker, 2007), 285, citing Samuel Eliot Morison, *The Founding of Harvard College* (Cambridge, MA: Harvard University Press, 1935).
3. Theme page from "Better Taught in English?: Institutional Language Strategies in European Higher Education," www.aca-secretariat.be/index .php?id=59, seminar of the Academic Cooperation Association, December 4, 2009 (accessed November 24, 2009).

RELAX

1. "relax," *OED,* draft revision, March 2010.
2. "relax(e)," *TLFi.*
3. www.zing.vn/news/dep/thanh-hang-dung-viet-ve-chuyen-tinh-cam-cua-toi/ a58901.html (accessed November 2, 2009).

SAFARI

1. For a brief account of Krapf as "the first Protestant missionary to East Africa," see M. Louise Pirouet, "The Legacy of Johann Ludwig Krapf," Henry Martyn Centre, www.martynmission.cam.ac.uk/pages/published-papers.php? searchresult=1&sstring=krapf (accessed May 5, 2010). The article was originally published in the *International Bulletin of Missionary Research* 23, no. 2 (April, 1999): n.p.

2. Johann Ludwig Krapf, *A Dictionary of the Suahili Language* (London: Trübner, 1882), 320.

DELUXE

1. "Nero," in Suetonius, *Lives of the Caesars,* Vol. II, ed. and trans. by J. C. Rolfe
(1914; repr., Cambridge, MA: Harvard University Press, 1997), 127–29.
2. *"de luxe," TLFi,* attestation of 1849.
3. Graham Robb takes a vivid look at the varied linguistic landscape of France,
and at efforts by some to "erase" it, in a chapter whose title envelopes diverse
words meaning "yes": "O Òc Sí Bai Ya Win Oui Oyi Awè Jo Ja Oua," in
*The Discovery of France: A Historical Geography from the Revolution to the First
World War* (New York: Norton, 2007), 50–70.
4. Roland Barthes, "Soap-powders and Detergents," in *Mythologie*s, selected and
trans. from the French by Annette Lavers (1957; repr., New York: Hill and
Wang, 1972), 37.

O.K.

1. H. L. Mencken, *The American Language*, 4th ed. (1919; repr., New York:
Knopf, 1957), 204, citing John S. Farmer, *Americanisms Old and New* (Lon-
don: privately printed, 1889), 1.
2. In 1815, the phrase "ok & at Trenton" was employed in a diary entry dated
February 21. But the *OED* has determined its sense to be uncertain. See
"OK," *OED*, draft revision, March 2010.
3. For O.K. as an abbreviation of "oll korrect" and similar intended misspell-
ings, see the articles by Allen Walker Read, who uncovered the first attested
OK of this kind in the *Boston Morning Post,* March 23, 1839. Allen Walker
Read, "The First Stage in the History of 'O.K.,' " *American Speech* 38, no. 1
(1963): 5–27; and "The Second Stage in the History of 'O.K.,' ibid., no. 2
(1963): 83–102.
4. For an account of Wolofisms identified in American English by David Dolby,
see Selase W. Williams, "The African Character of African American Language: Insights from the Creole Connection," in *Africanisms in American Culture*, ed. Joseph E. Holloway (1990; repr., Bloomington: Indiana University
Press, 2005), 410.
5. "o.k," *TLFi,* attestation of 1869.

6. FUTURE GLOBAL ENGLISH SPOKEN HERE

1. S. Robert Ramsey, "Chinese Writing Today," in *The Languages of China* (Princeton: Princeton University Press, 1987), 143–54.

2. Bruce Mitchell and Fred C. Robinson, *A Guide to Old English,* 7th ed. (1964; repr., Oxford: Blackwell, 2007), 292.

3. Johann Ludwig Krapf, *A Dictionary of the Suahili Language* (London: Trübner, 1882), xvi.

4. Ellen Contini-Morava, "Noun Classification in Swahili," Institute for Advanced Technology in the Humanities, University of Virginia, www2.iath .virginia.edu/swahili/swahili.html, n.d. (accessed October 13, 2009).

5. Rudolf P. G. de Rijk, *Standard Basque: A Progressive Grammar,* Vol 1: *The Grammar* (Cambridge, MA: MIT Press, 2007), 85.

6. Line 322a of Genesis B, cited in *Bright's Old English Grammar and Reader,* eds. Frederic G. Cassidy and Richard N. Ringler (New York: Holt, Rinehart and Winston, 1971), 303.

7. www.whitehouse.gov/issues/homeland-security (accessed March 5, 2010).

INDEX

Note: Page numbers in *italics* refer to tables/charts/maps/graphs

a (vs. *the*), 259–61
Academic Cooperation Association (ACA), 223
Académie Française, 237–38
ACT, 223*n*, 291
adobe, 245
Ælfred, king of England, 103, 106–107, 115, 154, 160, 275, *294*
Ænglisc, *49*, 99–116, 198, 266. *See also* English language: Old English; Germanic languages
Æthelstan, 107
ahoy, xix, xx
Aki na Ukwa (film), 77–78
Albanian, 52–53, 57–58, 86
alcachofa, 262
alcohol, 30, 31, 39, 41, 42, 44, 50, 91
algebra, 165, 254, 262*n*, 263, 276
Algonquian, 168
Alhambra, 262, 262*n*, 263*n*
al jazeera, 262, 262*n*
alkali, 254, 262, 262*n*
alleluia, 111, 257
Allen, Harry Nathaniel, 187
allô, xxii
al qaeda, 262, 262*n*
amen, 50, 111, 257
Anatolia, 60, *69n*
Angles, 99, 99*n*, 102, *110,* 114
Anglo-Saxons, xvi, 99, 112
annihilate, 165n
appendix, 176, 177

aptitude, 220, 222
Arabic, xi, xvi, xxii, 8, 10, 11, *27, 33,* 35, 84, 92, 95, 128, 140, 149, 172–73, *173n,* 175 *175,* 180, 184, 204–8, 231–32, 254–57, 256*n,* 262–66, 265*n,* 269, 278, *288*
argenteria, 136–37
Aristotle, 165
Armenian, 51,58, 94, 225
Armstrong, Neil, 97
artichoke, x–xi, 104, 188, 257, 262
ash-shāh māt, 175n
Asiatick Researches (Jones), 111*n*
Asimov, Isaac: *I, Robot,* 21
assessment, 220, 222, 223*n,* 276
aster, 94*n,* 98
Atari, 196
atom bomb, 4, 23–25, 26
Attila the Hun, 102
Augustine, Bishop of Canterbury, 102
Aymara, xiii, xiv, xvi, 12, 105*n*

Baker, Josephine, 37
banca, 136–41, 138*n*
bancus, 136, 137, 138
bank, 136–43, 138*n,* 140*n, 142–43,* 246–47, 247*n,* 248, 248*n,* 250, 283, 290, 291
banque, 248*n*
banquet, 141, 141*n*
Bardot, Brigitte, 25
Barger, Jorn, *90*

Barthes, Roland, 238*n*

Basque, 132*n*, 283–85, 284*n*

Batcave, x, 109, 259

Battlestar Galactica (TV shows), 19

Beach Boys, 26, 195, 234

Beatles, 27, 252

Beat poets, 195

Bechet, Sidney, 37

Bede, Venerable, 111

Bell, Alexander Graham, xix, xx, xxiii, 1, 64, 87

Bellamy, Edward, *Looking Backward*, 79–80

benc, 140–42, 141*n*

bench, 137, 139*n*, 140*n*, 141–42

Bengali, xvi, 29, *33,* 51, *52–53,* 59, 133, 140, *189,* 253, 264

Beowulf, xvi, 112, 141, 142, 160, 170, 290

Berlin Wall, 5, 16*n*, 88, 133

Bernardini, Micheline, 25

Berners-Lee, Tim, 86–88, 87*n*, 89

bhang, 142

Bible,
    King James Version, *161,* 168
    translations of, 54, 138*n,* 111, 160, *161,* 166, 201

bibliothèque, 90–91

bicycle, 45, 47, 48, 48*n*

bikini, 4, 18, 23–27, *27,* 50, 179*n,* 187, 257, 291

Bikini Atoll, 14, 23–24, 26, 93, 293

Black Death, 159, *161*

blog, 6, 71, 72, 86–90, 90*n*, 171, 171*n*, 179*n*, 285, 291

blood bank, *143*

blue jeans, 130

Bouly, Léon, 75, *78*

brand, 32, 45, 46*n*, 87, 131, 151–53, 157, 186, 222, 233

Brando, Marlon, *98,* 127

Britannia, 30, 101, 103, 245

British Empire, xxii, 1–2, 4, 29, 265

British Isles, xxiii, 1, 17, 29, 153, 254
    prehistoric, 100–101

Brittany, France, 101

Bruhn, Wilhelm, 186

Buck, Carl Darling, 177

Buffet, Warren, 252

bungalow, *33*

burnout, 118, 216

burqa, 27, 255

business, xv, 3, 29, 74, 93, 116, 117–22, 120*n,* *143,* 159, 182, 222*n,* 226, 241, 258, 272, 285, 287*n,* 291

bye, xiv, 88, 286, 293–94, *294*

C-3PO, 19

cab, 187, 188

Caesar, Julius, 101, *110*

Cairo Station (film), 77

California
    Anaheim. *See* Disneyland
    Castroville ("Artichoke Capital of the World"), 10, 11, 188
    Cupertino, 234
    fun in the sun in, 195–96
    Hollywood, 3, 47, 72, 76, 96–97, 126, 195, 291
    Los Angeles, 76, 96
    Monterey, 22
    Santa Cruz, ix, 195
    Sunnyvale. *See* Silicon Valley

"California Girls" (song), 26–27

Canada, xxiii, 9, 14*n,* 46, 47, bilingualism in, xvi*n,* 123, 148–49, 238

candy, 255

canoe, 233, 257

Canterbury Tales, The (Chaucer), 119, 160, *161,* 163–64

Cantonese, 42–43, 43*n,* 188, 249

Čapek, Josef, 19–20, 23
Čapek, Karel, 19–21, 22, *23*
card
  credit 4, 63, 72, 79, 80–82, 202*n*,
    243, 291
  wild-, 280–83
Carnegie Mellon University, 21
Carter, Jimmy, 16
cat, 242*n*
Catalan, *52–53*, 56, 83, 203, 284*n*.
    See also Italic languages;
    Romance languages
catch, 157
Catherine the Great, 200
Caxton, William, *161*, 163, 165
Celtic, 52–53, 56–57, 60, 80, 81, 94,
    100, 102, 103, 108, 109, *110*,
    170, 192, 202
Celtics (Boston basketball team), 57*n*
Celts, 101–102
CERN, 87, 87*n*
Chahine, Youssef, 77
Champagne, 238*n*
Chaplin, Charlie, 76
Charlemagne, king of the Franks, 15
chase, 157
chat rooms, 6, 132
Chaucer, Geoffrey, 119, 160, *161*, 162,
    163, 163*n*, 164, 170, 275, 290,
    294
check, 172–75, 174*n*, *175*
cheeseburger deluxe, 235
Cheke, Sir John, 167, 168, 282*n*
Cherokee, 94, 94*n*
chess, 173–75, *175*
chi, 249
chic, 4–5
Chicago Manual of Style, The, 291
Chinese, xv, xv*n*, 6, 9, 11, 13, *34*,
    42–43*n*, 47, 49, 95, 98, 123,
    132, 140*n*, 143, 149, 167, 180,
    188, 204, 208, 210, 211*n*,

    247–53, 247*n*, 248*n*, 250*n*,
    254, 260, 261, 264–65, 267,
    271, 286, *288*
Choctaw, 242
Christendom, 109, 111*n*
Christian Church, Latin in, 201
cinema, 25, *78–79*, 96, 255
coca, 50
Coca-Cola, 4, 50, 256, 263
cocktail, 18, 39–44, 42*n*, 43*n*,
    44*n*
COD, 240, 240*n*
Code of Hammurabi, *143*
coffee, 170, 254
cola, 257
Columbus, Christopher, 139, 246
Comanche, 12
communication technology, xiv, xx, 6,
    89, 133, 163, 170, 209, 249
compounding/compound words, ix–x,
    24, 42, *78–79*, *85*, *90*, 109,
    112, 120*n*, 123, 141, 142, 175,
    176–77, 179*n*, 180, 186–88,
    190, 216, 247, 247*n*, 250, 282,
    293*n*
computer age, 234
Contini-Morava, Ellen, 280, 281*n*
cookie, 172, 181–85, 182*n*, 257
cookies (in technological sense), 6,
    185. *See also* cookie
cool, 4–5
cotton, 254
crag, 109
Cran, William, 16*n*
credit, 63, 80–81, 82, 137*n*, 138–39,
    143, 246
credit card, 42, 63, 80–82, 202*n*, 243,
    291
Crusades/Crusaders, 206
culotte, 178
cuneiform writing, 60*n*, 128–29
cutting-edge technology, 22, 70*n*

Danelaw, the, 106
Danes, 103, 106–7
Dean, James, 127
Delacroix, Eugène, 236
deluxe, 214, 235–39, 237*n*, 238*n*
de luxe, 235, 236, 237*n*, 238, 238*n*
DeMille, Cecil B., 76
destresse, 216–17
détente, 3
Detroit, Michigan, 3, 144, 146, *149*
DiCaprio, Leonardo, 96
Dickens, Charles, xxi, *294*
Dickinson, W. K. L., 75
dictionaries, ix, 231*n*, 237*n*, 238, 287
  Age of the, *161,* 170, 276
dig, 242*n*
digit, 92
digital cookies, 185
digital technology, 92, 170, 249
diksi, 188
Dinesen, Isak, 233
Disneyland, 195
disaster, *98,* 215
disco, 4, 72, 90–93, 92*n*
distress, 216, 217, 269*n*
doctor, 231*n*
drunk, terms for, 43–44, *44*
duangdaw, 93
Duryea, Frank and Charles, 145

E= mc², 114
earth, 153*n*, 246, 267
earthquake, ix, x, 282
East India Company, 28–29, 32, 140, *161*
Eastman, George, 74–75
Edison, Thomas A., xx, 75
Eiffel Tower, 48*n*, 286, 290
Einstein, Albert, 114
Eleanor of Aquitaine, 156
element, 222*n*

Elizabeth I, queen of England, 28, 140, *161,* 166
Ellis, Bret Easton, 294
email, 6, 179*n*, 282
Empires of the World: A Language History of the World (Ostler), 204, 205
England, spellings of, 99*n*, 277
English language
  adding and deleting words in, 153–54, 170–71, 212, 245–46, 248, 253, 257
  alternate terms, 79, 156–57, 178, 253
  articles, 105–106, 259–64
  circulating, 153
  compounding, 109, 282. *See also* compounding/compound words
  contractions, 105*n*
  electronics and, 80, 83, 85, 135, 153, 249, 251
  future of, xiv, xvi, xviii, 16–17, 20, 99–100, 125–26, 157, 170, 200, 210, 212, 244–94, 250*n*, 269*n*, 281*n*
  genitive case, 105*n*
  historical events influencing evolution of, 1–6, 55, 100–103, 106–111, 154–168, *161,* 169, 200, 209–12, 248–49
  as an Indo-European language, 50–72
  inflection, 105, 108, 169, 207, 210, 268–69, 270, 273
  loss of inflection in, 105, 108, 169–70, 207, 210, 268–70, 273
  native vocabulary, 111–13, 115
  nouns, gender of, 104–105, 258–59
  nouns, plural-only, 95*n*
  obsolete words in, 153*n*
  order in sentence of, 272–75
  phases in evolution of:

Old English (500–1066), xvi–xvii, 56, 69, 99–115, 105*n*, 115*n*, 152, 153*n*, 154, 158, 162–63, 163*n*, 169, 210–11, 249, 266. *See also* Beowulf
Middle English (1066–1500), 108, 152, 154–164, *161,* 169, 273, 290, *294. See also* Chaucer
Early Modern (1500–1800), 151–153, *161,* 164–170, 170, 176, 227, 290, *294. See also* Shakespeare
Modern English (1500-present), xvi, 17, 105*n*, 108, *110,* 152, 153*n*, *161,* 169, 222*n*, 267, 290
Late Modern English (1800-present), 227, 290, 294
Global English, xiv–xviii, 1–49, 16*n*, 50–51, 58, 63, 84*n*, 153, 169–71, 198–99, *213. See also words and phrases* hello, robot, bikini, shampoo, jazz, cocktail, Made in China, film, credit card, lol, blog, disco, star, business, parking, T-shirt, free, bank, stop, check, penthouse, cookie, taxi, job, fun, stress, SAT, relax, safari, deluxe, OK, bye
phonetic alphabet of, 55, 109, 210–11, 222–23, 277, 279
plurals, 268–69
poetry, 112, 160–64, 163*n*
possessive case, 105, 268–69
pronouns, 107–108, 266–67, 269–71
as rejuvenator, 5, 84*n*
reshaping, 152–53
-s ending, 269
simplified, 154*n*
speakers of, 9, 16, 155, 156
spelling in, 48, 99*n*, 170, 203, 211, 238, 239, 241, 242, 276–78, 280

spellings of word for, 99*n*, 276–78
suffix, 109, 282–83
syntax, 187*n*
the (vs. *a*), 259–64
to be, 271–72
users vs. speakers of, 4, *9,* 13, 89, 154*n*, 179*n*, 185, 212, 253, 267, 278*n*
vocabulary, 170, 245
vowel sounds, 129–30, 278–80
who, 106
whom, 106
word order, 272–75
words borrowed into, 71, 107–108, 113, 115, 158–59, 162–63, 167–71, 210, 221, 244–45, 248, 257, 275, 290. *See also* robot, bikini, shampoo, credit card, disco, parking, bank, stop, check, penthouse, cookie, taxi, job, stress, SAT, relax, safari, deluxe
words native to, *49,* 73, *85,* 92, 109, 111–15, 140, 142, 151–52, 154–55, 168, 172, 178, 217, 227. *See also* hello, film, lol, blog, star, business, T-shirt, free, bank, bye
words now obsolete in, 153–54, 158, 165, 166–67
words redefined in, 152–53
you, 169, 269–71
Englishes, xiv
entertainment, 2–3, 16, 75–77, 80, 95–97, 145, 172, 188, 193, 201, 209, 237, 255
eschecs, 173–74
estrece, 217
estrés, 216
étoile, 94, 96
Europe, James Reese, 37

European Union, English speakers in, 13, 265
Eurostar, 98
Exekias, *48*

face-lift, 5, 289
Farsi. *See* Persian
father, 68*n*, 73
fell, 73
feng shui, 249
Ferry, Bryan, 134
film, 2–3, 72–79
film stars, 96
fire-new, 151–52, 155, 170, 198
Fitzgerald, F. Scott, 37
Ford, Henry, 144
fortune cookie, 182–83
Franklin, Benjamin, 44
free, 131–36
freedom, 34, 39, 46*n*, 109, 133, 134, 135
French, x, 3, 5, 6, 24, 27, 33, *33*, 35, 43*n*, 48, 48*n*, 51, 52–53, 56, 57, 72, *78*, 81, 83, 87*n*, 94, 96, *110*, 113–16, 115*n*, 120*n*, 122, 124, 128, 136, 143, 148, 154–65, 154*n*, 158*n*, *161*, 163*n*, 168, 170, 173, 173*n*, 174–76, 175, 178, 180, 186–87, 187*n*, 190*n*, 192, 200, 202, 203, 206, 208–10, *213*, 217, 219, 221, 224, 227, 229, 229*n*, 230*n*, *235*, 236–39, 237*n*, 238*n*, 239*n*, 243, 244–45, 247*n*, 249–51, 253, 256*n*, 261, 264, 271, 274, 275, 277, 278*n*, 279, 284, 288, 290. *See also* Italic languages; Romance languages
french fries, 46*n*, 239*n*
French Revolution, 148, 227

Friday, 134
friend, 134
Frisians, 54, 102,
fun, 4, 22, 28, 172, 193–97, 291
fuzz, 242*n*

Gaelic
  Irish Gaelic, 51, *52–53*, 57, *110*, 202, 274
  Scottish Gaelic, *52–53*, 57
  See also Celtic
galabiya, 255–56
galore, 235, 274, 276
gaoshou, 250–51
Garrick, David, 95–96
Gaulish, *52–53*, 56
George III, king of England, 47–48
George IV, king of England, 29
Germania, 101, 103
Germanic languages, 42, 51, *52–53*, 54–57, 55*n*, 61, 68*n*, 71, 73, *78*, 86, *98*, 101–103, 106–107, 109, *110*, 112, 113–16, 115*n*, 120, 123, *126*, 127, 133, 134, 135, 137, 138, 140, 140*n*, 141–42, 151, 155, 163*n*, 170, 172*n*, 177–78, 208, 217, 227, 245, 251, 257, 276
Gish, Lillian, 76
glasnost, 88
global culture, 1, 7–8, 11, 13, 225, 287, 291
Global English. *See* English language
Globe Theater, *161*
Globish the World Over (Nerrière and Hon), 154*n*
gobbe, 192
Godzilla (film), 77
Goethe, Johann Wolfgang von, *The Sorrows of Young Werther*, 216
Gorbachev, Mikhail, 88
gosu, 250, 251, 271–72

Grand Illusion, The (film), 77
graphos, 79
Great Gatsby The, (Fitzgerald), 194
Great Train Robbery, The (film), 76
Greek, *34,* 51, *52–53,* 54, 62, *67n,* 77, 80, *85,* 86, 128, 137, *138n,* 183–84, *189,* 207. *See also* Hellenic
    Ancient, 48, 58, 59, 78–79, 81, 91, 92, 93, *94n, 98,* 109, 111, 114, 128, 129, 130, 137, 164, 165, 166, 186, *187n,* 201, 204, 205, 209, *221n,* 231, 242, 245, 251
    Kione, 111, 138,
    Sanskrit related to, *111n*
groovy, 152, 153, 158, 165, 171
guerre, 158, *158n,* 165
gung ho, 249
guru, 167, 252
Guthrum (king of the Danes), 106
Guzārish (film), 77

hacienda, 245
Hagège, Claude, *61n*
ha ha, 83
Hammurabi, king of Babylon, *143*
hangover, 43–44
Harold II, king of England, 115
Harrison, K. David, *11n*
Harvard College, *221n*
Heaney, Seamus, 290
heaven, 97, *153n,* 178, 248
heaveno, *xxiii*
heavens, 70, *95n,* 248
Hebrew, xxii, *61n,* 111, *111n,* 128, 140, 201, *211n,* 231, 278
Hedd Wyn (film), 77
Heim, Jacques, 24
Hellenic, 58, 61, 108, 170, *187n,* 227
hello, xix–xxiii, *xxn,* *xxiin,* 1, 2, 6, 88, 93, 291, 293

"Hello Girls" (telephone operators), *xxn*
Hemingway, Ernest, 194, 233
Henry II, king of England, 156, 159, 160
Henson, Jim, 184
Heracles, *85*
hieroglyphics, 128
Hindi, xvi, 33, 50, *52–53,* 59, 83, 133, 143, 167, 208, 254, 264
Hittite, 59, *60n, 61n,* 67, 86
hliehhan, 83
Honda, Ishiro, 77
Hon, David, *154n*
honky, *242n*
hose, 178
hoshi, 93
house, 176, 177–78, *179n*
house cocktail, 42
Houston, Whitney, 91
Hrozný, Bedřich, *60n*
huddle, 178
Huns, 102
hutte, 178–79
Hyland, Brian, 26

Iceman, *96n*
Iheme, Osita, 78
iju, 93
Ikedieze, Chinedu, 78
Immortals, the, 237, 238
index, 92, *92n, 269n*
Indo-European language family:
    evolution of, 51–64, 71
    extinctions within, 59–61
    family tree of, 51, *52–53*
    linguistic archaeology and, 63–71
    meaning of "Indo-European," 51, 54
    Proto-Indo-European, 62–63
    prehistoric spread of, 68, *205n*

Indo-European roots of words in
        English, 69, 71, 72, 73, 81, 82,
        83, 85, 86, 91–92, 94–95, 98,
        113, 123, 127–28, 133, 135,
        147, 157, 159, 177, 178, 180,
        183, 217, 227
information technology (IT), 69*n*
Ingle, Dwight J., 215*n*
Inkhorn Controversy, 167–71, 275
inkhorn terms, 166–72
internet, xvii, xx*n*, 6, 16*n*, 83*n*, 89
        123, 179, 189, 204, 254, 258,
        283
    English as dominant language of,
        84*n, 288*
    free access to, 132, 133
    free stuff on, 135
    hyperlinks, 87
    new words related to, *85,* 170–71
    surfing, 196
Inuit, 14, 149
Inupiaq, 149, 199
Irish. *See* Gaelic
Italian, xxii*n,* 51, *52–53,* 56, 96*n,* 132,
        136, 142, 180, 200, 202, 203,
        206–8, *213,* 224, 226, 247,
        264. *See also* Italic languages,
        Romance languages
Italic languages, *52–53,* 56, 57, 61,
        68*n,* 108, 128, 170, 217,
        227
Italic Peninsula, 200
"Itsy Bitsy Teenie Weenie Yellow Polka
        Dot Bikini" (song), 26

James, William, 228
jasmine, 35–36
jazz, 4, 18, 34–39, 135
jeans, 5, 130
Jerome, Saint, 138*n,* 201
jĭnglĭ, 244, 247, 261, 285
jive, 242*n*

job, 172, 189–93
John, king of England, 159, *161*
Johnson, Samuel, *A Dictionary of the
        English Language, 161,* 170
Jones, Sir William, 62, 111*n,* 281*n*
judge, 92
Jutes, 102, *110*

Karlgren, Bernhard, 250*n*
kayak, 14, 50, 233, 257
Kelly, Bert, 36
Kerouac, Jack, 195
khartes, 81
Kiarostami, Abbas, 77
Kinetograph, 75
Kingsley, Walter J., 35
Kismet (film), 77
koekjes, 181–82
kola, 50
Koundouros, Nikos, 77
Korean, 83, 143, 180, 250–51, 253,
        283, 288
kowtow, 249
Krapf, Johann Ludwig, 230–32, 230*n,*
        231*n,* 281*n*
kuklos, 48
Kumar, Ashok, 77
Kurosawa, Akira, 77

language
    "click," 211n
    common. *See* lingua franca
    electronic influences on, 249
    magic glasses of, xiii–xiv
    planetary, xviii
    substrate, 192
    tonal, 211n
languages:
    dead, 61n, 201–2
    evolution of, xvi–xvii, 152–54, 157,
        164, 210–12
    extinct, 11–12, 59–61

learning, 131–33, 197. *See also*
  Lingua Franca *and individual*
  languages
local variations in, 265
numbers and varieties of, xvii
reconstruction of, 66, 100, 126,
  250, 281
speakers of, xv–xvi*n*, 155
spread of, 205–6
translations of, 164–65
See also specific languages
Latin: 11, 20, 42, 43*n*, 48, 48*n*, 51,
  52–53, 56, 57, 59–62, 67*n*,
  72, 81, 83*n*, 92, *98*, 101–102,
  108–12, *110*, 112*n*, 114, *126*,
  128–30, 136–38, 138*n*, 142,
  147, 156–57, *161*, 164, 165,
  170, 172*n*, 173*n*, 176–78, 186,
  192, 200–12, *213*, 214, 217,
  217*n*, 221, 221*n*, 222*n*, 227,
  231, 236, 242, 246, 247*n*,
  249, 250, 250*n*, 251, 254,
  275–76, 278, 283, 290. *See*
  also Italic languages; Romance
  languages; Lingua Franca
laugh, 82–83, *85*
Lauren, Ralph, 233
laxus, 227
lb., 43n
lingua franca, 198–214, *213*
  Arabic, 265
  French, 200, 208
  Global English as, xvii, 198, 204,
    208–14
  Indo-European, 205*n*, 207
  Latin, 200–4, 206, 208, 209, 249
  Lingua Franca, 206–7, 212, 214
  Mandarin Chinese, 208
  need for a global, xviii
  Phoenician, 204–5
  and religion, 209*n*
  Sanskrit, 209

spread of, 204–6
Swahili, 207–8
linguistic archaeology, 63–71, 111*n*,
  112
literacy, 129, 130, 164, 166, 221
Lithuanian, xxii, *34, 52–53*, 57, 132*n*,
  183, *189*, 190, 193
Livingstone, David, 231*n*
lol, 72, 82–85, 222*n*, 291
Lopez, Vincent, 35
L'Oréal, 32
London, England, 21, 30, 115, 139,
  140, 151, 155, 158, 159, 160,
  161, 168, 187, 188, 231, 249,
  287*n*
Louis XIII, king of France, 237
Lumière, Auguste and Louis, 75
luxe, 236–37, 237*n*, 238*n*,
luxury, 235–36, 238, 238*n*

MacNeil, Robert, 16*n*
Made in China, 18, 45–49, 291
Mahomet, Sake Dean "Dr. Brighton,"
  29–30, 32
make, 113, 114
Mallory, J. P., 57
Maneno, *235*
Mannyng, Robert, 216*n*
maquillage, 114
maritime powers, 206
Marshallese, 14, 24, 93, 293*n*
mason, 113
mass, 114
mass production, 3, 18, 32, 114, 228,
  229*n*, 291
McCrum, Robert, 16*n*
Méliès, Georges, 75
Mencken, H. L., 34–35, 240–41,
  240*n*, 242
meter, 109, 125, 163*n*, 186
Mikres Afrodites (film), 77
MIT, 21–22

Mitchell, Joni, 196
moccasin, 168
Model T Ford, 144, 146
mongrel, 113, 114
Monk, Thelonious, 34
Monroe, Marilyn, 25, 97
monte, 138, 139, 139*n*
moon, 134, 246
Mosaic (browser), 88
Motown, 149
mountebank, 139*n*
mouse, 69, 69*n*, 234
Mulcaster, Richard, *Elementarie,*
    161
multilingualism, 10–11, 15, 196
Murnau, F. W., 76
mushroom, x, 159
Mussolini, Romano, 37*n*
Muybridge, Eadweard, 75

nadir, 254
Nast, Condé, 180–81
Nero, Roman Emperor, 236
Nerrière, Jean-Paul, 154*n*
network, 6
New York City, xx, 3, 11*n*, 93, *180,*
    181, 182, 182*n*, 185, 187, 188,
    241, 278
news, 5
NG (no go), 242
Niagara Falls, xx, xxi
Nieuw Amsterdam, 181
Nigeria, filmmaking in, 78*n*
no-qui-si, 94
Normandy, 115*n*
Normans, *110,* 115–16, 155–57. *See*
    also Vikings
Norsemen. *See* Normans; Vikings
North Germanic, *52–53,* 106–107,
    110
nose, 104–105, 267
Nosferatu (film), 76

np (no problem), 242
nyota, 93

Official Languages Act of Canada,
    123
Ogden, C. K., 154*n*
O.K. (OK), 83, 239–43
Old Norse, *52–53,* 95, 106–108, *110,*
    112, 115*n*. *See also* Germanic
    languages; Scandinavian
"oll korrect" (ok), 242, 243
Olympic Games, 7
O'Neill, Jack, ix, 105*n*, 195, 247*n*
Open Sesame!, 10, 13, 156
Ostler, Nicholas, 204, 205, 221*n*
Ötzi, 96*n*
Out of Africa (film), 233
Ovid, *Metamorphoses,* 165
Ozu, Yasujiro, 77

park, 123–25
parka, 168
parking, 3, 116, 122–26, 291
parquer, 124
pater, 68*n*, 73
patio, 245, 248
PDQ, 240*n*
Pearl Harbor, 23
pellicula, 72–73
pellis, 72
penthouse, 172, 176–81
Penthouse (magazine), 176, 178
Persian, 35, *52–53,* 58–69, 172–73,
    175, 275
Persian Gulf War (1990–91), 5
philosophy, 245
Phoenician. *See* lingua franca
Phoenician alphabet, 128–30, 131,
    173*n*, 278
phonetic convergence, 173
phonetics, 129–30, 205, 210–11, 250,
    250*n*, 254, 278

Pickford, Mary, 76
pidgin, 199, 206, 207, 208, 212
pig, 56, 156–57
Playboy (magazine), 26
plaza, 245
pleasure, 120*n*, 226
Pontic Steppe, 68, 69*n*
populations, mobility of, 288–89
pork, 157
Porter, Edwin, 76
Portuguese, xvi, 51, *52–53,* 56, 94*n*,
        97, 175, 199, 203, 206–8, 210,
        213, 235, 253, 264, 271, 288.
        See also Italic languages;
        Romance languages
    Brazilian Portuguese, 143, 278*n*
post-traumatic stress disorder (PTSD),
        214–15
powwow, 168
precocious, 183
prestige, 217
printing press, movable-type, *161,* 163,
        164, 165
Private Life (film), 77
Proto-Indo-European (PIE), *52–53,*
        62–63. *See also* Indo-European
        language family
    chronology of, 82
    "linguistic archaeology" and, 63–
        71, 111*n,* 112
    reconstruction of, 66–71, 100
    related to English, *52–53,* 71–72,
        198

qanāt, 255
Quebec, Quebeckers, 123, 148–49

R2-D2, 19
Ra (Egyptian sun god), 129
Raizman, Yuli, 77
Ramsey, S. Robert, *The Languages of
        China,* 250*n*

rapprochement, 3
real, 158
Réard, Louis, 24, 25
Rebel Without a Cause (film), 127
Rebmann, Johannes, 231*n*
Red Sox (Boston baseball team), 136,
        141
Redford, Robert, 233
Reinach, Théodore, 187*n*
Reinhardt, Jean "Django," 37
relax, 225–30
Renaissance, 35, 152, 153, 156,
        164–68, 287. *See also* English
        language: Early Modern
        English
Renoir, Jean, 77
R.F.D. No. 3 (novel), 122*n*
Richard the Lionheart, 159
Richards, I. A., 154*n*
ring, 267
robot, 3, 18–23, 197, 282*n*
robotics, 21, 281
Romance languages, *52–53,* 56, 129,
        206, 212, 277. *See also* Italic
        languages; Latin
Roman Empire, 201, 202, 204, *213*
Romanticism, 216
Roosevelt, Theodore, 232–33
Ross, Diana, 149
royal, 158
runes, 55, 112*n,* 222
R.U.R. (Čapek), 20–21, 22
Rushani (language), 8

safari, 50, 230–35
Safire, William, 89
Sahara, 262
Sanskrit, 49, *52–53,* 59, 62, 67–68*n,*
        81, 86, 94, 111*n, 142,* 175,
        204, 205, 209, 252
sao, 93
SAT, 4, 87*n,* 218–25, 291

Saxons, 102. *See also* Anglo-Saxons

Scandinavian, *52–53,* 106–108, *110.*
    See also Old Norse

Schwarzenegger, Arnold, 19, 291

Schwarzkopf, Hans, 31

scip, 259

Scorsese, Martin, 188

scuba, 84

Seafarer, The (poem), 254, 254*n*

Selous, Frederick, 232

Semitic languages, 111, 278

Serbo-Croatian, xxii, *52–53,* 57, 57*n,*
    132*n,* 133*n*

Seven Samurai (film), 77

shāh, 173, 175

Shakespeare, William:
    and Early Modern English, 290,
        294
    free verse of, 163*n*
    Hamlet, 74, 120, 169
    Love's Labor's Lost, 151, *161,* 169
    Macbeth, 119–20
    new English words from, 152–53,
        286–87, 294
    Romeo and Juliet, 169
    spelling, 276–77
    Titus Andronicus, xxi
    view of English language in plays
        of, 168–70
    See also business; English language:
        Early Modern English;
        future of; you; film; fire-new;
        penthouse; Renaissance

shampoo, 28–34, 43*n,* 50, 238*n,* 256,
    276

Shaw, George Bernard, 21

Shelley, Mary, *Frankenstein, or The
    Modern Prometheus,* 18

ship, 267

ship's log, *90*

shirt, 127–28

shorts, 127

Siamak (of Bartang Valley, Tajikistan),
    8, 10, 15

Silicon Valley, 196

sitarih, 94

site, 6

skill, 109, 257

skirt, 127

sky, 109, 178, 179, 248

skyhut, 180

slack, 227

Smith, Ada "Bricktop," 37

"snow," and "words" in "Eskimo" for, 14*n*

soap, 31, 32, 257

Sophocles, 85

sorbet, 255

spam, 6, 185

Spanish, 52–53, 143,199, 210,
    245, 271–72. *See also* Italic
    languages; Romance languages

speech community, 115*n*

spelling, 99*n,* 276–78

spider, 177

spin, 177

star, 93–98, 246, 267

Stein, Aurel, 60*n*

stēlla, 94, 98

Stern, 95

stone, 267

STOP, 3, 143–50

Story of English, The (McCrum,
    MacNeil, and Cran), 16*n*

streak, 217

Streep, Meryl, 233

Streetcar Named Desire, A (film), 98,
    127

stress, 118, 214–18, 228

Sturm und Drang, 216

stuttbuxur relax, 230

Suetonius, 236

sugar, 255

Summer, Donna, 91, 290

Supremes, 149

surfing, 196
Swahili: *34,* 93, 97, 132*n,* 184, *189,* 204, 207, 208, 210, 230–35, 230*n,* 231*n,* 280–82, 281*n*

T, 128–30
Taklamakan Desert (Western China), 60*n*
taxa, 186
tax-free, 134
taxi, 185–89
Taxi Driver (film), 188
taxidermy, 187*n*
tea, 167, 249, 276
teach, 92
technology, 69–70*n. See also* cookies; internet; printing press; telegrams; telephone
    of agriculture, 205*n*
    communication, xx, 6, 89, 133, 163, 170, 209, 249
    and lingua franca, 209, 212
    military, 205
    words redefined by, 234
Teese, Dita Von, 41
telegrams, 148
telephone:
    cell phones, xx*n*
    conversation starters for, xix–xxii, 2
    distant contact via, xxiii
    technology of, xx
test, 222
Thanh Hang, 229
Thompson, Hunter S., 46*n*
Thousand and One Nights, The, 8, 10
tobacco, 50, 168
Tocharian 52–53, 59–60, 95*n*
Tokyo Story (film), 77
Toll House cookie, 184
trapeza, 138
Treaty of Versailles (1919), 3
tree, 246

Trip to the Moon, A (film), 75–76
T-shirt, 5, 126–31
Twain, Mark, xx*n*
tycoon, 257
Tyndale, William, 166

ulluriaq, 94
United States, influence of, 1, 2, 3–6, 15–16
U.S. Telegraph, xii

Van Buren, Martin "Old Kinderhook," 241–42
Vatican City, 201–2
Vedic Sanskrit, 52–53, 59, 205, 205*n*
vélo, 48*n*
Vermeersch, Jeannette, 25
video, 205*n*
Vienna Convention, 147, 149, 150
Vietnam War, 4, 130, 158*n*
Vietnam/Vietnamese, xvi, *34,* 93, 121, 158*n, 189,* 196, 229, 248*n*
Vikings, 106–107, *110,* 115*n,* 127, 140*n. See also* Normandy; Normans; Norsemen
Virgil, *Aeneid,* 165
Visigoths, 102
volume, 45
Voyager Golden Record, 16–17

waffle, 86
war, 158, 159
Washington, Charles "Chaz," 35
water, 246, 267
Watkins, Calvert, *53,* 69*n*
wave, 86
wawles, 176
We (novel), 19
weave, 69, 70*n,* 89–90
web + log = blog, 89, 90
web, 69, 86–88, 89
website, 6

weevil, 86
Welsh, *52–53,* 56–57, 101, *189*
Wertherfieber, 216
West Germanic, *52–53,* 54–57, 103, 123. *See also* Germanic languages
Wild One, The (film), 127
William the Conqueror, 115–16, 154, 155, 160
William IV, king of England, 29
Wilson, Thomas, *The Arte of Rhetorique, 161,* 166–67
wobble, 86
wok, 249
Wolof, 242
word-hoard, 112, 152, 170
workbench, 141
World Trade Organization (WTO), 45, 47
World War II, 4, 32, *33,* 122, 154*n,* 215. *See also* bikini; jazz; robot

World Wide Web (WWW), 71, 86–88, 221
wwwww, 83*n*
Wycliffe, John, 160, *161*

xǐng, 95

yellow cabs, 187
Yellowstone National Park, 124
yen, 249
yıldız, 93
yínháng, 247, 248, 250
Yogi, Maharishi Mahesh, 252

zenith, 254
zero, 254
zombie, 257
Zoroastrians, 58
Zulu, 211*n,* 225, *235*